Yellowstone Drift

Floating the Past in Real Time

John Holt

Yellowstone Drift

Floating the Past in Real Time

John Holt

CounterPunch
PETROLIA

PRESS

First published by
CounterPunch and AK Press 2009
© *CounterPunch* 2009
All rights reserved

CounterPunch
PO Box 228, Petrolia, California 95558

AK Press
674-A 23rd St, Oakland, California 94612-1163

ISBN 978-1904859895

A catalog record for this book is available from the Library of Congress.

Library of Congress Control Number: 2008927321

Typeset in Minion Pro, designed by Robert Slimbach for Adobe Systems Inc.; and Futura, originally designed by Paul Renner. Cover and Title Page use Hypatia Sans Pro designed by Thomas Phinney for Adobe Systems Incorporated.

Printed and bound in Canada.

Design and typography by Tiffany Wardle de Sousa.

Cover and author photo by Ginny Holt.

Books by John Holt

Table Of Contents

Acknowledgments

A number of people helped make this project possible and reasonably coherent. Among them are Louise Jones for encouragement; long-time friend and believer Jeffrey St. Clair who saw immediately what I was chasing with this one; Tiffany Wardle de Sousa for designing the manuscript; Doug Peacock for writing the evocative foreword; and my Mother who passed away before this one was published.

◆ ◆ ◆

Ten percent of the royalties I earn from sales of this book will be donated to the Greater Yellowstone Coalition.

◆ ◆ ◆

For Ginny

◆ ◆ ◆

There is a way to master silence
Control its curves, inhabit its dark corners
And listen to the hiss of time outside
Far From Why by Paul Bowles

ELK RIVER

By Doug Peacock

SHOULD YOU VISIT THE YELLOWSTONE RIVER COUNTRY WITH 13,000 years of human history in your head, the first thing you might notice is how little the landscape has changed. True, a few towns and ranches are now strewn about the topography. Yet, this thin cloak of agriculture falls lightly over the Yellowstone country; modern settlement can do little to flatter this lovely land. And it hasn't; the power and beauty of the raw habitat shines on through.

The native people, who lived here before the white man showed up, called this drainage the "Elk River." These hills and valleys were the best hunting country anywhere. The mountain man Osborne Russell passed along the valley numerous times in the 1830s. Russell wrote: "This is a beautiful country the large plains extending on either side of the river (Yellowstone or Elk River) intersected with streams and occasional low spurs of mountains whilst thousands of Buffaloe may be seen in almost every direction and Deer Elk and Grizzly bear are abundant. The latter are more numerous than in any other part of the mountains. Owing to the vast quantities of cherries and plums and other wild fruits which this section of the country affords."

In the second half of the nineteenth century, the last of the great tribes contested for the lush game habitat of the Elk River. Even later, after the turn of the century, the ethnographer and photographer Edward Curtis found the Elk River watershed "a veritable Eden of the Northwest, with beautiful broad valleys and abundant wooded streams, no part of the country was more favorable for buffalo, while its wild forested mountains made it unequaled for elk and other highland game."

And it was always that way. Our recorded European history, dating from 1805 when Lewis and Clark wandered through here, accounts for less than two percent of the time humans roamed the Yellowstone. That record, hinted at by archeological finds, places the first people here 13,050 years ago, in encampments just north of the great bend of the Elk River at present day Livingston, Montana. It was the last of the Pleistocene and one can now only imagine the richness of the country: blue ice of glaciers still capping the mountains and receding into the passes, revealing the topography we see today. The steppe land would have teemed with now-extinct species of camel, long-horned bison, tapir, deer, giant sloth and horses. Here and there, saber-tooth tigers, dire wolves and short-faced bears prowled the land, stalking the grazers. The valley would have been wet; the high benches pocked with pothole lakes, springs and ponds created by giant beaver. Mastodon browsed spruce trees at the edges of a boreal forest and, in the far distance, a line of mammoth might have paralleled a braided watercourse.

The first Montanans entered an uninhabited land with no human tracks, no smoke on the horizon. Think about it: coming into an increasingly hospitable land, open country in the last days of the Pleistocene, the wildest landscape on earth. It was truly the Great American Adventure.

These voyagers were called Clovis and they were big game hunters specializing in chasing mammoth. They were the first widely recognized archeological presence in North America. The near-synchronous appearance of the Clovis' signature artifact—a large, fluted, exquisitely-flaked projectile point often crafted from the finest cryptocrystalline rock sources—across the country, from Montana to Arizona to Florida and Panama within a few hundred years, is considered one of the most amazing events in the history of archeology.

It is quite possible that Clovis people emerged from the ice-free corridor out of Alaska and first appeared in the lower United States by way of Montana. It is also possible that their magnificent lithic technology was an American invention resulting from the necessity of big game hunters coming up with a weapon capable of bringing down shaggy elephants. The birth place of the Clovis complex could well have been in Montana, as the first quality lithic quarries you encounter coming south from the passageway between the great ice sheets are south of the Missouri River and in the Yellowstone River watershed. These claims, however, are contentious; conclusive evidence has yet to be unearthed.

Nonetheless, the fact is that the first appearance of Clovis was synchronous with two other occurrences: the opening of the ice-free corridor between the continental glaciers and the last fossil record of the gigantic short-faced bear, a swift predator and scavenger that stood seven feet at the shoulder. Were humans in the lower states and South America prior to the Clovis event? Probably a few existed here and there, but in any case, not many; the archeological record is very thin or invisible before to 13,500 years ago. There were surely not enough to slow down the Clovis hunters, who blitzkrieged across the continent in 300 years and probably none in the Interior West or Montana. At least there is no scientific evidence, no archeological finds. Paleontologists think the giant short-faced bear preferred higher, well-drained grasslands mainly west of the Mississippi River. In open country, these carnivores could have run down humans with ease. The most likely pre-Clovis sites in the contiguous states are in the East. Short-faced bears might have been a problem in the open western grasslands. It might have been easier to survive in the Eastern woodlands.

At any rate, the Yellowstone country looms large in the evolving story of the peopling of the New World. Arguably, the most important archeological discovery in American prehistory was unearthed on the Shields branch of the Elk River just south of Wilsall, Montana. Here, at the base of a small but imposing cliff on Flathead Creek, a one and a half year-old-child was buried, interred with nearly 120 of the most spectacular Clovis artifacts ever seen, all packed in consecrated red ochre and with great ceremony, evidenced by ritually broken spear-shafts. The antler tools dated back 13,040 years. Unlike other Clovis "caches," none of these artifacts were made of obsidian. This could mean the child was buried before other Clovis folk found the Obsidian Cliffs quarry seventy-five raven-miles upstream on the Elk River in present day Yellowstone Park. The lead archeologist has called this sacred site "America's first church."

The Clovis people spread out across most of lower North America in just 200 or 300 years. Then, beginning about 13,000 years ago, a series of extinctions swept over North America. The great Pleistocene mega-fauna disappeared. This paleoextinction is variously blamed on climate change, over-hunting by Clovis, introduced disease, or a combination of the above. Scientists like to point out that nearly every animal over 220 pounds died off and only smaller animals survived this wipeout of big mammals. A notable exception was the grizzly (along with bison and chunky humans). The force driving everything was climate. Recent dates on fossil bones suggest most of the megafauna started to drop dead about 13,400 years ago. In another 600 years, as indicated by the fossil record, the extinction was almost complete. The abrupt disappearance of Clovis in the archeological record is marked by a black, carbon-rich layer that dates to 12,900 years ago, a time of sudden chilling, also know as the Younger Dryas. What in turn might have generated the onset of this cold spell? Could it have been related to a reversal of world ocean currents? Perhaps a comet exploded in the air somewhere in Canada north of the Great Lakes bringing on the 1,300-year winter. There is evidence of both events.

At the end of this period, around 11,000 years ago, the flora and fauna of the Yellowstone valley began to resemble what we still see today. Cottonwoods and thickets of edible fruit shrubs occupied the flood plain and, beyond the grassy slopes, a succession of conifers climbed up the mountains towards timberline. Grizzly bears and native people shared the top of the food pyramid. These nomadic bands hunted big game, especially bison; there is evidence for systematic, communal hunting and the first jump sites, where bison were driven over a cliff, show up at this time. This pattern of big game hunting (known as the Paleo-Indian period) lasted 3,000 years, or until people began to settle down to a life-style of generalized hunting and gathering.

Unlike other parts of the country, the first availability of agricultural plants from Mesoamerica did not transform the human cultures of the Elk River valley into sedentary people. The land was so rich, and game so abundant, that the tribes never abandoned the hunting way of life. The Neolithic revolution of the Old World failed in the Yellowstone country, although the pre-historic Shoshone made pottery and stone bowls.

What did change the cultures of the Plains and inter-mountain West was the introduction of the Spanish horse after the Pueblo Revolt of 1680. Horses first arrived on the Elk River around 1720, reaching the Crow tribes by 1730. Some thirty different tribes adopted an equestrian society and became the fierce, warfare people we know from the movies. This caused massive cultural change among five different language families whose common tongue was sign language.

The Crow Nation, though a relatively recent tribe of the Elk River, perhaps arriving about 1600, controlled all the Yellowstone country before 1825. Through the familiar process of a litany of threats and deceptions, the white government took most of the land away; the Crow ceded the final piece of Yellowstone bottomland in 1899.

By this time, the buffalo had been slaughtered to near extinction, the 60 million at the time of Lewis and Clark reduced to 23 wild bison the government couldn't catch on the upper Yellowstone in 1902. Grizzlies and wolves too were shot on sight until only mountain populations remained. Today the wild bison and grizzlies mostly live in Yellowstone Park. The Elk River valley still contains habitat suitable for these animals, but our residual European intolerance has precluded re-colonization by bison and carnivores.

It is against this backdrop and history, that John Holt offers us his unique hit on the contemporary Elk River. Many people today know this river intimately. Some have spent a lifetime living and observing segments of this great river valley. But its entirety of 70,000 square miles escapes the individual eye; what we need is the collective phonologies of all the people, fishermen, ranchers, and Indians who live in this intact and rich country.

In the absence of this endeavor, John Holt is the man for the job, having devoted slightly less (we hope) than half of his adult life to this project. Of the many fine writers who contribute to the literature of American trout fishing, I have always found John among the least predictable and, for me, the most interesting. With *Yellowstone Drift: Floating the Past in Real Time*, he has written something more than a fishing book, bringing his flair for research and novelist's eye to produce the definitive study of the longest un-dammed river in the lower forty-eight states. The book, like the Yellowstone itself, is a big, sprawling work that blows its banks and meanders throughout the human and natural history of the region. Hovering over the 671 mile journey is Holt's own thunderstorm of a life; the man is not hesitant in taking a stand, whether it's a rage against the livestock-centric insanity of killing free-ranging bison that wander beyond Yellowstone Park's boundary or quietly summoning the 500 year flood that would wipe out all the garish trophy homes littering the river's flood plain. Holt's specialty is "nowhere" country and his accounts of the headwaters of the lower tributaries, the Tongue and Powder Rivers, constitute my favorite sections of the book. Here is Kerouac-style old-time adventure and exploration of a lonely, stark landscape, rich in history and rendered luminous by Holt's prose. At sunset, there's trout and catfish and grouse cooked over a cottonwood fire, washed down by many bottles of wine, with romance drifting on the evening air. This is a classic run down Montana's finest country and we are lucky to have such a guide.

Introduction

All of This Begins Here

BEING PART OF THE RIVER IS EASY. YOU JUST SETTLE INTO THE canoe, push off from the sandy, gravelly shore and begin paddling downstream, often letting the current take you where it will over the course of miles and hours while the sun seems to soar east to west. Cottonwoods with thick limbs supporting golden and bald eagles that resemble stoic statuary slide behind. Willows rustle in a warm breeze. Herons perch motionless on grey downfall, eccentric extensions of the dead trees, figures patiently waiting for small trout or sculpin to move into range of long, pointed beaks.

The quiet slip of the flowing, living current through a long, wide bend in the river, the enormous trees lining the grassy cutbanks, thick tangles of exposed roots dipping into the water, is disrupted by the sound of rushing, breaking water like strong wind working through the leaves of these watching trees, the broken water perhaps a quarter-mile ahead. Soon the silvery white crests of standing waves are visible and tangles of deadfalls and limbs slammed together during spring runoff line the edges of the main stem of the river. In a few seconds the pace of the current begins to accelerate, slowly at first, now rapidly and the strength of the Yellowstone is palpable, a force that is basic, direct and potentially overpowering. All effort is directed towards gaining a line through this rough cascade of loud splashing, a line that will hopefully track safely to one side of the three and four foot high humps of water that look like the hair standing up on the back of a starving mongrel dog. Paddling is fast and hard as the canoe tries to leak towards the center line of broken water. Time stands still while sun-sparkled water, glistening rock and deep green shoreline runs past in a blur of motion and sound. Then the river arcs to the left down below and the relative calm of the inside curve is visible. Hard pushes on the side of the rapids, with forceful J-strokes mixed into the action, maintain the course to smoother going. Then, like none of this ever happened, ever existed, the noise and whirling water recedes and sound vanishes from the senses.

That's being part of the river.

Becoming the river is not so hard, either. Those hours smoothly turn into days, weeks. The swirling and mixing determination of current leads inexorably downstream gradually, but sometimes abruptly, dropping through the country with still more splashing, crested waves and liquid sound and ever nearer to sea level. Paddling becomes second nature, repetitive—even Indian strokes and box-stroke pivots used to maintain course and position in the river are executed without thought. Muscles become routinized and mechanically perform their tasks without pain or fatigue.

Geese by the thousands honking with wild, natural insanity, are now almost subconsciously heard and appreciated, the shimmering vibrations of all those wings in the light have become part of the trip, the natural way of all of the motionless time, a part of the Yellowstone as all of this always has been.

The heat of mid-day, the afternoon upstream wind, the muffled grate of the canoe as it slips across a gravel bar covered with a few inches of water, the whisper of willow and Russian Olive leaves, the sound of a small fire crackling in the evening, the buzz of nighthawks feeding on insects and the yelps and howls of coyotes talking with the stars in the cooling air—all of this registers as elements of the river's life on a subliminal stage that has taken over and dominates a clear, basic awareness.

Now the river asserts benign control and draws me into its flow, just moving in and within the water's rhythms. I forget the enclosed, electronic life back home in Livingston. Everything is transformed to the elemental, second nature, happening without effort, without a need to learn or understand. The Yellowstone steadily flows down to the Missouri, then Mississippi and finally the Gulf of Mexico, always as gravity's companion—this movement is the essence of all rivers. The repetitive nature of the day to day routine out here is hypnotic, rapidly washing away anxiety and, finally, useless ego.

An unaccustomed serenity and well-being pervades as the canoe tracks its own way with slight help from me.

Everything is now the river and its fertile, riparian corridor with all of the creatures who depend on this water to live moving in synchronicity.

♦ ♦ ♦

The idea for canoeing the length of the Yellowstone River from below Gardiner on the northern edge of Yellowstone National Park down river to its confluence with the Missouri at Ft. Buford, North Dakota has been running around my head for a long time. Ever since I moved to Livingston from Whitefish a dozen years ago, During my daily walks on the levee along the river at Sacajewea Park I watch the water race and power its way to the east. Diverse currents rush around north and south sides of the Ninth Street Island and merge in a foam crested series of standing waves and foam flecked eddies. The river pushes against the flood-control riprap before plunging over an erosion polished upthrust of charcoal grey stone. From there the Yellowstone bounces and laughs its way past Mayor's Landing beneath ochre sandstone bluffs and then on down for several miles to the Highway 89 Bridge.

I'd floated this stretch in an Avon raft or McKenzie drift boat many times casting to large, and not-so-large, browns and rainbows over the years and had canoed this run a couple of times. Whether walking or floating my thoughts inevitably turned to imagining what doing the entire river would be like. What would I see. What kinds of fish, birds, animals and landscape would I encounter? What were the people like over in Forsyth more than 200 miles east or were there hermits and madmen roaming the banks along the badlands around Terry still further east?

Finally I made up my mind to make the journey. Floating in Yellowstone Park is not allowed and the Upper and Lower Falls are a sure death trip anyway, so I'd cover the 520-plus miles beginning just below Yankee Jim Canyon at Carbella.

I thought that I would complete my explorations in one season—pre-runoff spring then from mid-July when high-water levels have moderated until winter weather locked things up sometime in late October or early November. I progressed downriver in stretches, I did not do all of the river in one take. Obligations like maintaining my home, paying bills and completing writing assignments precluded this. With each trip, whether it was Mayor's Landing down 120 miles of river to Laurel or from Hysham to Forsyth or from above Terry to Glendive I learned more about the magic Yellowstone and about myself. And I realized that despite having fished the river for decades and walking next to it for years, I knew very little about the drainage—its moods, secret places, the wildlife and the people to name a few things.

By the first of October of that first season of paddling I realized that another year was needed. So be it. I was game. Another season spent floating in solitude through some of the most magnificent landscape on earth worked for me. The first year I covered all but a few of the shorter sections of the river—I divided the river into stretches based on location of diversion dams, changes from one type of water or landscape to another and overall river miles. Some the water was worked more than once. I did some this alone because my wife, photographer Ginny Holt, was attending to family business. During our second year exploring the river by canoe we covered a good deal of the river and I was beginning to feel that I knew the rhythms and pace of the Yellowstone to some extent. Ginny took thousands of photographs, I filled a couple of notebooks with observations, interviews and related research. I estimate that I did more than 1,100 river miles or the length of the proposed journey twice.

We'll be doing much of the river over and over in the coming years. We're enthralled with its power, beauty and serenity and there's so much more to learn, to discover.

Spending time in one certain section of landscape like the Yellowstone drainage or Canada's far north as we did for another book, leads me to research and try to understand specific elements of a given region. This book will describe the river as I experienced it from the paddling to camping to fishing and much more including people, the history—from explorers to development to Native People—the sometimes vicious, hell-bent weather—gale force wind, intense heat, rain, snow, sleet, hail, lightning—all of it, examinations of some of the flora and fauna that are an integral part of the Yellowstone corridor. And tributaries like the Stillwater, Bighorn, Tongue and Powder will be described as will some of the communities along the river that depend upon its flow for their existent. Every piece of good country is under siege and the Yellowstone is no exception. These concerns along with solutions and possible solutions will be shown. Curious experiences and weird happenings that are so much apart of Ginny's and my life edged their way into the narrative. The structure of the book is downstream all the way with side trips here and there and as far away as the Middle Fork of the Powder River in the remote canyon country of central Wyoming. Curious tangents that are part of how I explore, enjoy and appreciate the land. A few threats to the upper river are described just below as cautionary information showing that the best of our world is often the most threatened.

The Yellowstone is too good to waste, too good not to experience as fully as possible. As I say each morning while walking beside the water, "Thank you river for all you've given me, are giving me and hopefully will give me in the future. I'll do my best by you."

♦ ♦ ♦

The Yellowstone River is the largest tributary of the Missouri flowing from its headwaters below Younts Peak along the Continental Divide in the southwest quadrant of Yellowstone Park for 671 miles down to Ft. Buford, North Dakota. The drainage covers an area of more than 70,000 square miles or well over twice the size of Maine. The drainage includes much of the high plains of southern Montana and northern Wyoming. It is the longest undammed river in the lower 48, though there are a number of diversion dams of several feet in height beginning below Billings all the way to its confluence with the Missouri.

Dubbed with high originality by *National Geographic* as "the last best river," the Yellowstone initially flows northward, a true high country stream at this stage, emptying into and draining Yellowstone Lake. The lake is at 7,732 feet above sea level and covers an average area of 136 square miles, with 110 miles of shoreline. The mean depth of the lake is 139 feet.

It's deepest spot is 387 feet. Thermal pools and steam vents surround the lake and also issue from cracks below the surface along the lake's bottom. After Lake Titicaca in South America at 12,500 feet, Yellowstone Lake is the largest high-altitude lake in the world.

As the Yellowstone river flows north from the lake it plunges first over Upper Yellowstone Falls and then a quarter mile downstream over Lower Yellowstone Falls, where it enters the Grand Canyon of the Yellowstone, a spectacular and colorful gouge in the earth's surface that is up to 1,000 feet deep. The upper falls are 109 feet high while the lower falls are 308 feet high, or almost twice that of Niagara Falls—though the volume of water is in no way comparable to Niagara as the width of the Yellowstone River, before it goes over the lower falls, is 70 feet where Niagara is a half mile. The lower falls of the Yellowstone are still the largest volume major waterfall in the Rockies. The amount of water flowing over the falls can vary from 8,500 cubic feet per second at peak runoff in late spring to 700 cubic feet per second in the fall.

Many historians believe that Jim Bridger was the first white American to see the falls in 1846. The Folsom Party, a private group of explorers working in close relationship with the U.S. Government, named the falls in 1869. During the Hayden Expedition of 1870 to 1871, the falls were documented in photographs by William Henry Jackson and later in paintings by Thomas Moran. Today, there are numerous vantage points for viewing the falls. The Canyon loop road skirts the west side of the canyon with several vehicle parking areas. One trail leads down to the brink of the lower falls, a steep third of a mile. Another vantage point descends from the east down a series of stairs attached to the cliffs.

After passing through the Black Canyon of the Yellowstone downstream of the Grand Canyon, the river flows northward into Montana between the Absaroka Range and the Gallatin Range in the Paradise Valley. The river emerges from the mountains near Livingston, where it turns eastward and northeastward, flowing across the northern Great Plains past Billings.

East of Billings, it is joined by the Bighorn River. Further downriver, it is joined by the Tongue near the town of Miles City, and then by the Powder in eastern Montana. It joins the Missouri in extreme western

North Dakota at Fort Buford, upriver from the town of Williston at the Lake Sakajawea (there are a variety of spellings for this woman's name and one seems to be as accurate as another) reservoir, with the lower twenty miles of the river forming a narrow arm of the reservoir. At the confluence with the Missouri, the Yellowstone is actually the larger river. The river was explored in 1806 by William Clark during the return voyage of the Lewis and Clark Expedition, and the Clark's Fork of the river was named for him. The Clark's Fork collects drainage from the south side of the Beartooth Mountains, runs eastward through Wyoming, and then turns north to run through Clark, Wyoming, Belfry and Bridger, Montana, and several other towns before joining up with the main river near Billings, Montana. Clark's Fork (of the Yellowstone) should not be confused with the Clark Fork River that flows through Missoula in the western part of the state and is a tributary of the Columbia River.

The Yellowstone River was an important highway of transportation for Indians as well as for white settlers traveling by riverboat in the latter half of the nineteenth century. In Montana, it has been used extensively for irrigation for over 140 years. In its upper reaches, within Yellowstone Park then on downriver as far as the confluence with the Clark's Fork the river is considered one of the finest fly-fishing streams in the world. This includes the famous spring creeks of the Paradise Valley—DePuy's, Armstrong, Nelson's—that draw the celebrated, powerful and hopelessly addicted to fly-fishing among us from all over the world.

♦ ♦ ♦

Near the Yellowstone River's confluence with the Missouri are the sandstone bluffs that inspired American Indians to name the river "Yellow rock" or Yellowstone. That is also where William Clark reunited with Meriwether Lewis following his separate exploration of the river.

The Yellowstone is unique among rivers. It has been spared the fate of most other rivers in the U.S. Except for irrigation diversions, it is still undammed. In fact, it's the longest free-flowing river in the lower 48 states. The river has had its defenders since at least the 1920s, when irrigators downstream wanted to dam the river at its outlet from Yellowstone Lake. No doubt because of the then new Yellowstone Park's unique status as the world's first, lovers of the river found their cause supported by early environmentalists throughout the United States.

The 1970s brought further threats to the river. Efforts to impound the Yellowstone's waters behind a dam at Allenspur Gap, near Livingston, were turned aside when Montanans chose the Yellowstone's world-class trout fishery over the needs of coal-generating plants, the heart-stopping beauty of Paradise Valley over the desires of irrigators, and a free-flowing Yellowstone over the demands of flood control.

♦ ♦ ♦

From the first time I saw Yellowstone Park and the Paradise Valley in 1964, and every time since, I was in love with a land that is so far beyond anything I've ever seen anywhere else—the thermal features, the unspoiled forests, the pristine rivers, streams and lakes, the wildlife that includes grizzlies, elk, bison, pronghorn antelope and bald and golden eagles. The Greater Yellowstone Ecosystem (GYE) is unlike any other in the world. Development has always been a threat to the wild, free form nature of the West—gated communities, golf courses, ski resorts and the like threaten ranching, destroy wildlife habitat, disrupt wildlife migrations and compromise natural processes such as fire. The GYE is no exception when it comes to these dire problems. The Greater Yellowstone has the world's largest elk herd, the world's largest free-roaming bison herd and the world's greatest concentration of bighorn sheep. Grizzlies, wolves, along with the elusive wolverine and lynx are also found here. Because of all of this natural abundance and wonder many citizens in Montana and world-wide are actively involved in trying to preserve and even enhance the GYE.

I first moved to Livingston from Whitefish in 1996. The following spring saw the river rise well above flood stage. Standing above the Yellowstone, watching it roar and swirl with whirlpools, enormous standing waves and wicked riffs of current that carried away one-hundred-foot pines like they were twigs was awe inspiring, frightening. Landowners along the river, fearing that this immense power would wash away much of their lands, requested an unprecedented number of permits from the Army Corps of Engineers to build flood control structures along the river's banks. These concrete and stone structures, meant to stabilize the riverbank, appear to have unintended negative effects on the riparian or stream bank habitat, causing, in the words of the Greater Yellowstone Coalition (GYC) a "steady and rapid erosion of the natural qualities of the river."

A recent study by Montana Fish, Wildlife and Parks confirmed that trout populations had dropped nearly 60 percent in the most extensively rip-rapped sections of the river. Concerned over these losses and over the possibility that, because of a lack of planning, the structures could actually cause worse flooding downstream, the GYC and four other groups have filed suit to enjoin the Corps of Engineers from granting further permits until the effects of "canalizing" the river could be studied fully. In May 2000, a U.S. District Court judge ruled that the Corps had fallen short of its obligation to protect the river.

The Yellowstone has been named by the conservation group, American Rivers, as number five on its list of America's ten most endangered rivers. The Sierra Club's Kris Prinzing said that the Yellowstone is the "last river in America that Lewis and Clark would still recognize." Another couple of hours at this group's website proved this to me over and over again. During the winter of 2005–2006, out of the 4,900 bison in the park in the fall, close to 900 of them were killed by the Park Service or the Department of Livestock this winter. Another eighty-seven calves were permanently removed from the herd for research. The controversy over these bison is between the livestock industry, which wants to keep the bison numbers as low as possible and inside Yellowstone fearing an outbreak of brucellosis, and wildlife advocates like the GYC who support managing bison like other wildlife that migrate outside the park.

The GYC would like the Bison Management Plan amended to include: separation of bison and cattle by, among other things, improved fencing procedures and retiring current grazing allotments. In what the group terms the "North American model," sportsmen help wildlife officials manage wildlife populations through carefully designed hunts. Sportsmen by their very nature have always been champions of conservation and revenues from hunting licenses used to aid in this preservation are substantial. In Montana, big game species such as elk, moose, bighorn sheep, mountain goats, mountain lions and bears are hanging on in part because their habitat and conservation is supported by hunting.

♦ ♦ ♦

As can be seen by the above-mentioned issues, problems and contro- versy swirl within the Yellowstone River drainage like a mad whirlpool. How these issues ultimately are resolved will decide the fate of the river for centuries to come, and possibly serve as a model for similar disputes and contentions along other rivers.

Chapter 1

Gliding Through Paradise
Carbella to Mayor's Landing—46 miles

THIS IS THE HEIGHT OF SUMMER, LATE JULY AND THE UPPER Yellowstone running through the Paradise Valley is packed with rafts, drift boats, truck tire inner tubes looking like faded-black sausages, canoes like the one we're in and assorted other craft ranging from camouflaged duck boats to a large blue, green and white inflated plastic whale carrying a man wearing a Yankees cap, Bermuda shorts and nothing else and trailing a floating cooler filled with Tecate beer, the red of the cans unmistakable. There is also a listing log raft with Huckleberry Finn overtones spinning moribund in a near-shore eddy. Warm weather life on the river.

The reason for the appearance of this chaotic, serpentine armada is that grasshoppers are out in abundance, their numbers matching in apparent proportion the hatch of out-of-state and Montana anglers—people like myself who can't resist the marvelous fishing. Large trout—browns, Yellowstone cutthroat and rainbows—are smashing the hapless insects as they crash land with audible "splats" near grassy banks. Hayfields are being harvested for a second cut and the hoppers are fleeing the reapers as though their lives may be at stake, which they are. The fish are having a field day and one chunky eighteen-inch brown I bring to net is so full of grasshoppers that when I lift him some from the water by the belly several of the creatures are disgorged alive and kicking.

Even with the crowds, including plenty of individuals flinging live hoppers, patterns like Dave's and Joe's hopper and spin fishermen lobbing shiny lures representing nightmare visions of the large insects, roaming this stretch of the river is a blast. The Absaroka Mountains

1

dominate the eastern skyline in a series of rough-hewn peaks, ridgelines and deep canyons that stretch far into wilderness country before rising and curving out of view. The fishing is excellent. Great. Superb. Nearly every cast brings one or more fish to the surface in violent, slashing attacks. Ginny and I have caught dozens of trout from a foot to more than twenty-inches long using a pattern I've tied that looks something like a hopper on acid with yellow-gold dubbing and grizzly hackle for the body with a tuft of red yarn aft, turkey primary feathers for wings and brown hackle at the head. The more mangled and distressed the fly becomes the more the larger trout like it. We could do this for hours, days, weeks.

The island we plan to camp on is barely visible downstream about a mile away—gravel, rock, sand, some dense patches of scrub willow and alder and lots of beached cottonwood and pine trunks and limbs looking like carcasses left behind from a long ago battle between massive enemies. We put in at mid-morning near Carbella just below the rough water of Yankee Jim Canyon. We could do the fifty-mile float down to the Ninth Street Bridge in Livingston in two days easy or even one if we pushed hard, but we're taking a leisurely three-day cruise to enjoy the country, the fishing and the outrageous Montana summer that makes the cold, dark of winter a near-lost memory.

Despite all of the human traffic we've seen plenty of deer, a fox, a couple of raccoons, plenty of bald and golden eagles, red-tailed hawks, a skunk skulking along the bank near a bustling campground full of brightly-colored tents and happy campers building fires, cutting themselves with knives and axes while guzzling beer and cheap wine (the labels are clearly visible in the bright light of a truthful day)—the good life in full regalia. There have been a plenty of beavers along the way and their large stick, limb and mud lodges tucked away in calm backwaters not far from spinning, foam-flecked eddies.

And I'm always amazed and pleased at the way this section of the river holds up from a trout-population perspective, despite the non-stop fishing pressure and the environmental threats, particularly to the native Yellowstone cutthroat.

◆ ◆ ◆

Cutthroat trout have always been one of my favorite game fish. Their mixture of silvers, black spotting, shadings of golden orange ranging to crimson with aquamarine backs and the characteristic bright orange-red slashes on their lower jaws makes for a sparkling visual sense of wonder as they thrash a river's surface beneath a bright sun. There a number of varieties of cutthroat, but the two that I am most familiar with are the westslope and the Yellowstone. The westslope's range is along the west side of the divide. The trout, like all cutthroat, thrives in the clearest, coldest of rivers, mountain streams and lakes. The beauty of this is that these waters all lie in some of the most spectacular country in North America.

The Yellowstone cutthroat trout also prefers these waters and the upper stretches of the Yellowstone down all the way to Reed Point along with all of the tributaries in this stretch are prime habitat. Of all of the fish species in the upper river, no other more exemplifies or seems to represent its native habitat than the Yellowstone. The colors, the shape, just the feeling I get when I catch one vibrate with the resonance of the Yellowstone River drainage.

A member of the *Salmonidae* family, Yellowstone cutthroat trout were historically the most common and well distributed native trout in and around present day Yellowstone National Park. The origin and evolution of the Yellowstone cutthroat is associated with the Columbia River basin side of the Continental Divide and the Snake River system. The crossing of the divide and the establishment of the species in the headwaters of the Yellowstone River drainage occurred around 6,000 to 8,000 years ago, after glacial ice left the Yellowstone Plateau, and the waters became habitable to fish and other aquatic life.

Biologists estimate that Yellowstone cutts historically occupied 17,397 miles of habitat, ranging from the waters of the Snake River drainage (Columbia River basin) upstream from Shoshone Falls, Idaho, to the Yellowstone River drainage (Missouri River basin), including the Tongue River in eastern Montana, with small areas in northern Utah and Nevada.

Today this has shrunk to 1,300 stream miles, or around 17 percent of historically occupied habitat, a frightening loss of habitat.

The introduction of non-native species that include brook, brown, lake and rainbow trout, the loss of habitat through logging, mining and development and the invasion of disease such as whirling disease all threaten the survival of the Yellowstone cutthroat.

In 1994 lake trout were found in Yellowstone Lake. Biologists believe that the species was illegally introduced twenty-five years ago (bucket planting is the common euphemism here referring to days many years ago when anglers would carry their favorite game fish in tin buckets to their favorite water and dump them in hoping to create a new fishery). Lake trout are voracious feeders on other fish and the Yellowstone cutthroat is no exception. Officials are now gillnetting the trout and encouraging anglers to keep as many lake trout as they catch in hopes of diminishing the population. This is all part of Yellowstone Park's attempts to restore its waters back to native species that primarily include the Yellowstone cutt, grayling, and mountain whitefish. Many fly fishers oppose the plans to remove non-native species like brown, rainbow and brook. The Park's goal is an ambitious one, but reports and my personal experiences over the past few years indicate that it is making progress, albeit slowly.

In 1998, *Myxobolus cerebralis,* a microscopic parasite that causes whirling disease, was found in Yellowstone cutthroat trout. The parasite was introduced from Europe through shipments of frozen fish in the 1950s. Reports from the Teton River in eastern Idaho and from Yellowstone Lake and its tributaries indicate significant declines in populations, to the point of a complete loss of a fishery at Pelican Creek. The disease is easily transported between stream systems, mostly by other wildlife species such as pelicans, and by anglers. There is no known effective way of dealing with whirling disease, and a number of others that may make dramatic impacts on fish populations.

◆ ◆ ◆

Between drought, floods and temperature extremes, early settlers were faced with choices regarding their homes and livelihoods that determined if they and their families would perish or prosper. Nowhere was that early pragmatism more evident than the choices made in riverside development in the Yellowstone Valley. With a few exceptions, these pioneers avoided placing their homes or businesses in areas where the next high water would wipe out all that they had worked for. Experiencing just a single flood during spring runoff is sufficient to understand the power of the river, the destruction it is capable of and the foolishness of building along the river's floodplain.

Recently, increasing numbers of homes and businesses are placed in harm's way along the Yellowstone. This seemingly fatalistic development along the floodplain is putting a growing number of lives and properties at risk during the Yellowstone's floods. Current floodplain development regulations do not sufficiently protect lives and property. What is needed is a rational approach to floodplain development that incorporates both voluntary economic incentives and clear regulatory guidelines.

A 2002 poll commissioned by the GYC and Montana Smart Growth Coalition found that 83 percent of residents in Beaverhead, Carbon, Gallatin and Park Counties supported limiting development in areas that are vulnerable to floods or forest fires in order to protect life and property, while only 12 percent opposed such restrictions.

Personally I would like to see a 500-year flood event that would wipe out all of the garish trophy homes littering the Yellowstone floodplain (and all other rivers in Montana). Not that I wish for any loss of life, and I certainly hope know that these careless home owners have adequate insurance.

♦ ♦ ♦

Aside from bison no other mammal has had a greater impact on the exploration and settling of the Yellowstone region than the beaver. Trappers with traders hot on their heels explored every river and side drainage, no matter how small, in search of beavers and their valuable pelts. This all began two centuries ago and ran wildly until the numbers of the animals begin to decline rapidly around the middle of the nineteenth century.

Over the years I've had countless experiences with beavers on the lakes of northern Ontario, in the Upper Peninsula of Michigan, Wisconsin, Colorado and many, many times in Montana.

I almost stepped on a submerged one as I tried to leap-frog across a Yellowstone River tributary. The animal was as large as a Springer spaniel. I was surprised and leaped backwards to the muddy bank. The beaver smacked his tail on the stream's surface and raced in full panic downstream.

Beavers are best known for their natural trait of building dams in rivers and streams, and building their lodges in the eventual pond. They are the second-largest rodent in the world, after the capybara.

The rodents continue to grow throughout life. Adult specimens weighing over 55 lb are not uncommon, larger by a number of pounds than the one on which I almost stepped. While often a nuisance, this dam building also provides a venue for new wetlands to form over the years as eutrophication (the natural evolution of a lake into marsh land and finally grassland and/or forest through siltation) occurs. Wetlands provide key habitat for countless animals including waterfowl, songbirds, deer, bats, amphibians, fur bearers like raccoons and mink, damsel and dragonflies and so on. Abandoned ponds provide habitat for numerous species including owls, hawks and reptiles. Most of us think that the damage their natural behavior causes is far outweighed by this fact.

The beaver's ability to build dams almost overnight is astounding. They do this to provide habitat, to safely access food sources such as the sweet bark of willows and alders, and I sometimes think out of some neurotic urge to keep busy. On a favorite trout stream not far from Livingston, I returned one fine fall day to fish for brown trout after an absence of two weeks. Rounding a cottonwood and aspen-lined bend, the trees already flaming orange and gold in their fall coloration, the river seemed different, changed. Looking upstream and to my left, I saw why. Beavers had built a dam of sticks, logs, and mud more than six feet tall blocking the entrance of a small creek. Clambering up and around the sturdy structure I looked over the top and saw an impoundment that must have been three or four acres. It was full of brown trout. Little ones, Medium-sized ones and some cruising big boys. They attacked my madly-cast bugger as though they hadn't eaten in weeks. Fishing that was just too easy so I exercised a modicum of restraint and quit after three hours. The browns then switched over to small mayflies (*callibaetis*?) and I bushwhacked back down to the river. All of this change took place in just fourteen days, the time I last fished here. Amazing.

I've talked to ranchers who were forced to hire trappers to rid their land of beavers because the animals dam building had flooded fields, barn yards and even the basements of their homes. I've seen the animals' dams dynamited and come back a month later to discover an even grander structure in place. Along the river in Livingston it seems like small cottonwoods and willows are gnawed down in the dark every night.

Beavers used to drive me crazy when I was fishing. There would be times on the river when large browns were lined up beneath grassy banks like marauding wolves as they fed voraciously on wind-blown grasshoppers that blew into the water from adjacent hayfields. Just as I would be about to make a cast to the first trout on the downstream end of the feeding pack a beaver would appear near the fish and slap his tail on the river's surface in alarm and warning to others of his kind. This turned me manic until finally with the passage of time I realized that this was merely another manifestation of the arcane humor bestowed upon me by the fish gods. Being the Zen master that has proven to be my destiny, I accepted things as they were and moved on mumbling "Form is emptiness. Emptiness is form" or maybe it was "Viva Wrigley Field!" Now I laugh and acknowledge the fact that the rivers are the beavers' home and I'm nothing more than an interloper, a mere tourist.

Beavers were almost trapped to extinction in Montana during the first the nineteenth century, but as anyone who lives along the Yellowstone will tell you, they're back. Big time.

♦ ♦ ♦

In the area surrounding where I live in Livingston no single issue has caused as much debate, anger, confusion and overall insanity as the shooting of bison that wander from Yellowstone Park and cross over into private land in the Paradise.

Those opposed to the shooting of the bison say that the animals were here first and have a right to roam as they please and that killing any animal is just plain wrong. Those in favor of the hunt, mainly ranchers, say that the roaming animals destroy fence lines and other property, graze down land meant for beef cattle and carry the threat of brucellosis. No one is really giving an inch so far in this acrimonious confrontation that has at times led to fistfights and may grow into something far more sinister and violent.

Bison, by nature, wander vast distances in search of food as the seasons spin around us. Containing them within the Park is probably impossible. Ranchers, who raise the cattle that provide the steaks for so many of us, raise legitimate concerns, concerns about issues that may curtail their way of making a living and ultimately destroy western tradition, romance and a large segment of the economy. What? No more dude ranches? Bison once ranged from the eastern seaboard to Oregon and California; from Great Slave Lake in northern Alberta to northern Mexico. I've seen hundreds of the animals on my trips to the Northwest Territories. Larger than their southern brethren due to the cold climate, the bison leisurely graze along rough dirt and rock roads or drift ghostlike through the boreal forest.

Population estimates of the peak numbers of bison range from 25–70 million. William Hornaday, a naturalist who spent considerable time in the West, both before and during the most severe years of the slaughter, comments on the seemingly infinite bison population and the impossibility of estimating their quantity: "It would have been as easy to count or to estimate the number of leaves in a forest as to calculate the number of buffaloes living at any given time during the history of the species previous to 1870."

The growing middle and upper classes had a nearly insatiable appetite for beef, and the post Civil War economic boom gave them the buying power to satisfy it. Texas alone could not feed the demand. In response ranchers turned to the western plains, a vast area that had already demonstrated its ability to sustain large and healthy populations of ungulates.

As these ranchers moved in with their enormous herds of cattle, the need to extirpate both the bison and Indian become obvious to all of those greedy for the profits the protein-rich grasses of the high plains promised. The establishment of reservations was an attempt to confine the Indians from their natural movements, centered, like and because of the bison, on the seasons.

White settlers wished to imposed the ways of living they'd grown accustomed to back East on this wild unsettled land. This included the elimination of the herds of bison that often were so large they took days to pass by. But to the Indian the bison was the ultimate resource. It provided not only food, clothing, and shelter but nearly every material need. Plains Indians depended on the bison for their existence, their religions were centered around the buffalo. This interdependence between Indian and buffalo is exemplified in the words of John Fire Lame Deer. He was born in 1906 on the Rosebud Reservation in South Dakota and died in 1976:

> The buffalo gave us everything we needed. Without it we were nothing. Our tipis were made of his skin. His hide was our bed, our blanket, our winter coat. It was our drum, throbbing through the night, alive, holy. Out of his skin we made our water bags. His flesh strengthened us, became flesh of our flesh. Not the smallest part of it was wasted. His stomach, a red-hot stone dropped into it, became our soup kettle. His horns were our spoons, the bones our knives, our women's awls and needles. Out of his sinews we made our bowstrings and thread. His ribs were fashioned into sleds for our children, his hoofs became rattles. His mighty skull, with the pipe leaning against it, was our sacred altar. The name of the greatest of all Sioux was Tatanka Iyotake—Sitting Bull. When you killed off the buffalo you also killed the Indian—the real, natural, "wild" Indian.

In the 1870s, more buffalo were killed than in any other decade in history. The three years of 1872, '73 and '74 were the worst. According to one buffalo hunter, who based his calculations on first-hand accounts and shipping records, 4.5 million buffalo were slaughtered in that 3-year period alone.

Influenced by forces discussed above, the U.S. government pursued a policy to eradicate the buffalo and thereby extinguish the Indians' very sustenance, forcing them onto reservations. The following speech, recounted by John Cook—a buffalo hunter, was delivered by General Phil Sheridan to the Texas legislature in 1875. The legislature, as the story goes, was discussing a bill to protect the buffalo when the General took the floor in opposition:

> These men have done more in the last two years, and will do more in the next year, to settle the vexed Indian question, than the entire regular army has done in the last forty years. They are destroying the Indians' commissary. And it is a well known fact that an army losing its base of supplies is placed at a great disadvantage. Send them powder and lead, if you will; but for a lasting peace, let them kill, skin, and sell until the buffaloes are exterminated. Then your prairies can be covered with speckled cattle.

This testimony, spoken by an Army leader in the Indian wars, spells it out: The buffalo and the Indian were in the way of civilization's onslaught. Kill the buffalo and not only would the Indian wars be won, but the vast tracks of public land would be opened for cattle.

◆ ◆ ◆

The Ponderosa pine is the state tree. Often well over one-hundred feet tall with trunks several feet in diameter, the Ponderosa is not just majestic, it's regal as it holds sway over the land. Walking through and beneath large stands of them at our dry camp—no water nearby, so you bring your own in—is peaceful, almost surreal and a bit humbling when one considers that some of these trees have been growing since before Lewis and Clark. The sound of a soft afternoon breeze slipping through long green needles is intoxicating. The rough, thick rust-colored bark glows softly. As the sun lowers in the west all of those needles turn the golden light a radiant emerald that deepens as the suns colors move through stages of orange, crimson and then the final burst of quicksilver.

Pinus ponderosa, Western Yellow Pine, Western Red, Ponderosa Pine—the Ponderosa has a long list of names. Still the tree will always be Ponderosa to me. I've hunted Merriam's turkeys hunkered down beneath one during a freak May snow storm. (If you're ever up eastern Montana way and the day is in the eighties and the northern lights blow the sky away later on, pack your gear and head for hard road. Winter is making a madman's slight return. A lunatic blizzard is riding down on you. I've learned this from days-at-a-time snowed-in experience.) The tree kept me dry and broke the icy wind and I did shoot a big bird for an uncommon spring feast.

The power of the Ponderosa in a curious way can be far reaching. In what is now South Dakota, Lewis and Clark first observed the ponderosa cones that had floated that far on the currents of the Missouri River.

Today the tree may be found in most parts of western Montana. Its range includes the entire West, from the plains to the Pacific Coast. On the average the tree reaches maturity when 60 to 125 feet tall (about 150 years old) and approximately 20 to 30 inches in diameter. The largest Ponderosa pine on record live along the humid Pacific coast, where around 1870 John Muir measured a Ponderosa that was 220 feet tall and 8 feet in diameter. The largest I've ever seen were perhaps 150 feet tall and 5 feet thick.

I can think of so many things that symbolize Yellowstone country and the West in general—Yellowstone cutthroat, elk, open spaces, antelope, grizzlies, cottonwoods, mountain peaks—but the Ponderosa has no peer in this land.

♦ ♦ ♦

What first drew me to the upper Yellowstone almost forty years ago was the legendary fly fishing for large rainbows and browns. I'd read articles and books about this and heard stories from my grandmother, who loved to fly fish and had fished all over the world since the late 1920s. Places like Norway, Alaska, northern Canada, the West back when fly fishing was considered by the few who even knew about the esoteric and arcane pursuit as something practiced by those who were at best eccentric but more likely mad. The more I fished here the more I learned about the hatches, an obvious key to successful angling.

The Yellowstone is open to fishing all year, and except for the dead of winter and during spring runoff offers good options for the angler. In February, as days lengthen and warm, fish become more active. Nymph fishing works well in deeper water along to riffles. Trout are still using the insulation of the deeper water and saving energy. Midges will start to appear during this time creating some dry fly action. Midge clusters, midge emergers and small parachutes can work well. A midge pupae just a few inches below a dry may work on trout feeding just below the surface. Foam lines and back eddies normally hold quantities of insects blasted into them by the area's strong and common winds. Rainbows become active prior to spawning and can be caught in riffles and runs with attractor nymphs. March through runoff, which is around the first of May, is one of the best times to fly fish on the Yellowstone. The midges and nymph fishing continues, but around the end of March and first of April, baetis will begin to appear. These are blue wing olives in the #16–18 range. The hatch seems to progress along the Yellowstone. Parachute Adams or BWOs with black or white wings help the angler follow the fly in tough visibility situations created by flat light or glare from the sun. When wade fishing to a pod of trout, smaller, imitative flies, such as small Elk hair caddis, that seem to mimic about anything in my experience and emergers will work. The greatly under-appreciated and little-used soft hackles fly imitates active nymphs and when allowed to swing below and out from the angler can be most effective. I've often tied three along the last few feet of the leader, the first two as droppers and sometimes have had three eager trout hooked at once a few times, though through a prodigious exercise in skill and delicacy I always manage to snap the leader above the fish. March Browns also appear and dwarf smaller insects.

Around the end of April, the famous Mother's Day Caddis Hatch will occur. Actually if you are there Mother's Day, take Mom to dinner because you are too late. This hatch of brachycentrus-cased caddis can be amazing. During my thirteen years in Livingston, I've managed to hit this one only three times when the caddis were present and the water wasn't a roiling, turbid mess carrying entire trees, small sheds, rusting Buicks and the like far downstream for destinations only imagined. The number of caddis on the water and whirring through the air is amazing. They are often thick outside our home six blocks from the river. I live and die by Elk Hair caddis and a size fourteen in brown or tan works just fine. Before the hatch begins the trout work on the nymphs. Hare's Ears do the job here. In the mornings a Glass House Caddis pupae of Prince Nymph will fool fish feeding on drifting larvae. The late Gary LaFontaine's sparkle pupa and emergers have caught a lot of big trout for me. Runoff usually ends around mid-July, and depending on the year salmon-flies coincide with the rivers clearing. Around Livingston and Paradise Valley fishing rubber leg nymphs is the most productive fishing, while on the upper Valley to Gardner there is more dry fly fishing. Accurate casts into the willows can be more important than the exact fly. Stimulators are good choices. At this same time, golden stones, Yellow Sallies (small golden stones) and caddis are present, also. In some sections of river the smaller flies will work better, and these hatches will be there long after the salmonflies are gone. Yellow Sallies and Elk hairs are sound choices.

A number of mayflies hatch on the Yellowstone through the summer months. Pale Morning Duns to large Grey and Green Drakes are seen on specific stretches of the river. Parachutes or Wulffs in #12–16 work for searching likely-looking places.

Grasshoppers are a summertime tradition. Patterns are up to the individual and his or her own esoteric even arcane tastes. I just tie something with a yellow body, scarlet tuft of tail, brown turkey primary feather for wings and brown hackle. The rattier the better. Late June through mid-September is the season. Casting the bugs so they ricochet off banks or splat on the surface attracts the trout who can be anywhere in the river depending on the number of hoppers and the strength of the wind.

Large brown stoneflies are also found on the Yellowstone at this time. A Foam Wing Hopper or a Parachute Hopper are good imitations of both. Woolly buggers, always woolly buggers in my angling life, will turn large fishing before surface activity begins. Bank-tight casts and rapid, medium-length strips are needed.

Fall fishing begins around the middle of September. Baetis are key players, especially along bank-side runs, riffles and slow spinning eddies. A seven or eight-weight nine-foot rod with a seven-foot 1x leader tippet is my setup. I use brown, weighted woolly buggers palmered with Cree hackle and a medium piece of shot clipped on at the head. I have a strange, perhaps twisted, aversion to beadhead patterns, and I like the action created by the slight separation of the weight from the bugger.

The weather this time of year is often gorgeous and the surroundings are divine. The Absaroka, Crazy and Bridger mountains rising severely along the horizon. Cottonwoods going madly yellow. The intensity brought on by a barely perceived compression of time created by winter waiting impatiently up above the border in Canada along with fewer anglers turns this into a special time of the year.

♦ ♦ ♦

Another dozen trout are taken before making the island. We beach the canoe, haul all of our gear and goods well back from the water to a sandy rise where we set up camp next to a modest, well-used fire ring. Tent, cooking and gear storage areas are established and within thirty minutes a small fire is going, steaks are seasoned. Ginny and I recline against a smooth, grey cottonwood trunk. A steady but diminishing stream of anglers drifts past. The browning grasslands of covering alluvial fans that poured out from Absaroka canyons lead smoothly to steeper slopes covered in dense pine forest then sheer granite cliffs and sway-backed escarpments connecting ragged peaks and finally a darkening blue sky.

We enjoy the view comfortable in the easy silence that comes from countless days sharing good country together. We are comfortable on this river that is so much a part of our home that waits for us only a couple of dozen miles downriver.

Chapter 2

Out Into The Open
Mayor's Landing to Big Timber—39 miles

> …every water is the same water coming round. Everyday someone
> is standing on the edge of this river, staring into time, whispering
> mistakenly: only here. Only now.
> — From *The Mississippi Empties Into The Gulf* by Lucille Clifton

THE RIVER FLOWS RIGHT BEHIND TOWN WITH POWERFUL ELEGANCE, heading toward the immense caldera south of here just beyond Paradise aiming towards the Missouri free flowing for hundreds of miles not damned, yet. This river is a mirror for a town with wild character. A nexus for drifters, loners, ranchers, rails, drunks and worse—writers—and the stream keeps going regardless of all this and more. Mayflies, stoneflies, caddis, cutthroat, browns, rainbows, whitefish, geese, ducks, cranes, eagles, deer, beaver, moose, bear.

The cool water sweeps along easy bends through warming spring days, sizzling thunderstorms, buffeting winds. The swelled stream levels rise like hell during runoff slamming against levees, soaking Sacajewea Park, shrinking islands, piling up deadfalls and sweepers, until calmed by mid-summer's long days of heat that slows all this down—not the momentum only the amount of water. This diminishment brings on an armada of dapperly clad sports flogging the river with flies more vainly than not in hopes of fooling large fish, all of this herded along by too many guides chasing too little money for the wrong reasons through autumn. Finally the process turns back in on itself when winter blasts home from the Canadian north locking the current up for the year, like a tired vagrant who's lost all sense of purpose, in thick anchor ice, narrowly channeling the remaining flow through the dark months before the circle spins round once again.

Livingston is a place of many personalities—railroad, ranching, small town, tourist destination, home to boozers and drugged-out wastrels, hideout for crazies, and if nothing else, is old-time fly fishing personified. Still a small reminder of a period when eccentricity and casting artfully to trout went hand-in-hand like new lovers. The town is the center of the western world when it comes to fly fishing. All the big boys come here, have been here, even Tiger Woods, a few presidents, and Hollywood types. Forget about Jackson, West Yellowstone, Manchester, anywhere in Colorado. Drift boats are parked in alleys, on front yards, packed along streets like cabs in New York at rush hour. Guides, outfitters, fly shop owners bump into each other on every corner searching madly for misplaced clients who have usually found themselves in a bar tossing down shots and gabbing about fish yet to be caught. There's a museum (though Colorado money wants to move this venue down its way) for this once arcane pursuit now spun big business just down the street. In the warm months, peak time, out-of-state fly fishers cluster along the streets like a blizzard hatch of whirling caddis or perhaps spinning mayflies—Vermont, Texas, Maine, Wisconsin, Washington, California—of course, Japan, England, Germany, Tasmania, Alberta—of course, even Key West (foreign enough). Restaurants are filled in season with individuals clad in waders, bonefish scrubs, vests, weird hats, Stetsons adorned with pheasant skins, elk horns, Montana vanity license plates, air horns, plasma TVs, whatever. The fish are all over the place—up in the Park, in the river, in lakes, cruising drainage ditches within one-hundred miles. There are so many quality streams that learning all of them would take several lifetimes, lots of flies, plenty of gas, a nothing job like mine—"*Keyboard for hire, have own camera, works cheap.*"

Like any northern high plains town, there are quite a few bars here. Some have the expected names like The Mint and Stockman's. And then there are a few others like The Owl, where the former owner, Dana, made an honest drink at a fair price, a place gone to youth and no style. And the always constant and debauched Murray. Sometimes I'll wander in here during the weekday afternoons. Especially on a burning hot, forest fire smoky August day when few people are on the streets and I have the place mostly to myself. I'll work on a couple of beers or maybe a brace of

Beams. This is the best time for me, before other writers and such stroll in to have their cocktail-hour belts and tell worn out stories to worn out friends. And then there's the Murray's wall of fame. Many dozens of photos of local crazies, famous and otherwise, hanging from the walls, including me right next to one of the real writers, Peter Bowen. (The guy doesn't talk about doing a book. He does it and like many of us he isn't getting rich at it.) Maybe a poker machine chatters away, maybe some pool balls click against one another. This is well before things begin to get locally loony with a naive mix of out-of-towners thrown in for grins. Not my style and a couple of nights I've seen things going down here, literally defying explanation, actions that don't deserve description due to their base nature. Like I said, not my style—anymore. Much too cool and adult for such behavior, and it's not my time of day-night. There are others, but the Murray works for me And sometimes, so does the Stockman's, though not often. But what the hell, for the very few times I wander into one, a bar's a bar.

So naturally because of the wind-blown irresponsible pace of the western terrain, nearly every high plains town's has one of these—a drinker's bar. A place for professional slammers to slouch and kill off a morning, an afternoon, a night, a lifetime. This one's called The Mint. This version is no better or worse than all the others around the state. Somewhat dark, dullish neon, long wooden bar, mirror back, scarred linoleum floor, jukebox, gaming machines, pool table, booths, opens early, closes late. The usual stuff drawing the expected crowd of local hard-core drinkers who pass the dragging, near-dead moments working on draughts, shots, shooters, red beers, while smoking steady chains of cigarettes as they talk about all of it over and over, day after day, rain or shine, wind or snow...or both. The place smells of booze, Mr. Clean, drunkenness, some sad happiness. There's a lot of disappointment, traces of loss, tragedy and desiccated dreams. Yeah, every town's got one. Killed my share of time in plenty of them.

By late March I'm wading some of the waters not far from home with only a passing interest in catching anything, just happy to have sur-vived another winter. For now I'm wandering along killing time with sandhill cranes. We clack and chatter back and forth with each other, our necks craning for a better view. This silliness rattles onward for all but the coldest days of the year. One early-spring morning along the Yellowstone behind home I spotted a drift boat wedged among the rocks in fast water, partially submerged, abandoned, wrecked—a March outing gone astray with a lone Budweiser beer bottle still in its holder. Another year of angling madness makes an early appearance.

♦ ♦ ♦

The hypnotic fascination of wild, pulsating water thundering eastward carrying downed trees, parts of streamside structures and a hapless deer to certain death is overpowering and frightening on this warm day in early June. Many feet of last winter's snow is still piled up in the alpine country of the Absaroka, Bridger and Crazy mountains that frame Livingston to the south, north and east. Obviously much more water and higher river levels are on the way from up on high.

Strolling along the levee that runs along Sacajawea Park on the south side of town the pull of all of this roiling, churning muddy water is intoxicating, tempting me in the deadliest of ways and reminding me of Poe's short story "The Imp of the Perverse," a cautionary tale about humans' inability to stave off yielding to temptations that will do them serious, even lethal harm.

Standing waves several feet tall curl hump-backed along the rip rapped bank. Whirlpools spin fifty-foot tree trunks like matchsticks before sucking them from sight in a brown, frothy *whoosh,* only to see them shot out of the water like berserk Trident submarines a hundred yards down river. The water moves with such velocity and force that it draws the air with it rustling new green leaves and grasses in the process.

The pull is immense. I experience a crazed desire to jump into the river. Shades of Kesey's novel and the inspiration from "Good Night Irene" by Leadbelly—

"Sometimes I get a great notion

To jump into the river…an' drown."

And this urge feels oh-so-much like the first time I looked over the edge of the Hungry Horse Dam and its 500-foot dance through free-fall madness many years ago in northwest Montana. Some arcane force far beyond my comprehension called strongly and clearly to me to climb the ledge and leap into space for the insane joyride to the South Fork of the Flathead River a lifetime below me. The strength and the unknowable finality of that height and this river now in full spate as it rages madly with the freedom of spring runoff is nearly too much for me to resist. I shake my head and tilt away from the Yellowstone, regain composure, before continuing to walk with some trepidation a dozen feet above and back from the roaring current along the walkway.

This annual mayhem coupled with an eagerness bordering on manic frustration to begin floating the river from the upper Paradise Valley for more than 500 miles downstream to its confluence with the Missouri in North Dakota, to just begin working on this book, to be out in the fresh-air wildness of the drainage, all of this fuels a mixture of anxiety and futility. This is a trip—or rather series of trips—I've wanted to make and a book I've wanted to complete for years. I finally said enough pro-crastination and decided to make the leap. Patience is a virtue I have in meager supply, if at all, and none this year. I want to head down the Yellowstone to camp on isolated islands, drop down the rapids that run along Greycliffs and drift out onto the prairie to completely lose it with the coyotes and turkey vultures along the hard sage flats. All this is fantasy for now. The violence of all of this chilled chocolate water is the reality for today and at least the next few weeks.

I check the real time USGS stream flow data for the river several times a day. Have done so for a couple of weeks. Three-thousand cubic-feet-per-second (CFS). Then 4,500 cfs, 6,470 cfs, 8,390 cfs, 10,550 cfs and ever upward. Hope is not springing eternal here. It's drowned.

When will the flood end and the river recede to a level that I can negotiate with at least the illusion of confidence and safety? Late July? Mid-August? October?

Growing up in the Midwest gave me little preparation for spring runoff. The Rock River running south from Wisconsin into Illinois and the Mississippi River would rise a few feet, but it was always muddy all day, all year so any change went largely unnoticed by me and the carp. Kinnikinnick Creek that flowed beneath limestone bluffs below our home in the country would shout and roar diminutive-haystack-flourish for maybe a week, but that was the extent of the runoff festivities.

When I came out to Missoula, a long time ago, one robust June I expected to hit Rock Creek and the upper Clark Fork in their placid, clear blue magnificence, to cast delicate dry flies to eager rainbows, cut-throats and browns, to wade shallow riffles and work quiet pools. I was to be disappointed. All of the rivers and creeks were blown, blasted brown and overflowing their banks. The Bitterroot was a debris-filled mess. So was the Clark Fork. Rock Creek and the Blackfoot were disasters.

Out of desperation and perhaps latent intuitiveness I stopped into Streamside Anglers one morning back when the then small shop was located along the Clark Fork just east of the Holiday Inn. It was an eccentric but honest place back in those peaceful times when Missoula was a small mountain/college/pulp mill town and not the chaotic madness that it proudly exhibits today. The establishment was noted for its gigantic iron sculpture of a Royal Wulff fly mounted on the roof above the door and a small trout pond with circulating water and a few fish located in one corner of the shop.

As I walked in, the owner, Glenn West, was busy tying something that looked like a small butterfly and taking sips from a bottle of Jack Daniels. A bushy-haired, bearded man sat across the counter from West talking about entomology and helping drain the Jack. I was soon to learn that this guy was Harmon Henkin, author of books on fishing tackle, wry essays on our curious avocation, book reviews, a novel titled *Crisscross* and political commentaries—a fine friend who died some years back in a car accident. Within an hour we were all cruising on the whiskey, with another bottle and a six pack of Rainier appearing as if by some secret form of collective prestidigitation. Three free-form crazies babbling away like old friends—the spontaneous comradeship that was once fly fishing but now has nearly vanished in what has become an industry-driven hustle instead of a sporting way of life.

Diatribes be damned and back to the matter at hand.

I explained my disappointment with the out-of-sorts water conditions. Both of them glanced at each other and exchanged knowing smiles.

Glenn said, "Spend the next few weeks in here with us shooting the breeze. A little of the whiskey and some useless conversation will help pass the time until the water is right again. Harmon can teach you about the bugs that make our life interesting. Beats staring at the river right now."

I did just that, showing up far more often than not, getting to know both Glenn and Harmon along the sodden way. Talking with them was a graduate course in fly fishing. I learned nuance, artifice and lore in a few weeks that would have taken years to discover on my own. Harmon helped me pick out my first cane rod, a beautiful piece of fired Tonkin cane that still glows red-brown in the Montana sun. Those were glorious days that moved seamlessly into an even more pleasant summer and fall. Glenn eventually landed an enormous rainbow along the Interstate in the Clark Fork up by Turah with his butterfly concoction, I actually caught a few trout over twelve inches, we all became friends, and I learned a little bit about the fine art of patience and waiting out the floods of spring.

So where is that restraint now? Seems like this useful quality should be present in great quantities considering all of the confusions, delays and disappointments I've experienced over the ensuing decades in the not-so-magical realms of writing, romance and acquiring a vast fortune—experience equaling at least a battered semblance of wisdom, perhaps.

Not so in my latest pathetic waltz with spring meltdown.

Runoff. Damn runoff. Drives me crazy every year. The angst and restlessness of this natural condition never seems to go away or even diminish. The condition feels significantly worse this time around, like nothing I've ever experienced before and bearing no resemblance to that…

…relatively halcyon period in early June of 1997 when I drove past Butte, south and west up through the Big Hole and on down to the Bitterroot River to spend a few weeks with a long-time friend of mine. He'd called one night and said in his always optimistic voice, "Holt, come on down and ride out the flood with me. You can still get across Tana Creek to the lodge," he said. "I've got cases of Henry Weinhardt's root beer, gallons of ice cream, geese, elk, pork chops, steaks from Terminal Meat Locker, mallards—we'll eat ourselves silly watching the flood and the NBA and NHL playoffs."

Blowing out of Livingston the morning breeze, I made it to the lodge, just barely, through the rising water that turned my friend's property into an island as the river roared by in a constant thunder of crashing waves, boulders exploding into each other beneath the surface and the odd afternoon thunderstorm. We filled a bunch of sandbags to slow the rising water that crept up the dusty road to his place and placed rocks at the edge of the liquid to mark its progress—submerged rock followed submerged rock and a gradually slowing but still nerve-wracking pace.

I remember throwing a Woolly Bugger into a shore side eddy of chocolate milk for the hell of it only to have a four-pound rainbow latch onto the pattern as though it were a lifeline. The trout leaped onto shore in the fresh green grass and looked at me with an expression that said, "Oh Lord, please don't throw me back into that watery hell. I beseech thee. Please."

I did and the rainbow most likely drowned within minutes.

Later that night my friend and I destroyed an eleven-pound Canada Goose that he'd grilled to perfection, six one-inch-thick pork chops, and a brace of two-pound Idaho bakers loaded with butter and sour cream. One chop remained quivering in fear and pleading for its life much as the trout had done earlier in the day. We spared its life, for the moment, retired to couches in front of the TV and knocked ourselves senseless with hours of sports and a continuous stream of root beer floats.

A few days later we rowed across Tana Creek to head to the Bank restaurant in Hamilton for a green salad and two-pound steaks, returned home and watched more sports, drank more floats.

The flood eventually subsided. Tana Creek went dry as it always did in the heat of summer. I returned home and life rolled on in its curiously haphazard way...

...and that was one of the finest spring runoffs I've ever drifted through.

But what to do about this one and my lunatic eagerness to start moving on down the Yellowstone madly North Dakota bound?

Strolling along beside the ferociously chaotic Yellowstone I notice a wooden bench beneath an old cottonwood just ahead. The seat offers a fine view of the Absarokas to the south and right below my feet a large maelstrom that is spinning wildly and audibly sucking air, leaves, low-flying private jets and unlucky swallows into the dark vortex and down into the bowls of the savage river. I sit and watch—mesmerized. For some inexplicable reason the spinning puts me at ease and sets me free from the neurotic weight that is my obsession to be on the water.

I recall that Miami and Detroit are on TV in about thirty minutes in the NBA Eastern Conference Finals and that there is a six-pack of Weinhardt's root beer and a half-gallon of Wilcoxin's French vanilla ice cream. Life begins to offer intriguing possibilities of the most delightful stripe.

Spring runoff be damned. The float and the book will come in due time. Right now sedate pleasures are calling me with a vaguely-remembered seductiveness.

♦ ♦ ♦

Shadowed familiars ghosting within dazzling bright waves along a July afternoon's river that cuts through the Yellowstone valley in a timeless present. The wooden canoe moves through the uneven patterns with determined ease as eagles—bald, golden—and dozens of herons peer from limbed perches down through the entwined currents. Kingfishers plummet seeking small rainbows.

Hot. Breezy. Swift. Alone.

Trout, some big ones, slam and crush wind-blown grasshoppers whose only real mistake in life is or was an unconscious insect desire to soar over the always moving sapphire current with no particular destination in mind. A flight that is death on this alive afternoon. Thoughts of casting to these fish are everywhere—thirty to forty feet of line tossed on seams and in foam lines ahead of the canoe, watery variations that flash and disperse in light that sparkles golden-green through the rustling cottonwood leaves. Casual fishing with mixed results. Sixteen inches. One missed. Another. Seventeen inches. Ten. Broken tippet. Set the rod down on the canoe's braces.

The Yellowstone slaps and whispers against the cedar as the craft slices downriver. The paddle pushes through the river sometimes with no resistance as standing waves shaped like loose-jointed pyramids appear to move upstream. These are crested as the tall sandstone cliffs block everything but the deep blue as the day slides along.

For a few days at least I'm on the run from my hometown that is the center of the western world when it comes to fly fishing.

I've found that convincing the large trout to take is even harder than they tell you. Matching the hatch jive doesn't really get it much of the time nor does artful casting over classic water with a dainty piece of pretentious fluff. The ones that matter, those worth the effort, rarely buy the obvious con of this artifice.

Learning to see without looking, understanding how to chase without wanting, because the trout know when they're being hunted, makes hammering an offering of substance tight to a sweet lie just barely possible with my laughable stealth and dark humor. Why would anyone want to do any of this to begin with I think sometimes, but accept that the primal urge and wonderful country and the crazy fish are answers enough.

♦ ♦ ♦

With all of the manufactured hysteria, including former TV news anchor Tom Brokaw hosting a vaguely restrained and entertaining PBS special about the possibilities of the Yellowstone caldera going ballistic, and the nearness of all of this to my home—a mere fifty miles to the south up the Paradise Valley—it's difficult not to think about a cataclysmic event of a magnitude none of us can truly imagine. Living at ground zero does this to a person. Should the big one happen, and this event would make Mount St. Helens look like a backyard barbecue, a pyroclastic flow—high-density mixtures of hot, dry rock fragments and hot gases that move away from the vent that erupted them at high speeds—would reach our home in less than an hour with temperatures that may exceed 1,200 degrees. Like I said, ground zero.

The super volcano of Yellowstone National Park poses a threat to the world. Current research shows the potential magnitude of this latest in a seemingly never-ending series of threats to our species' existence—

meteors crashing into us, hurricanes, madman terrorists, corrupt administrations, bad TV. Today's spectacular geysers and hot springs at Yellowstone are the most visible part of the volcanic system there. They are charged with heated snow and rainwater which leave a geochemical record that provides insight into the region's geologic activity.

Reading the record found in tiny crystals of the minerals zircon and quartz, scientists are now forming a new picture of the life history—and a geologic timetable—of a type of volcano in the western United States capable of dramatically altering the global climate sometime within the next 100,000 years. These are volcanoes that occur over "hot spots" in the Earth and they erupt every few hundred thousand years in cataclysmic explosions, sending hundreds to thousands of cubic miles of ash into the atmosphere. A little Google search action on the Internet turned up a synopsis of a series of papers by UW-Madison geologists Ilya N. Bindeman and John W. Valley that present a life history of the hot spot volcanism that has occurred in the Yellowstone basin over the past two million years. Their findings suggest a dying, but still frightening cycle of volcanism, and a high probability of a future catastrophic eruption sometime within the next million years, and possibly within the next hundred thousand years.

"Today's Yellowstone landscape represents the last in a sequence of calderas—the broad crater-like basins created when volcanoes explode and their characteristic cones collapse—that formed in regular progression over the past 2 million years. The near-clockwork timing of eruptions there—2 million years ago, 1.3 million years ago and 600,000 years ago—suggests a pattern that may foreshadow an eruption of catastrophic proportions," said Bindeman and Valley in their lengthy report.

Beneath Yellowstone and its spectacular landscape of hot springs and geysers is a hot spot, an upwelling plume of melted rock from the Earth's mantle. As the plume of hot, liquid rock rises in the Earth, it melts the Earth's crust and creates large magma chambers.

"These magmas usually erupt in a very catastrophic way," said Bindeman. "By comparison, the eruption of Mount St. Helens sent about two cubic kilometers of ash into the atmosphere. These catastrophic types of eruptions send thousands of cubic kilometers of ash skyward."

When I watched the PBS show on this situation, a possible scenario played out, and the outcome is frightening. Volcanic winter. A dark, ash-choked hell with little sunlight, the whole thing reminding me of the relentless setting in Cormac McCarthy's novel *The Road*. I'm glad I'm close to this one if it goes off in my lifetime. I don't want to live to experience the hellish aftermath.

There are so many death trips waiting for me out there—our country's foreign policy (read: arrogance, greed and gluttony), avian flu scare tactics, melanomas caused by my canoeing and fly fishing under a harsh Montana sun, drive-by shootings by crazed teenagers, strokes, heart attacks and related maladies brought on by our frenetic lifestyles and the insipid madness foisted on us by puerile TV programmers—that I figure an eruption of Yellowstone's super volcano really doesn't warrant much concern on my part. Hell, as I've said, I live at ground zero and will be ashes-to-ashes in a very short time if the caldera blows its lid.

The Yellowstone caldera is an extraordinary, close-at-hand, tangible reminder of how transitory life is. I worry about money, relationships, world affairs, getting good book reviews and other sillinesses. Often when I'm camped far out on the high plains on some wind swept grassy ridge where the lights of civilization are out of sight I look up into a sky so full of stars and galaxies that the entire world around me seems to hum and vibrate as the universe descends and envelops me and my little campfire. I take a sip from my drink and look up once more. "Why bother with any of it?" I say out loud. "What's the point? Really, what's the damn point?" And slowly and powerfully it always comes back to me. This sky, the Yellowstone Caldera, the natural world—these are all object lessons in the subtle art of learning to be humble with the distant goal of catching a glimpse of true humility.

That's how one madman looks at all of these forces that are at once awesome and terrifying—concrete visions to draw intrinsic meaning from.

You know the drill—"*Such is life.*"

♦ ♦ ♦

Running a fast line of current that slices along the north edge of this midstream island, the canoe slides easily over a two-foot standing wave formed by the river's channels merging in a raucous V at the gravelly downstream end of the land. Willow, cottonwood, aspen, alder and pine shoot by in a multi-shaded blur of warm green, white, buckskin and burgundy. The cedar strip craft rides up on the crest, gains its bearings from this mild increase in elevation, then shoots down onto smoother water with the aid of a few directional strokes on my part. The sounds of rushing water fade behind us as we cruise down stream.

The canoe, called a White Guide and lovingly constructed by Newfound Woodworks of New Hampshire, seems completely at ease, happy, in her new western surroundings, the Adirondack waters of her youth turning swiftly into memories.

Through the years I've acquired several canoes including a sixteen-foot Mad River Explorer, a twelve-foot Old Town Pack (I still have both of these) and heavy, unwieldy and noisy aluminum and fiberglass ones that are long gone though memories of their ungainliness still linger. Each had and has its own distinct and palpable personality that becomes apparent within minutes of setting out on a river or lake. The Explorer is a capable, sturdy yet sporting individual. The Pack is like a British sports car, say a 1966 Triumph Spitfire, full of spirit and out for a good time. The Explorer reminds of that long-ago, fine machine, the BMW Bavaria—speed, power to spare, durability. The canoe we are in now is all of this and more. At eighteen-feet, six-inches she radiates meticulous craftsmanship, beauty and the wilderness lineage that can only come from centuries of canoeing by explorers and trappers. Experiences that ultimately lead to her perfect design. The northern white cedar stripping, ash gunwales and cane seats, the perfect fit of all of this, her fine lines— I've never been in a canoe of this quality. The White Guide handles standing waves, whirling holes, rapids—all of this and more—with a solid grasp on the water. I feel like I'm king of the river totally at ease, secure in my place as the three of us—Ginny, the canoe and I—travel the river corridor at peace within the timelessness of a perfect setting that is beyond my imagination.

Finally the Yellowstone is clear, cool aquamarine after weeks of muddy, debris-choked, snowmelt runoff turbulence roaring through the canyons and racing out along the wide-open valley floor. Along this stretch a few miles below the ranching community of Big Timber the water is halcyon perfect rolling easily under gravity's influence. The river drifts west in a series of serpentine loops and bends punctuated with deep runs that are separated by wide, shallow riffles where the liquid sparkles and splashes over the streambed of salmon, bronze and ochre rock and stone. Long lines of foamy bubbles stretch out like phantom fingers beneath this faster water as it slows down entering the upper ends of the deeper, darker sections.

Puffs of wind billow and gust warmly from the southwest as it pours down off the high, ancient volcanic plateau that is Yellowstone National Park seventy miles away. Puffy cumulous clouds race off towards Billings. Large cottonwood shimmer in the day's glow, the millions of leaves whispering and laughing in the swirling air. A band of antelope works a nearby grass and sage bench—black masks, dusty tans and browns of sides and backs, white rumps clearly visible. A golden eagle holds on a rotting fence post that drips rusting strands of barbed wire. The bird is motionless, stately. The Crazy Mountains rise fiercely above the north-west horizon, all but the highest peaks now barren, without snow.

This is late July. Hopper time. The large, clumsy insects leap, clack and crash among the tall, already browning fields of grass that cover the banks rising more than ten feet above us. The wind blows many of the bugs out over, and eventually onto, the water's surface. The ungainly creatures smack into the water with audible "splats." These disturbances do not go unnoticed by the large rainbow and brown trout holding barely out from the shadowy shelter of the undercut banks. The fish are lined up like marauding wolf packs as far as we can see up and down the river. This is a period of gluttony for the browns, not only on the Yellowstone but along many other western rivers as well. The trout, some of them weigh-ing more than five pounds, slash and rip through the insects trapped in the surface tension. The sound of tooth-filled mouths crunching down on the hoppers is steady, voracious. Sprays of water flashing prismatic variations of the sun's light explode in gem-like micro-bursts all along the river as the feeding frenzy grows in intensity.

This is too much for an inveterate fly fisherman such as myself. I connect the two pieces of my already-rigged rod and yell to Ginny who's enjoying the day in the bow, shooting photos, gazing at the wild country as it wanders past us.

"Hold about twenty feet from the bank if you can. I'm going to take a few casts."

She turns, smiles, laughs.

"I was wondering how long you'd last," she says. "Go ahead. Enjoy yourself."

She casually works the water when needed with her paddle, feathering the blade to cheat the wind on her back strokes.

I've tied on a large, ratty-looking tan Elk Hair caddis, a pattern that mimics many things, among them the grasshoppers. I work out sufficient line to both reach downstream ahead of us to avoid spooking the fish and also to cover the additional distance into the bank where the fish are feeding. Each puff of wind knocks bunches of the hoppers onto the water. Big trout, little ones, too, go crazy as they charge down on the feebly struggling insects. If you're a lover of grasshoppers, the carnage is horrific. If you like to connect with big browns and rainbows, this is a magic time of the day and the year. Pure paradise. A quick backcast and a little line haul forward to help power across the breeze is all that's needed. The fly unfurls with a slap on the water. A pair of browns race towards it, backs and dorsal fins slicing the surface. The larger of the two engulfs the Elk Hair in a splashing swirl after only a few feet of drift. Pulling back on the rod slightly sets the hook. The brown turns and runs downstream for cover at the restraint of the alien pressure of the line. We follow easily in the canoe, Ginny back-stroking to slow our progress and to keep us a few feet from shore. I notice that she also manages to shoot a series of photos while all of this is going on. Multi-tasking. I gain line rapidly. The fish leaps once, twice, its tail standing on the river's surface. It sounds then releases its hold on the water down below and blasts out of the water in an arc of silvery spray, crashes back into the Yellowstone and sounds once more. The brown holds along the bottom for a minute.

The vibrations of it shaking its head are clearly transmitted through the taught line. Suddenly the fish quits the fight, tired. I pull the fish to me. The trout's gold, rich brown, yellow, bronze, blood crimson, white, and jet black colorings flash and flicker beneath the sun. The brown is eighteen inches, maybe a little more, thick, healthy. I reach down into the water and grab the hook. A quick twist sets the fish free. Before I am able to grab its tail to gently revive it, the fish shoots out to mid-stream and the shelter of deep water.

What can I say? Nothing. We smile at each other. Paddle away from the bank and repeat the process. Another cast. Another brown. This goes on for an hour or so and a few miles. Mainly browns with a few vermilion flanked rainbows. The trout run from twelve inches to twenty. The fishing is so good it is almost frantic. Near ridiculous in its ease and joy. Days like this, despite what the slick travel brochures fabricate, are not everyday occurrences. My right arm is tired from playing all of the fish. As good a stretch as I've ever experienced on a river in Montana. I've kept four of the smaller ones for dinner tonight. Sautéed in butter with salt, pepper, a squeeze of lemon and slivered almonds along with grilled zucchini and corn and some Merlot, maybe a cigar and a sip of cognac after dinner as the stars come out—yeah, we can handle this. Makes the dark, mean, cold winter seem worthwhile.

Our focus has been down river as we targeted prime spots to catch the trout. The sky as far east as we can see is deep blue with rafts of fluffy clouds drifting towards North Dakota hundreds of miles distant.

I turn and check out the weather behind us.

Not so good. Slight understatement surfacing on the high plains.

A dense wall of deep purple, nearing black, clouds is bearing down on us. The entire system is anvil shaped with the mixture shooting billowing clouds tens of thousands of feet above the land. They appear illuminated from within as the sun's rays are refracted and reflected by the moisture creating the illusion of internal fires raging out of control as the layers of cloud constantly shift and turn in the wild updraft that varies the light's color and intensity. As we watch, the cell expands and towers above everything, dwarfing even the Crazies. The dark mass appears to be walking towards us on legs of lightning. We have perhaps fifteen, twenty minutes to find shelter or risk being knocked senseless by what will no doubt be enormous hailstones. After this indignity our unconscious bodies likely will be fricasseed by a relentless series of white-hot lightning bolts that ignite the canoe. Life is indeed good right now. The possibilities seem cheerful and limitless.

Perhaps a mile ahead a series of low hills with gentle notches in them created by centuries of erosion appears like a beacon to desperate sailors. Ideal protection all things considered, including our lack of options way out here in the open landscape. There is a band of haystack whitewater guarding the shore, but we'll have to risk this tumultuous uproar to gain shelter.

"Up ahead," I yell, pointing out the structure.

The wind is increasing steadily and growing cool. The air smells of rain with a delightful hint of ozone. One last look behind reveals that the entire storm is rotating very slowly in a counterclockwise direction. Forget the hail and the lightning. A tornado is going to do the job with a flurry of insanely punishing, wind-driven jagged sheets of demolished feed silos, doublewides, abandoned Packards, and airborne derelicts swept from the streets of Livingston by the maelstrom. I recognize a couple of them and wave. They wave back then set their sights on Reed Point.

"Go like hell, Ginny."

She already is.

We close in on the perceived sanctuary as the thunderstorm-slash-tornado closes in on the canoe. Lightning strikes behind us, the light flickering across the sage hills up ahead. Thunder booms with a clarity that indicates that our demise is at hand. Hard driven raindrops mixed with pea-sized bits of hail bang against our backs and splatter and bounce in the canoe sounding like small marbles that have been mysteriously cast from the heavens. The wind is screaming now and actually helping our pathetic survival efforts by pushing us towards our goal. The bank passes by like a fast-forward, out-of-focus movie. I catch glimpses of lone cottonwoods, a Russian Olive with its branches of silver-green leaves bending in the gale as though in prayer, a herd of black Angus cattle munching bunch grass while clearly oblivious to their potential barbecue fate. I imagine, I think, the smell of roasted beef. A bunch of antelope running over a far hill.

Craaack!

The sound is deafening. Everything goes silent. Numb. Then a ringing in my ears, my head.

A bolt of electricity hotter than the sun's surface nailed an elderly tree on the other side of the river. The top of the cottonwood disintegrates in a mad mixture of shattered, smoldering wood and leaves. The mayhem is right behind us—lightning, thunder, hail, chaotic wind—all of it beating down, around and through us. I cut the canoe at a 45-degree angle through the rough water, aiming at the first miniature valley. The White Guide rocks from side to side but pushes safely over and through the sizeable chop. The motion is a bit unnerving, but I've learned to give the craft her head in broken water and she sees us through the turbulence. I turn the canoe abruptly and continue to push with violent strokes. It pounds up on the shore of mud, snake grass and sand. We leap out and pull it all the way up onto dry land, then flee for the shelter offered by the small depression that is rounded enough not to be a lightning magnet. We're drenched, getting pelting with ever-larger hail, and wired on an adrenalin rush spawned by stark, raving terror.

"That was close," I say while sucking in air to catch my breath. "What is it with lightning? The stuff tracks us wherever we go—the Missouri Breaks, the Ram River in Alberta, even along the Olgilvie in the Yukon. We must have done something horrible in a previous life. And whoever said that being a damn Mayan princess was easy."

"Don't start with that nonsense," says Ginny. "Here. Maybe this will calm you down." She hands me a bottle of Anchor Steam Ale.

How she had time to grab this during our manic, pell-mell landing, I'll never know. This type of thing reminds me of the antics of a character named Dirt Tidrow who roams the pages of an unpublished murder mystery of mine. He's always producing silver flasks with single malt scotch, Cuban cigars, bottles of ale like the one I'm holding, other stuff, as though out of thin air. Why argue? I twist off the light blue cap. The liquid foams cold and light brown. I take a long drink and enjoy the sensation of the icy brew working its way to my stomach.

Not all that far above us the storm is completely out of control, having its way with the landscape. Lightning sizzles in psychotic lines across the base of the tumult or arcs down into the ground, tops of trees, mountain peaks, all over the place. The pungent smell of ozone is thick. I expect to begin catching that earlier-imagined aroma of torched cow, for real this time, at any minute. We have a bottle of Open Pit or Bulls Eye sauce in the cooler in case this spontaneous steer fry should manifest itself nearby. The detonations of thunder make any fireworks display I've ever witnessed seem pale, without force. The concussions compress and rock the air punishing my eardrums. Dark masses of cloud roll, spin and explode in enormous flowers of bubbling condensation resembling mammatus. These normally form in sinking air while most clouds form in rising air. Although mammatus most frequently appear on the under-side of a cumulonimbus, they can develop underneath cirrocumulus. Sometimes very ominous in appearance, they are harmless, victims of ugly and unfounded rumor, and seeing these does not mean that a tornado is about to form, a commonly held misconception. They are usually visible after the worst of a thunderstorm has passed. For a mammatus to take shape, the sinking air must be cooler than the air around it and have high liquid water or ice content. They derive their name from their appearance. The bag-like sacs that hang beneath the cloud resemble cow's udders.

Why I know all of this is not much of a mystery. Ginny and I spend a great deal of time out in wild, remote country. We are frequently hammered by weather like this dandy little storm dancing just above the river. The research and resulting information helps me to understand the possible means of my death.

We are on the lee side of the valley and pretty much sheltered from the rain, though the wind whips and back tracks, swatting us with cold drops of rain and rogue hailstones. The storm is moving off as the mammatus were trying to tell me moments ago. The sky is growing lighter, an eerie yellow-green radiance works its way across the native grasses and clumps of sage sparkling with the rain dripping from them. Even the reds, pinks and yellows of the surrounding bluffs are shaded by the green luminescence. The temperature has fallen into the upper sixties. I'm wet,

chilled. I finish off the cold ale. This helps a good deal. I shiver and antici-
pate the warmth of the late-afternoon sun that will appear shortly. These
bursts of heavy weather are nearly clock-like in their predictability in the
heat of summer that draws moisture rapidly and far up into the chilled
atmosphere triggering the thunderstorms. Around two or three in the
afternoon the cells burst forth and pound across the prairie. Normally
I'm prepared for this, but the lunatic hoppers and attendant carefree
trout feeding like there was no tomorrow diverted me.

The rain is almost over. In a few minutes we'll be back on the river.

Looking uphill I see an open cut of greenish rock studded with dark
chunks of another mineral. This is a slice of the Livingston formation, a
thick accumulation of late Cretaceous sediments that is mostly volcanic
debris. The greyish chunks are pieces of andesite, a rock common to large
volcanoes. I still have difficulty imaging this entire region as a hot bed of
ancient volcanic activity despite the awareness that Yellowstone Park is
perched on top of an ancient crater that will one day erupt again with a
force and magnitude that will render existence as far away as Minnesota
something of a moot point. Seismic activity has increased slightly in the
area and hot water jets are appearing an increasing rate through cracks
on the floor beneath Yellowstone Lake. The volcano has erupted several
times over the eons in a path that seems to be gradually moving mainly
east and slightly north. Look out Glendive.

I learn these curious and probably useless bits of information while
examining a collection of field guides we've accumulated over the years
and miles: *The Complete Guide to Rattlesnake Raising, Tall Grass Prairie
Wildflowers I've Known and Loved, Rocky Mountain Geology High, Birds
You Won't Be able to Identify, The Same Goes For These Trees Guide,
Native Grasslands I Refuse to Mow* (this one is out of print, hard to find,
but worth the effort), etc. I do this while Ginny waits for the light of
any given day and time to take on the arcane dimensions she so loves
in her photographs. This process often takes hours, if it happens at all,
giving me plenty of time to chase trout, smoke cigars, watch ants crawl
about between prickly pear cactus growing in the parched soil at my
feet, try to sharpen one of my knives (a pointless study in futility) or
read a book. I've discovered more on our trips than I ever did in nearly

a decade of stumbling through academic programs at universities and colleges in Boulder, Colorado; Rockford, Illinois; Beloit, Wisconsin; and Missoula, Montana. A late-blooming student way too far along the road of Bukowski-esque set-in-his-ways stubbornness to do much with all of this knowledge.

Back on the river we push along, the storm is now long gone over the eastern horizon, disappearing in a diminishing cacophony of lightning-fueled thunder. A double rainbow, with soft hints of an inner third one, arcs across the sky from north to south. At its apex the colors are bright and clearly separated. It grows in luminosity showing no sign of dissipating. We watch for long minutes and several casual river miles. We surprise a pair of mallards who break from the water and flee downstream in a flurry of quacks and beating wings.

A whitetail deer stands in the tall grass looking down on us from the cutbank, its tail flicking nervously back and forth. The paddling is easy in the smooth water. We make good time, maybe six miles per hour. According to the river maps I've brought along, and a corresponding topographic map that I've loaded into a GPS I can sometimes use with at least a suggestion of accuracy, a series of islands ranging in size from about two acres all the way to thirty or forty acres lies just above where Bridger Creek, the stream, that heads in the Absaroka Mountains, enters the Yellowstone about nine river miles away. I'm hoping for an open campsite near the water so we can hear the current gliding along throughout the night. And a location that looks out and up to both the Beartooth and Absaroka mountain ranges on the southern horizon would be good. It's now 4 P.M., so with a bit of luck and due diligence we should make camp on one of these within ninety minutes or so. The river flows silently and swiftly with only occasional stretches of broken water that would be classified at most as vigorous Class I rapids. The canoe rides over and through this with no effort. I find myself seeking out broken water, searching for silvery-white crests of the tops of small waves that indicate the rapids. Rushing and bouncing along at an increased pace is fun, at times exhilarating.

♦ ♦ ♦

Rising to their own eccentric rhythm in the north are the Crazy Mountains. They're one of a kind, one of us, we are them, rising up northeast of town shoulder next to Sheep Mountain, a small band of outlaw mountains hiding out like many of us. An island range some call them. They climb thousands of feet above the breezy high plains, but seem happiest when the sky is dead clear blue for dozens and dozens of miles all around them. Yet their mad summits are obscured by dark, ragged sheets of swirling storm clouds. Tiny creeks run down from the high country eventually becoming streams with wild, native Yellowstone cutthroat trout in them. Further down in the wide, open valleys rivers hold browns, rainbows, brookies, whitefish. This is what draws me to these isolated ranges—the aloofness, the trout, the strange weather, the lack of people, the high peaks. I'll walk off from old logging roads and catch trout the length of my index finger and maybe see a grizzly or a wolf that biologists say aren't here. Hard to argue with hard headed science, though. Stands of old Ponderosa survivors rise thick-trunk, red-bark, banged up from centuries of wind, cold, heat, drought, fire. On the north end of the unchecked madness lies the Mussellshell and prime grassland. To the east is an openness that measures itself in the Earth's curvature, south past the Interstate and whizzing traffic stretch Absaroka and Beartooth peaks. West is the Shields Valley, then the straight-up Bridgers. Yes, and right in the damn middle of all that's right about this place stand the Crazies, if only they'll let you really see them on a clear day.

◆ ◆ ◆

Immediately below Sweet Grass Creek bubbling in from the north and Lower Doe Creek merging from the opposite direction, we begin to pass through the Grey Cliffs, a stretch of more than a mile of exposed, eroding Livingston formation that towers over the river for a couple of hundred feet. Gary LaFontaine, along with partners Stan and Glenda Bradshaw, published a couple of my books years ago at Greycliff Publishing, named after the geologic feature we're observing now. The wind has died and the sun is still high in the sky. The air becomes trapped, shiftless between the cliffs turning hot and close. Small stones and rivulets of dirt slide into the water, clattering down the face. The sound echoes within the confines of the cliffs. Ginny spins back and forth from side to side in her seat taking photos. I do little but keep the canoe pointing downstream trying to give her a consistent, stable platform to shoot from. Interstate 90 follows the course of the Yellowstone. I hear the growl of semis and the whooshing of tires along the highways hot pavement. Anomalous sensations of contemporary freneticism out on the river.

In another hour we approach the islands. The first three are small and not suitable for camping, consisting of jumbled piles of rock and scraggly trees. I decide to risk finding a good spot on the last one, also the largest, that sits in the middle of the river directly across from Bridger Creek entering from the south. Perhaps some fishing will make an appearance, goes my predictable thinking. We stay between the islands and the southern bank of the river. From upstream, we both simultaneously spot a clearing in the aspen and pine midway down the last island.

"There it is, John," said Ginny. "It looks perfect."

The current is moving at a good clip, but right before we need to beach a large eddy swirls ideally like a benign foaming galaxy offering shelter for the slightly weary. We drift below the landing spot, swing smartly around and ride the reverse current in natural parking valet-style right up to our camp for the night—or maybe the next two or three evenings. Who knows? We're in no hurry to be anywhere. The shore is largely tan-grey sand mixed with rounded stones of muted jade, rust, orange, charcoal, brown ranging in size from three inches to a foot in diameter. There is plenty of dry, weathered driftwood scattered about, a level spot for our tent that is also open to the breezes on two sides to help mitigate the mosquito factor, and an old, modest-sized fire ring located about twenty feet below this. Grass is growing from the middle of the pit. Tall stalks rise from the stones.

We gently ease the canoe to the sand, step out into the warm water along shore and unload our gear. We then haul it well up from the river and secure it to a cottonwood with a length of rope before turning the craft over bottom side up. Setting up the tent takes only a few minutes. I arrange it so that the main view is across the river to Bridger Creek that cascades down a fall of copper-colored rocks and farther over and well above the island the Absarokas. The highest peaks still have a covering of last year's snow. By the time I'm finished laying out the sleeping bags, Ginny's gathered a large pile of wood, started a fire that is crackling and shooting sparks, and purified a couple of quarts of water.

About 6 P.M. I build us each a drink of Jim Beam and cold water in large tin cups. We lean back in the padded canoe seats we use to give our aging backs a break and enjoy the view—the gradual play of light and color across the land, the sound of murmuring water, the booming of nighthawks already feeding on insects and the pleasure that a modest fire always gives to any camp.

The sky is clear.

The air is soft and warm enough.

Trout are rising along an easy glide not far from shore, the fish sipping in small mayflies, the circular rise forms vanishing downstream.

Two red-tailed hawks work a ridge not too far away.

We smile and nod to each other.

We're home.

◆ ◆ ◆

The next morning the river changes abruptly. No more Mr. Nice Guy. The stream begins to tumble and fall down elongated stairways of rock and boulder with tall grey cliffs rising one-hundred feet and more on the north side. Standing waves and broken water that is foaming white plunge down to fields of grazing Angus well below us.

On the first drop we ride slowly on a smooth gathering V of narrowing river current. The Interstate is visible several miles distant, the sound of traffic inaudible; the cars, campers and semis look like toys escaped from someone's basement HO scale train set. I guide us to the shallow inside of the rapids and we race down, banging over slightly-submerged stones and bouncing over small waves. Standing waves of several feet crash and cascade down along with us next to the cliffs. This dangerous water is only yards from us and its hydraulics try to suck us into what surely would be capsize disaster. In minutes that pass like seconds but feel like hours, we are down and out cruising over a long level stretch of choppy, mingling currents. Graceful banks zip by in a bright green blur.

The bawling of steers starts weak, grows loud, and weakens and deepens in pitch in Doppler effect as we sail past the mindless beasts. The drone of trucks reaches us from the highway, muted by distance and the soft grasses. A pod of large rainbows sips small Trico mayflies near shore along a glassy slick. We're a bit wet but exhilarated from the wild dash down the rapids that are more like a staircase of minor waterfalls.

Before this trip I'd studied two guidebooks that had sections on floating the Yellowstone. Both authors said that the river is easy and that a beginner could float it with no trouble. It would seem that neither one of these guys had ever run the Yellowstone and had, instead, relied on eyesight of the river as they roared by in their cars on I-90. Or if they actually did do the river along this stretch their memories must have come equipped with the optional, and I hear quite expensive, turn-bad-trips-into-halcyon-moments attachment. I wonder what other misinformation is proffered in these two books concerning other Montana rivers and wonder how many trips were ruined, how many people were injured and if any paddlers drowned because of these fatally inaccurate guide books.

♦ ♦ ♦

How in the hell did I get here? I've fished this stretch of the Shields River many times, but everything seems madly changed in the most unnoticeable of ways. I've been here spring, summer and, finest of all, autumn.

Early October is when large browns lose their secretive, shadowy behavior. The trout, now driven by the spawning urge, are roaming the shallow, gravel runs where the females will build their redds in earnest in a week or so. In summer they are holding-out way back in the darkness of brushy, undercut banks. Most times browns are secretive, loners. Even the chaotic splash of a suicidal grasshopper a few feet out in the open water rarely causes them to move. Nymphs, minnows, smaller trout, any of these that happen to wander in front of the large predators will be killed quickly, but otherwise they won't budge. I know. I've tried launching everything from woolly buggers to hefty nymphs to saltwater patterns like Deceivers. Rarely will one of the browns take my offering, one made with the most honest of intentions. I want to connect, to feel a wild fish as it runs for cover at the bite of the hook or walks and crashes along the surface. The trout's fight for survival makes me feel alive. Perhaps a cruel way to get one's kicks, but I'm a predator, too—an emotional one above all else.

So after taking a half-dozen browns, a small brook trout and a Yellowstone cutthroat, everything is pretty much as I've always remembered it over the years. I notice this as I sit down on a fallen tree trunk along the bank. The stream is low and clear. The streambed sparkles in gem-like colors beneath the gold-copper light of the fall sun. The leaves on willows, birch and cottonwoods are going brilliant yellow, manipulating light in carefree ways. The undergrowth is a mixture of colorful life and death—the buff browns of dying grasses swirled with riffs of crimson and purple from wild berries and rosehips. The freshly-white peaks of the Crazies are visible over the ridge in the east and the Bridgers glow dark-blue, grey and white. Shadows tinted in the same shades creep down the mountain cirques and valleys as the sun moves west. A pair of sandhill cranes clacks away in that dying grass. I see their heads and necks bobbing and lurching as they strut away from me. Strings of geese are moving south with their common cries. Pairs of mallards whistle through the air. Deer silently observe my movements from a distance, as do Angus cattle that pause from their loud munchings to check me out. The last dregs of this year's mayflies bounce above the river's surface. Ahead I see an oval depression of newly cleared stone. The first brown trout spawning bed. One of many that will be dotted along this isolated stretch of water before much longer.

Yeah, all of this seems the same, but just like the end of last season and the one before and so on, everything is different in ways that are visible, but not to the eyes. This valley and everywhere else I travel in Montana at this time of the year seems to have shifted to a slightly different slice of time than the one I'm buzzing in. There's just enough of this movement to make me feel as though I'm in the middle of the gentlest of earthquakes or passing through a mild moment of dizziness. I feel like I'm in a room where the furniture has been subtly rearranged with such sophistication that I can't notice the changes.

I know I'm crazy. Have been as long as I can remember. I once had some concern about this to the extent that I used to down large quantities of whiskey to try and feel sane. Didn't work. Drunk is drunk, and hungover is hell growing ever larger as I get older. A pair of situations I now avoid. Time and the river flowing once again. The changes I'm experiencing aren't associated with being loony. They seem to be more involved with experience and the smallest of advancements in awareness. One would think that an individual as self-absorbed as myself would see any growth in perception as enormous, but it doesn't work that way. And I've noticed all of this for years in a number of places. Fishing's to blame. Hanging out in undisturbed nowhere is at fault. Casting to trout or bass or pike is strong stuff, much stronger than the whiskey I mentioned. The power has little to do with landing a large trout, though, like sex, following fly fishing to its commonly accepted conclusion is of brief satisfaction.

I first drifted through this mild oddity in vision a dozen years ago down in Tongue River country, the home of my heart. The coulees, eroding rock, native grasses, turkeys, coyotes and the vast aloneness are sensible to me. One October I'd shot a pair of sharptail grouse on a flat just off the red-dust two-track that winds to a dry camp I have near a bunch of old Ponderosa. There were lots of the birds feeding on fat crickets. When they took wing at my approach, their flight was labored. The shooting straightforward. Next I drove to a pond that used to hold rainbows, still does in a non-fishing way. An hour of relaxed casting netted me several trout. I killed one to go with my grouse/baked potato/ roasted-onion dinner. As I was cleaning this fish I felt as though the landscape slipped sideways. I put the rainbow in the cooler on ice, opened a Pabst, lit a smoke and looked around. The land was silent. Nothing but yellow sunlight shifting towards orange moving over the country dragging purple shadows with it. This was as alone as I'd ever felt. Like the only person on the planet. In some ways I was terrified. Then giving in to the unnamed but obviously deep fear, a sense of power ripped through me. The rush faded. I have no concept of what is meant by serenity, but I felt at peace for the first time in I don't know how many damn years. What had I done to earn this respite from the day-to-day anxiety? Well,

I'd walked a windy flat, killed a couple of birds and then fished for some trout. Nothing more or less. Not one for examining my psychological navel, I finished my beer and moved on.

Since that little country ditty there have been many other moments of oh-so-modest revelation. Fishing the Yellowstone here in Livingston with a longtime friend. Hooking a brown and then slipping on a rock, falling in and gaily floating downstream with the angry fish pulling on my line as I tried to keep the rod above water and avoid drowning. I lost the fish, but saved my life. I remember the sound of my companion laughing from his vantage point on a high cut bank and his yelling "Holt, I can't understand why Orvis won't send you any more stuff. You're fly fishing's poster child." And then that slight lateral shift of reality, life, whatever, materialized. A touch of fear, aloneness (not loneliness, that's something else) and then happy calm. I doubt I would have felt this way at a sports bar or a concert or a restaurant.

I've never been much for fishing with guides or doing the "in" thing like traveling to the latest hot river or lodge. I did some of this about fifteen or twenty years back, but was so uncomfortable I rarely enjoyed myself. I'm a true loner, like the browns, and simpler is better. It avoids confusion and eventual torment. This is how fly fishing, bird hunting, any outdoor avocation, was shown me. Catching fish—yes, that's nice. Killing a few pheasants—not bad either. Owning quality gear that makes all of this easier and more enjoyable—nothing wrong here. But that's not really the point. Those who have patiently guided me along a life that centers on good country have all said in their own curious ways, "That's cool that you made that cast that caught that fish, but that's not what's important. What counts, kid, is that river you're standing in. Those mountains over there. That blood-red prairie we crossed at sunrise— how all of it makes you feel. That's the game you're really after."

And I finally grasped the natural concept. Basically it's brain-dead simple. Lose the ego. Submit to the land. Connect with the feral buzz, then recognize my insignificant yet worthwhile place in the untamed, unfathomable scheme of things. None of the good stuff is related to fancy clothing, pricey fly rods or $5,000-a-week lodge gigs. Get wet and a little muddy. Then feel good enough to slide along in a strange dance for no good reason.

The light of October is special. It glows with an amber influence. I look up from my tree-trunk seat and spot a brown holding in a soft run about forty feet upstream. Only its fins and slight flicks of its tail reveal motion. Slowly I work out line to cover the distance, make the cast and start the retrieve. The fish hits the pattern with its head once, then again. It circles back and slams the streamer. The white of its mouth flashes. This fish thrashes across the surface, tires quickly and comes easily to me as I kneel in a few inches of water. Reds, browns, blacks, pale greens and bronze flanks. The lower jaw is formed into a hook or a kype. A male. I twist the hook free and watch as the trout swims slowly across stream to a deep hole beneath the tangled roots of an old cottonwood. And my fragile, lunatic world shifts casually out of kilter. I'm a bit afraid, then serene again, then laughing. "Completely nuts, Holt," I say out loud to no one, and feel good about it all.

♦ ♦ ♦

All of what transpired above is the wild mixture of natural experience that orbits around the Mayor's Landing to Big Timber stretch of the river. If I were, due to capricious or inexplicable reasoning of the powers that be, confined to this part of Montana and no other for the rest of my life, I would be admittedly a bit confused or even perplexed as to why such a seemingly draconian decision had been made. But in a short period of time, I would be completely content, spending my remaining years floating this always changing stretch of river, wandering its tributaries, fishing for trout, laughing with Ginny, camping, reading guide books, upland bird hunting or just hanging out in this remarkable landscape. This thirty-nine mile run of the river is one of the reasons that I'm seriously addicted to the Yellowstone.

Chapter 3

Whitewater Slide
Big Timber to Stillwater River—43 miles

THE RUN DOWN FROM WHERE I CAMPED LAST NIGHT WAS FILLED with broken water and swift glides that zipped me past stately cottonwoods as the Crazies faded in the western distant. Herons seemed to be standing on nearly every downed tree, looking for careless Longnose dace and Mottled sculpins and small trout. Pairs of sandhill cranes clacked from near their nests hidden away in the tall grass—the clacking a familiar yet prehistoric sound. The rhythm of the river, my paddling, the afternoon arrival of the wind and often thunderheads—all of this now seemed familiar, part of my life. All that happens is unexpected in an anticipated way.

♦ ♦ ♦

I seem to encounter the most interesting souls in the most curious of places. A casual, lovely late July afternoon. Typical Montana grace riding a sweet wind. On an island twenty miles below Big Timber and not too far above the small town of Reed Point, I'd set up camp—sleeping bag and tarp on the sand, cooking area with small fire pit, folding chair and attendant cooler. I am sitting in my chair taking in the view of the river, holding solitary court over green fields and the distant purple Crazies, when a bright red canoe comes into view—Mad River with the classic logo of a white rabbit smoking god-knows-what in a small pipe. The guy paddling the craft appears to be in his late-twenties, and familiar with canoes, judging from the J-strokes and draw strokes he used to work the current for a smart landing in front of me.

"Mind if I stop and rest a bit?" he asks in a cheerful voice. "I've got beer."

I'm easy and the beer is a sure come-on, so I wave him in with the aplomb of an airport tarmac worker. He's tall, tanned and wearing ragged cutoffs, like me, and a white T-shirt, also like me, although his is cooler. A small logo reads "Joe Jackson." Haven't thought of that musician in years. *Beat Crazy* races through my head. In fact, he looks a good deal like I did twenty-five years ago. I brush my hand back and forth in front of my face to check and see if any residual effects from an abundance of late-sixties dalliances are making an appearance. No trails. No electric colors. I'm as okay as I get at this stage in the passage of the years' proceedings. Apparently this guy is legit and not some maverick hallucination. He hands me a cold Molson's ale, pulled from a cooler filled with ice and brown bottles, then sits on a weathered, grey cottonwood trunk that's doing double duty as a windbreak for my modest camp.

We chat about the state of the river and the level of water—ideal for floating and high enough to be entertaining. And about the easy fishing for browns and rainbows on hopper patterns. Then Mike, that's the name he gives me—I tell him mine is Joe Graves (a character from my novel *Hunted*)—looks at me with an earnest and worried expression.

"I hope you don't mind this, but I've got to tell someone."

Confessions normally bore me, but what the hell? I'm not going anywhere—surprise—and I have nothing particular planned for the rest of the day other than some fishing in a side channel below camp, cooking dinner and working over a few drinks.

"Go ahead."

"I'm on the run," he said.

"Who isn't?" I said with a touch of cynicism, a rare state in my life.

"No really, from the Nebraska cops. I side-swiped a squad car in Hyannis out in the Sand Hill country. I wasn't paying attention. Well, actually I'd had several schooners of Grain Belt, four as I remember, cold and bubbling," a fond glow flashed across his face, one I was all too conversant with, "at the Hyannis Hotel, and when I went down Main to get back on the highway I swerved a little and hit a cop car. The door was open. Last I saw it was lying on the road. I panicked and took off down dirt and gravel roads then through a two-track next to a cornfield, before working my way up through South Dakota, the Badlands, Rapid

City, then Wyoming, Yellowstone and down to the Rainbow Motel in Livingston. I don't think anyone followed me or got my license plate number."

I almost dropped my beer, a most unusual occurrence. Parallel universes. Quaint coincidences. Synchronicity.

I'd had a remarkably similar experience back in 1986 just up the road apiece from Hyannis at Alliance. I was on my way back from an Outdoor Writers Association of America convention that had been held somewhere in Iowa. That was back when I thought being a member of that slap-happy group of hacks was of value. But I mean just how damn many camo-colored suede sport coats is one person expected to endure in a seventy-two hour span? I quit the bunch as soon as I got back home to the Flathead Valley in northwest Montana. Anyway, following a sumptuous meal and a pair of gin and tonics at the Porterhouse Chinese Restaurant (how can a person go wrong at a place with a name like this?) and with a meal of egg rolls, wontons, a porterhouse steak and the aforementioned cocktails, I continued on my lazy, leisurely back-road drive towards home. But before traveling one-hundred yards, I managed to drill a Box Butte County squad car parked in the middle of the main drag with lights and siren going loud, bright, insanely and the driver's side door wide open. The cop was probably busting a farmer stoned on Everclear at The Dew Drop Inn bar across the street from me. The squad's door, like Mike's, wound up lying mortally wounded, glass pulverized, metal crinkled, in the street along with my now-mangled side mirror.

Not wanting to take up the good officer's time and definitely not interested in an all expenses paid sojourn in the Box Butte County slammer, I high-tailed it through back country fields and along old roads until dark set in. I was out of sight before the officer discovered the damage to his cruiser. I hid in a dry irrigation ditch for a few hours before creeping and sneaking my way along nearly the same track my friend had taken, this surreptitious flight made all the way back to Whitefish. Stopped for gas south of the Badlands at an old-time station, one of those numbers with the gas pumps that had the spinning glass-encased orange balls that showed that fuel was actually being loaded into your tank. Had a couple of drinks with an old boy wearing worn bib overalls and long johns. He owned the joint. Chewed tobacco. Dipped snuff. Listened to Conway, Hank and Johnny Horton. Liked bonded bourbon. Clearly a relative of mine. As the sky turned black-purple a trio of silver-white tornadoes played pinball with the rolling hills north of the station. Spent the night in my sleeping bag on his wrap-around porch. Demolished ham, eggs, biscuits and gravy and strong, strong coffee with the guy at sunrise and struck off for Potato Creek an hour or so northwest on BIA Hwy 2 on the southern side of the Pine Ridge Indian Reservation. I planned on reassessing my position at this Spartan location.

I'll never forget that little Nebraska-Dakota road show and the adrenalin rush that resulted from acting the bit part of a small-time outlaw as I motored across the high plains into Wyoming and finally back in home sweet Montana and over the Continental Divide at Pipestone Pass.

I finished the Molson's and grabbed a pair of Miller longnecks from my cooler and offered Mike one.

"Thanks, Joe."

I looked around then remember my new identity. Right. Joe. Nebraska. Battered cop cars. Lord, none of this ever goes away. What past? It's all the present to me.

"Don't sweat it. They aren't going to spend time, money or energy on you. Nothing more than Hyannis bar talk by now for a few days, and off and on during the winter," I said. The banged-up, derelict sage holding court in the middle of the Yellowstone River on some nondescript island. "I've been there, almost the same road, so to speak."

We chatter away about my related experience and this seemed to calm him down a fair amount. We go fishing. Catch some trout. He stays for dinner—game hens, potatoes and onions wrapped in foil, same method with corn on the cob, lots of butter, salt, pepper—a couple more drinks over a modest fire and then off to sleep on an air mattress near his canoe and me in my bag. Earlier Mike told me that he'd rented the canoe from some goofy-named hustle joint back in town.

In the morning I help push Mike off. He waves his paddle back and forth in goodbye as he moves downstream and yells, "Take care, Joe."

Joe it is or was for the rest of this/that trip on the river. Hadn't thought about my great Nebraska squad car fiasco in years. Oh, to be young and carefree once more. Never saw Mike again. Still, a little lunatic parallel experience shared along the Yellowstone felt good. I like things like that.

I decide to remain Joe Graves for awhile longer.

♦ ♦ ♦

When I wake up in the morning these August days of dead heat, when I walk around town, when I go to bed at night, smoke is all around me, burning my eyes, filling my lungs, and obscuring my vision, some days so much so that I can't see the Crazy Mountains only twenty miles away. The Yellowstone is obscured by the smoke and ash as I walk along the levee in Sacajawea Park or float a half dozen or so miles every few days. There are wildfires burning in the Crazies, fires in the Stillwater drainage below the Beartooth Mountains south of Big Timber, wildfires burning in the southwestern part of the state nearly 200 miles away over several mountain ranges, wildfires burning 300 miles away in the northwest corner, and all the smoke, it seems, has converged here in Livingston, Montana.

When the air is still, everything in town looks like it's cloaked in singed fog.

Forest fires in the West are a natural phenomenon. They occur every year and sometimes, as in 1988, they blow up and scorch hundreds of thousands of acres of spectacular country. That's the year Yellowstone National Park burned live on global TV. The attempts to control the blazes and to save important man-made structures like Old Faithful Lodge were valiant and costly. I talked to one of the firefighters after the rains and snows of September finally put an end to the burning, and I remember his wry smile, the trace of frustrated anger and a shrug of his shoulders when he said, "Hell, there was nothing we could do with those. They were out of control. It was a big waste of money and manpower to keep the public happy. We had to damn well pretend that we could do something. No one could stop those fires." And now Yellowstone is showcased as an area that demonstrates the benefits of forest fires.

Out of the ashes, I suppose.

I walked through some of that burned-over country the next spring. The day was warm and the sky blue. My boots kicked up clouds of grey ash as I walked. Nothing was growing. Nothing was green, though I knew that, over the years, the land would come back to its wild radiance. When I reached the small mountain stream I'd fished so many times in the past, the place resembled the scene of a natural holocaust. Blackened stumps that had once been graceful pines, stood at odd angles or lay scattered across the ground like corpses. The stream was choked with black silt—no mayflies dancing in the air, no Yellowstone cutthroat trout, no birds singing. I looked for a bit before turning around and returning home. That was a dozen years ago. I have not returned.

The firefighter's words say it all: No one can really do anything when fires of this magnitude touch off in densely-timbered, tinder-dry mountain country. The Flathead Valley in Montana, wilderness country in Idaho, rangeland in Wyoming, all of it is burning this scorching season.

That's the natural way of it out here in the West, especially in years of low to average snowpack, drought and high heat, and in the long run it does more good than harm—or so I tell myself. Then I call my Mom in Whitefish in the Flathead Valley, less than a dozen air miles from the blazes around Glacier National Park and along the west side of the North Fork of the Flathead River. I think about all of this in a different, eerie light. Empirical experience alters one's vision.

"It's like *Apocalypse Now* down here," says Mom (who did the unexpected and died at the youthful age of eighty one week before Christmas. The world seems a far lesser place for all of us.). "First the floods of a couple years ago, now this. What's next? Hordes of locusts? Last night was spooky. Around six it was like dusk. The smoke turned the sun into a dull, orange ball. A band of dry thunderstorms rolled in and the lightning made everything look surreal and it touched off more fires. The North Fork of the Flathead River is ashes in many sections. Fish Creek campground is gone. The Wedge Creek fire is out of control. The Roberts fire is 40,000 acres. And if all of these fires hook up, we could go. I haven't seen the mountains in weeks. I can stare directly at the sun all day. It's just a blood red ball up in the sky. The smoke and the neverending heat—it's like hell."

We talked some more and then Mom hung up with an ironic laugh. She's a good, strong woman who knows this particular disaster is part of the West, part of living out here, but it's tough on those whose homes and lives are linked to some of the best country left on the planet.

I think about natural process, the firefighter and my mother this morning while I walk through the smoky haze along the Yellowstone River near town. The water level is as low as I've seen it, caused by the drought and ranchers sucking water out of it for yet another cut of hay. The nearby Shields and Musselshell Rivers are less than a trickle for the same reasons.

Fly fishing guides are floating their clients along promising stretches of the Yellowstone. The trout are having a tough time surviving the low water and increased temperatures but the steady stream of drift boats continues, turning a buck from the stressed fish. Life goes on and, anyway, the fires aren't burning along the river, yet. They're up in the foothills along Livingston Peak and cruising along up Mission Creek, burning thousands of acres in east of the Paradise Valley, but they're not down here in town, not yet.

Many of us are hoping that the August Singularity will arrive on schedule near the end of this month as it always has in Montana in the past. This first cool sweep of moisture wandering down from northern Canada normally brings with it a couple of days of light, though steady rain, enough to cleanse the air and slow the fires until the snows of late September. If this system fails to make an appearance an ugly situation could turn deadly. Homes will burn. Cattle, antelope, coyotes, grouse, a lot of animals will cook. And people will probably die.

All of this makes for a great thirty-two second visual bite on the nightly network news, but it's a lot different when a Crow fire races through the tree tops at over sixty miles-an-hour, flames spinning and roaring in glowing orange tornadoes hundreds of feet high and bears down on where you live. As the conflagration closes the gap to where you're standing, the distance between life and death, there is a roar beyond sound. Breathing becomes labored as the flames suck up all the available oxygen. The fire draws in the air and creates its own wind that rushes to fill the infernal vacuum, doing this with such vehemence that leaves are torn from trees and any birds that have not left the area fly crazily.

The scene looks good on TV, but it's terrifying to experience first-hand, as my mother is doing now. While walking through town, I picture her out on her deck above her smoke-clogged, burning valley and I can sense her concern as she stares at the land in smoke a lot thicker than I'm walking through here in Livingston. She knows as well as I do that the wildfires do some good—the elimination of piles of deadfalls, the destruction of harmful insects, all of the bright green, new growth in the coming seasons—but for those like her trying to live through all of this, it's hell.

◆ ◆ ◆

The dog days of summer are a dangerous time for some of us. The sun and the heat and the languid nature of the high summer season produce a lethargy that is punctuated by sitting in the bright light, drinking too many beers and practicing the high art of exquisite procrastination. This period of the year is defined as "the interval between early July and late August when the hot sultry weather of summer usually occurs in the Montana;" and/or "a period of stagnation or inactivity."

Both definitions work for me. But how did this term originate? A quick check on the internet reveals that in ancient times, when the night sky was not washed out by artificial lights and smog, different groups of peoples in different parts of the world drew images in the sky by "connecting the dots" of stars. The images drawn were dependent upon the culture: The Chinese saw different images than the Native Americans, who saw different pictures than the Europeans. I found all of this on a website designed with the slow of wit in mind, but to continue blithely along this moronic, pedantic path, these star pictures are now called constellations, and the constellations that are now mapped out in the sky come from our European ancestors.

They saw images of bears (Ursa Major and Ursa Minor), twins (Gemini), a bull (Taurus) and others, including dogs (Canis Major and Canis Minor). The brightest of the stars in Canis Major (the big dog) is Sirius, which also happens to be the brightest star in the night sky. In fact, it is so bright that the ancient Romans thought that the earth received heat from it.

In the summer, however, Sirius, the "dog star," rises and sets with the sun. During late July Sirius is in conjunction with the sun, and the ancients believed that its heat added to the heat of the sun, creating a stretch of hot and sultry weather. They named this period of time, from twenty days before the conjunction to twenty days after, "dog days" after the dog star. The conjunction of Sirius with the sun varies somewhat with latitude. And the progression (a gradual drifting of the constellations over time) means that the constellations today are not in exactly the same place in the sky as they were in ancient Rome.

Today, dog days occur during the period between July 3 and August 11. Well, enough of this. The following entries from a haphazard diary I kept in a vain attempt to divine the reason(s) for my annual squandering of these days give some insight into my malady(ies). I should have been on the river, but as the following clearly shows, I wasn't. The dates are accurate give or take a week or two.

TUESDAY JULY 11—Sat in the backyard working on cans of very cold Icehouse beer drawn from an ice-filled cooler nearby. Was reading Bowles' *The Sheltering Sky* when waves of medium-sized caddis appear suddenly from out of somewhere. The creatures whirred and hung in desultory fashion perhaps laid borderline comatose by the thick, hot, still air. Thousands of them. What were these bugs, species unknown to me and what were they doing here so far from the Yellowstone? They're tan so I guess they're tan caddis. I go inside and grab Dave Hughes' useful *Western Streamside Guide* and thumb through the fine little book. Near as I and Dave could figure the insects were indeed tan caddis, genus *Hydropsyche*. I probably should've gone upstairs and tied a few of these in Elk hair fashion and then wandered down to the river and to see what they might have produced. Not likely. Too hot. Too lazy out. I grabbed another beer and lit a La Escepcion Baltasar Series VI EMS wrapper. Routinized exercise for now. I understand little when it comes to Latin names of bugs or figuring out what each one is in terms of species. Caddis, mayfly, stonefly, grasshopper, damselfly—these I can tell one from the other, but that's about it. Cigars are another matter. I know wrappers, styles, binders, fillers and makers. The phone rang and rang. I opened another beer. The afternoon glided by. Dusk. Grilled steaks, beer, a cigar and some visiting with my neighbor Murphy. No writing accomplished. None.

FRIDAY JULY 14—Drove up past Wilsall north of town and turned towards the Crazies coming to the Shields River in five miles or so. The water was already low, but I rigged my delightful Redington 7-0 three-weight with a weighted Hare's ear nymph. I walked downstream well away from the bank to avoid spooking trout, through marshy areas with thick bright green grass and some jointed stalks of snake grass, cow pies and angus cattle that actually appeared to be at least as alert as I felt, not a Crowing achievement by any of us. The air was scented with the evaporating fecundity of the wetlands and with the decay of last years cottonwood leaves. Approaching the river I passed a Great Grey Owl that is standing motionless on a limb on a foot higher than me. Neither of us was startled by this occurrence. I stopped and looked at the bird. Its yellow eyes fixed on me. We killed a few minutes with this friendly inspection. As I moved on I watched over my shoulder as the owl's head rotated silently and smoothly following my passing. Never been that close to one of these before. The river was cool, refreshing. I worked the mile or so of stream that is more creek than river catching a few browns of modest size, a suicidal brook trout then inhaled the nymph (I cut the tippet and let the fish deal with the hook which it will with its digestive juices doing the job in a few days), and a sixteen-inch Yellowstone cut-throat. Bright oranges, cerise, green bordering on viridian, black blacks and white whites. Made the day. I pulled a now less-than-cold beer from my day back and drank in the day before driving back to town. Grilled steaks, beer, a cigar and some visiting with my neighbor Murphy. No writing. And like the long-hoped-for rain, none was in sight.

THURSDAY JULY 20—Checked out the Shields. Way too low. Gave the trout a break. Drive another hour to the Musselshell River near Martinsdale. Way too low. Gave the fish a break. Stopped in at JT's Bar in Ringling for a couple of beers and a burger with fries. Killed time talking with a couple of ranchers taking a break from the heat and the cloudless blue sky. Grilled steaks, beer, a cigar and some visiting with my neighbor Murphy. No writing. Still none of this silliness in sight.

WEDNESDAY JULY 26—Ginny and I spend the day driving up the Paradise Valley. Armada of floating fly fishers entire length of river. Enter Yellowstone at Gardiner, then cross the high bridge just southeast of Mammoth and headed for the Lamar Canyon. Farther on in the openness of the Lamar Valley, lots of bison wallowed in the mud and dirt next to the Yellowstone or stood in the water to cool off. Mid-morning and already hot. The sky was washed out silver from the glaring sun. Hordes of tourists photographed and observed the animals through a staggering array of high-powered, high-priced optical devices. Ginny shot a few hundred pictures with her digital camera. Driving along Soda Butte Creek, a Yellowstone tributary, towards Cooke City and the Beartooth Highway we saw dozens and dozens of anglers lined up in angling gridlock casting in extremely low water conditions to trout that were no doubt traumatized, long gone, already caught or no longer with us. All of the anglers were dressed in chest or hip waders to weather the one-foot flow of warm water. None of these guys was smiling. Looked like fun. We cruised through the jam-packed Pebble Creek Campground. Hundreds of anglers perched at picnic tables, or slumped into chairs or standing around. Grim faces. Bad fly fishing vibes. The Park in summer. Gunfire loomed in the pines. We drove through a tourist-packed Cooke City and began the easy wind up to where the Beartooth Highway starts in earnest. I turned the driving over to Ginny. Don't like heights or precipices protected by rusting guardrails. We came to the first acrophobic moment on the road. I muttered "Oh God!" while working on an Icehouse and staring at the floor promising myself that I'd never do this road again. Ginny pulled into the campground at Glacier Lake and got out to stretch her legs. I crawled out of my side of the Suburban and had some sharp white cheddar, sourdough bread, Kalamata olives, sliced apple and another beer. The rest of the drive down to Red Lodge was more of the same stoned-out, high mountain, blown away landscape. Not quite real. Other worldly. By now the beers had quelled my terror and I enjoyed the drive, but still rode the remains of a fear-charged adrenalin rush. Ginny said that she would pay for hypnosis to try and lessen my abnormal fear of heights. We'll see. The drive back on I-90 takes us through rolling black clouds mammatus style—hail, thick rain, clearing skies, double rainbows. Grilled steaks, beer, a cigar and some visiting with my neighbor Murphy. No writing. No words staggering across the crests of distant ridges.

SUNDAY JULY 30—Hanging out on a weathered bench fronting the Yellowstone River in Sacajawea Park on a lazy, hot Sunday afternoon. Felt like one of the old boys you always see playing dominos in some city park in some near-dead movie. Maybe I am one of the old boys. Time passes. Brought a couple of Icehouse and one of my cigars. River was low. Storm clouds rattled and hummed (slight apology to U2) along the south over the Absarokas. Lightning, rain in curtains that never reached the ground. A small rainbow sipped mayflies beneath me in light water. Guides guiding sports passed by in a steady stream of rafts and drift boats. None of their clients caught fish. I spotted large trout holding out from me along gravel shelves below riffles sixty yards opposite of where everyone was so madly casting. Trout aren't completely dumb. After the fiftieth drift boat passing overhead and the same patterns cast over and over they flee their trout ghetto and move into quieter water. We passed the time together. Groups of people behind me. Families, church groups grilling burgers and hot dogs, playing horseshoes. Sounds of children raising hell. Having a good time. The beers and cigar were perfect. The beer cold, bubbling, yeasty. The cigar rich, smelling of the tropics and the earth, tasting rich. Pleasant afternoon doing nothing. Grilled steaks, beer, another cigar and some visiting with my neighbor Murphy. No writing. No how.

MONDAY AUGUST 7—Smoke from the fires over in the Stillwater drainage south of Big Timber clogged the air in the oppressive heat. Many thousands of acres burned. One fire blew up in the southeast looking like a mushroom cloud before flattening to anvil shape and pushed northeast by strong winds. As the day turned to dusk a slight suggestion of orange flame showed through the smoke clouds. Murphy and family not home. Order pizza. Writing not an issue at this point.

FRIDAY AUGUST 18—Ginny and I drove over east to Reed Point and spent the late morning and early afternoon fishing the riffles and side eddies along the gravel cobble next to Indian Fort Campground. We caught some fat rainbows on hoppers, and a couple of Yellowstone cutts.

Then we packed up and headed into Reed Point a mile away for burgers, fries and draft beer at the Waterhole Saloon. Cool, quiet. Draft beer a nice change of pace from a summer of the canned stuff. Several ranchers sat at a long table playing pinochle while working on pitchers and shots of bar whiskey. A biker couple, their Harleys reclining outside, played the Keno and poker machines. We chatted with the bartender about this and that. She told us she wanted to move to the coast. Which one? Headed back home. Grilled steaks, beer, a cigar and some visiting with my neighbor Murphy. Words wandered in my head. Perhaps prelude to writing. Illusions of productivity.

THURSDAY AUGUST 24—The August Singularity arrived in the night. Annual weather shift bringing cold, rain, even sleet and wind. Arrives sometime around the 22nd of the month like casual clockwork. Dog days are dead. Summer's pretty much shot though still plenty of fine autumn weather ahead. Time for canoeing the lower Yellowstone, working for large browns and kicking up grouse. Rain and wind turn nasty. Murphy not in view. Head indoors and began working on a magazine column.

That's down-time summer style for me all too often. Maybe this will change next year. Maybe the Cubs will win the Series. Maybe.

♦ ♦ ♦

The heron stood on a grey, weathered log. Motionless. Looking like the fractured protrusion of a broken limb. Invisible. The bird's long, pointed beak was aimed at the heart of a small eddy swirling at its feet. The Great Blue's eyes bored into the clear water, through the bubbling surface down where small rainbows were holding just above the graveled streambed. The bird saw only those wild trout, never noticing the white-tail deer feeding beneath the pine trees across the river, or the skunk as it pushed its way along the bank, nose down sniffing for food. Mayflies lifted from the river's surface. Trout rose to eat these insects. A cluster of yellow butterflies gathered on a patch of moist silt nearby, wings lazily opening and closing in the light. A bald eagle soared by far overhead using the soft force of a warm breeze to cover distance swiftly, effortlessly. The heron noticed none of this, only the small rainbow gliding slowly upwards towards the center of the swirling water, opening its jaws to take an emerging mayfly trapped temporarily in the eddy. As the fish sipped in the insect, the heron's neck shot down, its beak spearing the trout in the back and through its white belly. The small fish wriggled to free itself causing the large bird's head to jerk back-and-forth and up-and-down. Then the trout quivered briefly and died. The heron moved silently from the log on its long legs, back into calm, shallow water sheltered by over-hanging brush and grass. The bird made short work of the rainbow, then swished its beak rapidly in the water, shook its feathers back in place and resumed its place on the log. Motionless. Dead still eyes peering through the water.

The Great blue heron has always been one of my favorite birds. Long, graceful and prehistoric, all encased in a stealthy feathered package set off by a long pointed beak designed with spearing little and sometimes not so little fish in mind. The Yellowstone River proffers visuals of these magnificent creatures at nearly every bend in the river. Perched on logs, along muddy banks, hidden within tall grasses above the water, the herons wait with what seems infinite patience for a meal to swim by. They never acknowledge my presence as I sweep by in the canoe. They're occupied with far more important doings than gazing at mere humans.

Other names for them include blue crane, grey crane, grand heron and Treganza's heron. The taxonomic name for the graceful creature is *Ardea herodias* or Heron heron. *Ardea* means "heron" in Latin. *Herodias* means "heron" in Greek. According to the USGS's Integrated Taxonomic Information System (ITIS) four subspecies exist in the world and all occur in North America. *A.h. wardi* occurs from Kansas and Oklahoma to Florida and *A.h. herodias* occurs over almost all the rest of North America, including southern Oregon. *A.h. fannini* is found on the Pacific coast from southeastern Alaska to the coast of Washington and *A.h. occidentalis* occurs in the extreme south of Florida. The birds are most commonly blue-grey in color with a black stripe above each eye extending to the back of the neck as a plume.

Most of the herons I've seen on the river appear grey with just the faintest, if any, hint of steel blue. Black streaks occur on a white neck. The bill is long, large and yellowish. The legs are long and greyish with reddish thighs. Great blue herons are between thirty-eight and fifty-four inches in length. Watching these birds take flight is impressive as they lift off their perches near the water, working wings that span up to six feet, the sound of the increasing flapping make loud "whomphs." Though the herons look like they are moving through the air slowly, an illusion probably due to the large wing spread, they have been measured at speeds up to twenty-nine miles per hour. The birds weigh between five and eight pounds, but to my eyes they seem much larger. Perhaps this is a result of being at near water level in the canoe as I pass by them. Often as they turn their heads my way and follow my course down river they seem to be looking down at me from an angle to suggests superiority. Life for the birds, for any bird in the wild, is tough. Sixty-nine percent of the newborn die in their first year. Two of the oldest known great blue herons have lived twenty-three years and three months, and twenty years.

Towards sunset down below Big Timber I passed beneath a stand of towering cottonwoods, limbs arcing out over the river far above me. Dozens of huge, irregularly shaped nests, that may have been heron attempts at circles or ovals, were constructed at the tops of the trees. The birds were quiet as I passed by their rookery, but I could see many elongated heads and beaks swiveling atop gangling necks. The feeling was eerie to say the least as the herons peered down at me from far above, silently monitoring my passage. To be watched in this way by birds that have inhabited the Yellowstone corridor for thousands of years was impressive, an avian statement that I was only a transient drifting by on some fancy-looking log and that the river belonged to the herons.

♦ ♦ ♦

Last night was one of those "I've got to get off the road and get some sleep" 3 A.M. landings. I'd been driving around the state enjoying the first bloom of spring and time slipped right on by me until I realized that it was getting late out. So I drove down a little-used two-track that led to the river and thankfully a nice smooth meadow. I dragged a tarp and sleeping pad out, tossed the stuff on the ground, pulled my waxed cotton poncho over my head and collapsed on the ground in exhausted synchronicity with a setting quarter-moon. Nighthawks boomed above me hammering mosquitoes, moths and other bugs. I don't remember falling asleep, but I assume the act was near instantaneous.

"Clack, clack, ratchet, squawk-clack, ratchet," in a roar that sounded like something bad was happening again in Beirut. Wave upon wave of this sound coming not from a singular source but from the throats of a modern day Mongol hoard. I sat up, back and knees cracking with sounds like very dry larch being tossed on a very fire. As I looked around me my neck made similar popping, cracking sounds. The joys of creeping age and senility. Over my right shoulder, across the river I beheld an other-worldly, out-of-time vision. Hundreds, maybe a thousand, big, tall brown birds that resembled mutant herons, were bobbing and weaving up and down. Occasionally this odd dance was augmented with displays of huge wings stretching far out as these birds craned their lengthy necks to the heavens and arched their backs.

I wasn't fully awake and could only utter the most profound of questions.

"What the hell is going on?" and isn't it joyous to behold a college-trained mind firing like a finely-tuned Formula I racer?

And it dawned on me, the pun not completely lost in the early morning light, that these were Sandhill cranes. I'd seen them many times before, singly, in pairs, maybe six at once, but never this many.

The sight of these large and also prehistoric-looking birds as they fed on insects, grubs and worms in a newly turned-over field on the other side of the Yellowstone was other-worldly especially when coupled with the clacking of hundreds of the birds as they communicated with each other or just liked to hear the sound of their own voices. I'll never forget later that morning wading up a small side-channel catching medium-sized brown trout in the dissipating mist with the cranes standing tall, erect or bending and stooping as they gathered food from the earth. Montana seemed a very ancient, primitive place that day.

The Sandhill crane (*Grus canadensis*) is one of only fifteen species of cranes in the world and is one of just two crane species native to North America. While the Whooping crane is highly endangered and restricted to only a few areas of the West, the Sandhill is more widespread and in most areas is more abundant.

The birds I was looking at were four to five feet high, with wing spans of six to seven feet. Sandhill cranes are Montana's largest bird. Long, skinny legs and neck give a false impression of size; the males weigh an average of about twelve pounds and the females around nine and a half pounds, which dwarfs the heron.

There is limited hunting in many western states, including Montana, and Canadian provinces, as the cranes return south each fall. I'm not opposed to hunting. I take my share of upland birds, but shooting the cranes strikes me is greedy, moronic and just plain wrong. I'd like to see all hunting of these birds cease.

The annual return of Sandhill cranes is a sure sign of spring. When I hear their distinctive "clacking" during my walks along the Yellowstone in late March and early April I know that I've survived another winter. Cranes are famous for their courtship dance, though I've never been fortunate enough to view this in the wild—only on the Discovery Channel. The dance consists of a series of bowing, jumping and stick-tossing movements. When it occurs in a flock, it often begins slowly with one bird, then increasing in tempo, the excitement of the dance soon spreads to others until many are dancing at the same time.

I ease myself into a standing position and totter down to the edge of the river stepping from one large stone to another until I'm actually about fifteen feet away from shore. The water gurgles and bubbles at my feet. The sun begins its crimson ball rise, then smoothly shifts to orange then hot yellow. The intensifying light sweeps across the land and the sandhills. The congregation now washed in a timeless glow.

♦ ♦ ♦

There is no doubt in my mind that the Ponderosa pine is a regal tree, but to my way of thinking the cottonwood could share the honor with the Ponderosa as Montana's state tree, if indeed such things matter and more and more I'm prone to believe that they don't. When the trees first leaf it in the purest of deep greens along the Yellowstone, when an evening breeze rustles their millions of leaves or when they stand dead still in the stifling heat of an August afternoon or, most dramatic of all, when they go completely berserk and turning every shade of electric, flaming yellow, gold and orange imaginable in early October, there is no sight more magical. Not towering the peaks of the Absarokas. Not the Yellowstone gone insane with spring runoff. Not deadly thunderstorms tearing across the Missouri Breaks.

Everything that says Montana to me, the trees say and they say it with an visual eloquence that leaves me speechless.

There are still plenty of cottonwoods remaining, but the great stands of trees that line Montana's streams and rivers are getting older. New trees appear slowly, haphazardly if at all. I've wondered why this is so and research by the University of Montana's College of Forestry and Conservation offers some answers.

In the spring, fluffy cottonwood seeds drift in the breeze and pile up against rocks and grass along stream banks. Cottonwoods require bare, moist mineral soil to grow, primarily gravel bars that form on the inside of river bends. Controlling a river's natural flow or movement reduces the gravel bars deposited by the stream. Buffeted by high water and chewed on by beavers and other animals, a cottonwood's early years are full of struggle. Once established, however, they anchor the stream edge, providing food and shelter for dozens of bird and mammal species.

Cottonwoods also have a well-understood relationship to stream dynamics, says Mike Merigliano, a UM research associate who studies river systems in Montana and surrounding states. He explains that cottonwoods are a natural clock for creating a timeline of river changes.

"Because they establish and grow on new but stable gravel bars, you can age a tree [determine how old it is] to find out when the bar was deposited," Merigliano says. "Then if you map the aged-tree patches, some of which are quite far from the present river course, you can see how the river has changed over time."

One study has focused on the Redwater River near Circle in the eastern part of the state where young stands of cottonwoods are few and far between. Merigliano's guess as to why this is happening is that a combination of ice jams, which scour the river bed and nearby vegetation, plus a general change in climate that is leading to a less active stream, are making the difference. New tree generations also may be impacted by naturally occurring salt concentrations—particularly along the upper portion of the stream—and the many small water developments that together may be reducing the incidence of big floods required to deposit new gravel bars.

All of this concerns me, of course, but when I'm paddling down a placid stretch of the Yellowstone in autumn with the images of the trees reflected with liquid perfection on the river's surface, well, that's all I can focus on for the moment, in the moment.

♦ ♦ ♦

The trail keeps climbing. No end in immediate sight. I continue to hope that over the next steep pitch or around the next pine shrouded bend I'll break out into the open and enjoy a Crazy Mountain, snowy, high country panorama.

A curious aspect of this part of the Yellowstone is that on an October day I can be paddling the river wearing only a T-shirt while if I'm up in these mountains at the same time of day I'm dealing with early winter. In the summer through mid-September this is a pleasant hike of several miles that expands into a rich meadow with several ponds holding nice Yellowstone cutthroat. With all of this snow nothing seems familiar and all sense of distance covered is inaccurate or nonexistent. I've recognized the pair of wood and metal bridges that pass over Big Timber Creek so I figure that I'm about two-plus miles up the path to my destination. There must be several feet of snow on the ground, some of it powdery from last night's fall and some windswept and crusted over.

Small squirrels chatter away out of sight in the woods, as do mountain chickadees. Grouse tracks, feet and tail feathers, wind to and fro across my way. I see what could be wolverine tracks. I've only spotted a couple of these ill-tempered animals in the wild and have no desire to encounter one today wearing cumbersome snowshoes. The official line is that there are no grizzlies in the Crazies, but some people I respect have told me differently, that the bears sometimes use these island mountains as a sort of refuge as they move from one place to another. It's nice to think that these mountains are wild enough to hold grizzlies, if only for brief periods.

Tree wells, bare or mostly bare patches of ground shelter from precipitation by the layers of pine limbs, look to be at least this deep. Trying to move through this in boots would be impossible. Each step would sink more than waist high. The new snow is still resting thickly on the tops of the branches. A quick brush of wind knocks some of this down onto me covering my hat, chilling my face and arching my back when some of it goes down my neck and back.

Snowshoes make this jaunt possible sinking only an inch or two into the powder and breaking through the hard-pack sufficiently to gain traction along the steep stretches. Uphill is uphill and this is not that much more strenuous than walking on bare ground.

Ice locked along boulders and gravels of both banks of Big Timber Creek narrow the visible flow of water to a few feet of silvery, crystal splashing that slides over copper and dark brown cobble with the diminished sound of medium-pitched bells. The breeze, what there is of it, rustles the tops of the pines making a gentle moaning sound as perhaps the trees bemoan the harsh winter weather fate yet to come their way from up North. The air smells lightly of pine and snow, crisp and clean. I'd cross country skied in from the last gate before the Half Moon Campground, shoes and day pack linked together. The skis are left behind leaning on a battered, brown trail sign. I use the poles for balance and push.

I've never combined skiing and snowshoeing before. The idea of doing so in October amuses me for some reason. Winter recreation surfacing in the height of a glorious fall. I've considered combining the two pursuits before but that's as far as I've ever gotten until today. The roundtrip will be about twelve miles—an hour in and out on the skis, and hopefully two hours each way on the shoes with an hour to enjoy the mountains on top. An early start this morning offers the slight chance of a daylight return to the Suburban, but if this finely-tuned, exquisite itinerary fails to manifest itself, I've packed a headlamp for an early evening landing. No big deal either way. I've got water in a plastic jug, cocoa-and-brandy in a bota, sharp white cheddar, sour dough bread, a half-dozen of my beloved Mounds Bars and some good cigars. Plenty of matches. Zippo lighter. Space blanket. Binoculars. Spare wool and cotton socks. Xikar knife. There's water in the creek and temperatures are not predicted to fall below 20 degrees, although I can still see a headline in the *Livingston Enterprise*—"Aged, Crazed Hipster Found Frozen Stiff in the Crazies," followed by a short rundown of my productive life, surviving relations, one or two friends that will own up to actually knowing me, and a funeral attended by perhaps five people if the weather's not too bad. Again, no big deal either way.

The snowshoes that I'm using are high tech—Atlas Elektras—maybe a light year leap in evolution from the ones the Ojibway and western Cree used centuries earlier. Theirs were narrow shoes, like mine, designed for maneuverability, less finely laced due to denser snow in their lands. A number of researchers believe that a form of winter walking device was developed in central Asia around 4000 B.C. Some speculate that the first shoes were inspired by animals that had adapted to moving over the snow—species that may have included moose, woodland caribou, snowshoe hare, lynx and birds like the spruce grouse, which grows scaly fringes on its toes in winter to increase the surface area of its feet.

Makes no difference, really, where all of this comes from or leads to. I've used snowshoes during every month of the year in Montana. There's always snow someplace out here. Every day I paddle this stretch of river I can see vast snowfields and icefields in the Beartooths and the Abasarokas. One of the reasons I've taken a break from canoeing this stretch of the river is because the juxtaposition of hot and cold, early fall and early winter all within a few miles of each other on the same day, appeals to my sense of a disrupted perceived order. A silly notion I'm sure, but that's the way it is sometimes.

The Crazies along with the Bridgers are the only mountains in central Montana to exhibit such spectacular glaciation in the form of these walls, cirques and carved valleys. These two ranges were able to capture sufficient snow during the last ice age (the Wisconsin that began 70,000 years distant and ended 10,000 years back ago) to build the dense pack that later turned to ice and sculpted the landscape, as the glaciers moved out onto the prairie. The Crazies sit in the center of the Crazy Mountain basin and are a part of the crust that folded down not up like most other igneous intrusions (the forcible entry of molten rock or magma into or between other rock formations). Crazy Peak is the highest point at 11,178 feet and is a tertiary intrusion of granite and alkaline rock. The summit rises more than 7,000 feet from the valley floor. Conical Peak rises over 10,000 feet due west.

This time of year the sense of being alone up here, having all of this good country to myself, is overpowering. I feel euphoric, very alone and at peace at the same time. The sun beams down with intense radiance and, despite the altitude, wind and time of the year, provides a palpable warmth.

I work my way over to a boulder that overlooks one of the ponds. This one is several acres. I gain the top of the rock from an easy slope in the rear and stand on the edge about fifteen feet above the floor of this bowl. There are several dark, snowless patches on the ice. Indications of springs. An open area of maybe fifty feet is not far from the near shore. Looking through the binoculars I scan the surface and am surprised, no, stunned, to see cutthroat cruising no more than a foot or two below the surface. I can clearly see their jaws opening and closing as they turn on their sides at times feeding on some type of nymph. This holds my interest for a long time. I could watch the trout until dark. I'd considered bringing a light-weight pack rod, a box of flies and small reel but figured the outing promised to be strange enough without hauling fishing gear up into the mountains in winter. I regret the decision. Next time. And there will be a next time.

This landscape is magnificent in a way that surpasses that of summer or early fall. Maybe this is due to the fact that I've only been to the high country in cold-weather conditions a few times and those were in the Mission, Whitefish and Swan mountains west of the divide in the Flathead Valley.

Unscrewing the plug of the bota, I squirt a long stream of the fortified cocoa into my mouth. Swallow and have another. The liquid is still warm and the brandy burns as it should in my stomach. Clipping the end of the cigar I flick the wheel in my old lighter that ignites as expected. The cigar soon burns smoothly. I lean against a small slab of rock and enjoy the day, the solitude, the sense of accomplishment, though modest, a vast improvement over sitting in front of a keyboard or reading a book.

The cocoa continues to taste good, Some cheese and bread go well and the cigar smokes to its own tune. I'm saving the rest of the water and the candy for the return trip.

The unmistakable sharp cry of a bald eagle whistles down to me, cutting through the distance and wind clear and strong. The bird soars a thousand feet above circling and no doubt trying to figure out what this creature is on the boulder. White head and tail and the long separated feathers at the wing tips are visible through the glasses. Deciding that this particular meal is maybe too large, the eagle shifts course slightly, stretches its wings and sails off down the drainage I've just climbed. He'll cover the distance in minutes. I'll take hours.

I spend another forty minutes smoking and sipping from the bota, then pack load my pack and move off from my perch. The sun is beginning to dip behind the southwest ridge. Time to move. One last 360-degree scan of the alpine bowl and then its time to push down to the trailhead and then ski the few miles back to the rig.

Worth doing all of this again. Tomorrow I'll fish for large browns.

♦ ♦ ♦

I continue on downstream riding the broken water and ripping along the fast-current flats. In no time I'm at the take-out near the Reed Point bridge. I unload our gear, set up camp and walk the mile down a gravel road to the small ranching community, and past the twin grain bins at the north end of town. Reed Point is a town that has a genuine feeling of the old, unspoiled west, and is one of the smallest communities along the Yellowstone River. It was a booming little town in the early part of the century with fifty-four operating businesses. Most of the surrounding area was homesteaded, and after a 3-year drought and realization by the homesteaders that they needed more than the 320 acre allotment in order to make a living in this area, they picked up and moved on further west. The little town began its slow demise at that time, though over the past years there's been a resurgence with the renovation of the Hotel Montana Bed & Breakfast, the steady business at the Waterhole Saloon and at Indian Fort Campground. Small town Montana is alive and well on this stretch of the river.

I walk another block or so and push through the door into the venerable, rustic Waterhole.

The woman behind the bar brings me a cold bottle of Miller's. I order a cheeseburger with homemade french fries and another round. Some older ranchers are working on shots of Rich & Rare whiskey and pitchers of beer while playing cribbage and shooting the breeze about how the hay is doing, cattle futures, Bob's pickup that broke a rear axle when it slammed through a broken cattle guard, last night's hail storm and life in general out in the country.

The place felt good, comfortable, familiar. The cheeseburgers was excellent as were the fries and a couple more beers. I had the bartender load my daypack with a six of the frosty bottles and a pint of Lewis and Clark vodka. Horrible, cheap stuff, but the brand name seemed appropriate for the excursion. I walk back to camp bucking a warm wind that brought an overcast sky and some spitting rain. I build a fire in the growing dark. Worked on the beer and vodka and thought some about the river, the BS guidebooks, and the fishing that was always good on this stretch.

While this was going on, a ranching family—Dad, Mom dressed in designer jeans and high heels, two kids and the old boy who was fat and sported worn bib overalls battered boots and little else—unload near us, cast some lures for a few minutes and then pack up to head to town. The old boy returned from fishing somewhere out of sight, soaked to the shoulders. Belches and farts resounded in the gathering gloom. Quite the crew and we laughed in spite of ourselves. They pulled out in a spray of wet gravel and a cloud of dust when they hit the rod. Then a group of teenagers powered up from somewhere downriver in an aluminum boat with a large outboard motor that bounced, grated and ground along the rocky stream bottom. After what seemed to be six or seven hours and three cases of Keystone beer they finally secured their boat to the trailer that was backed well into the river as was the rear end of the pickup. The two girls screamed and swore in mad glee as the boys roared and spun the tires in four-wheel-drive as the rig finally dug its way up to high, dry ground and on out to the gravel road and then roaring across the tall bridge into Reed Point.

Saturday night is Saturday night whether it's Elizabeth, New Jersey, Old Towne Chicago or right here in downtown Montana nowhere. Life seemed good to the people I'd just been with and to me as well.

Chapter 4

The Modern World Surfaces Then Fades Away
Stillwater River to Pompey's Pillar—83 miles

KNEW THAT REDHEADS WERE CAPABLE OF LAUGHTER. I'D WATCHED
Jill St. John laugh at a bumbling James Bond in *Diamonds are
Forever*, and I'd observed Shirley Maclaine laughing at all sorts of
things—including nothing—in a variety of movies. Well, Ginny wasn't
laughing. She was too busy being herself, but she managed to break me
up with comments, questions and smiles. Close enough. Celtic. Ginny
was standing off to one side of the Suburban in high good humor,
making laughing sounds like crystalline water sailing over a high mountain precipice.

We are camped downstream of this mountain cirque lake on the
Stillwater River, one of the larger tributaries to the Yellowstone located
about forty miles west of Billings. We reached this place by taking a
highway punctuated with long, sweeping curves that climbed through
steppes and bench land of hay, native grasses, sage and tumbleweeds,
thousands of them bunched up in ditches and caught in rough tangles
along barbed wire fence lines.

The Stillwater River plummets and rushes down from snow fields,
sapphire tinted ice fields and mini glaciers more than 12,000 feet above
sea level—the highest country in Montana—in a stark, barren, remote,
awesome landscape that seems both alien and fantastic. Canyon walls
and rough mountains composed of 2.7 billion year old grey granite
gneisses rise precipitously, thousands of feet above us. The gneisses are
coarse grained metamorphic rocks that resemble each other in having
a streaky or banded appearance. The rocks form through re-crystalliza-
tion, at high temperatures, of sedimentary and igneous stone. The clear

water drops in silvery cascades from shelved ledges, and swirls and spins over and through the colorful boulder streambed. Small Yellowstone cutthroat dart here and there, rising swiftly to take small stoneflies and caddis. Shadowy forms of larger trout are visible darting from rock to rock, dredging up nymphs. The air smells richly of pine from the forest that drapes the gentler slopes and clings to the thinnest of ledges in the cliffs. Eagles circle high over head. Mountain Chickadees chatter in the woods and small squirrels ratchet away in annoyance at out intrusion as they watches us from the tops of the pines. The air is cool and warm as it mixes and moves down the valley.

What apparently seemed so damn funny was the sight of an aging, derelict crazed sports fan hopping around on one foot simultaneously swearing in long, darkly-glittering strings of invective at the latest loss by the Chicago Cubs, as relayed by a too lengthy story and tragic box score in the *Billings Gazette* sports section, and the same fool also cursing both his apparently-fractured big toe and the steel wheel that, when recently kicked, caused the injury. I'm working on a can of Pabst, after reading the paper then kicking the Suburban, while sitting on top of a large boulder covered with orange and light-green lichen. The stone leans out over the water and is now in the sun. I lean against my daypack and enjoy the day, but not the results from Wrigley.

Just another Cubs' loss in a staggering continuum of thousands that has rained down on me over the years. How any collection of even marginally-talented professional athletes could kiss away a 7-0 lead in two innings is amazing. I'd been through this a thousand times over the years that stretched painfully across decades of failure, some I only recall in dim, grey shapes that vibrate morosely as infantile memories. This time it was against the Padres who won 8-7 by scoring five runs in the eighth and three in the top of the ninth on just three hits—a bunt and two Texas-League singles. Six Cub errors—a ghastly combination of dropped pop-ups, misplayed grounders, and a pair of throws by second baseman Ryan Theriot to first that wound up high in the Wrigley Field grandstand (one scintillating toss knocked an Old Style beer vendor unconscious, though the lad gamely returned to his duties minutes later to a standing ovation), two balks, six walks, a hit batter and two passed balls led to this. The *Gazette,* along with whiskey, steaks and other assorted vaga-ries—all of this was acquired in a brief, well-coordinated shopping foray in town following our return from several sublime days of fishing the upper Yellowstone in the Absaroka-Beartooth Wilderness for browns, Yellowstone cutthroat and rogue mountain whitefish. Yellowstone cutts— glorious fish of riotous coloration reminding me of their even higher mountain waters cousins, golden trout, except that the Yellowstones feed and take flies much more readily than their high-altitude relatives.

Ah yes. Alpine splendor accented in a delightfully crazy woman flashing crazily about a place where the water was so damn clear the trout seemed to be floating in midair a few feet below me far above tree-line. Yellowstone cutts (*Oncorhynchus clarki alvordensis* for those interested in such matters) are related to Westslope, Snake River, Rio Grande, Paiute, Bonneville, Lahontan and several other species of cut-throat. Like their brethren, they rise readily to a fly, any fly, fight a little, are marked with dark spots, bright reds, yellows shading to orange and aquamarine. They live in only the purest of waters in the best of the Northern Rockies. The fish glided silently about their isolated domain, occasionally tilting skyward with wild nonchalance, rising effortlessly to sip tiny insects trapped in the surface tension of the ice-water. I have no idea what the bugs were. Midges? It didn't matter then, any more than it does today, though at least now in frighteningly-brief moments of clarity, I can sometimes tell a caddis from a mayfly from a stonefly from a grasshopper from a Woolly Bugger from a Royal Wulff from an Outlaw Hopper. That's as far as that foolishness goes, at least as far as I'm willing to admit to at this point. It makes no damn difference anyway. Matching the hatch through specious employment of vaguely-understood, Latin-based entomology—that's what grabs my attention.

"John. Look. A blizzard hatch of *Paraleptophlebia bicornuta.*"

"What the hell are you talking about? Isn't that what killed Nixon?"

"Mayflies, John. They're all over the place."

"Whatever you say. Think I'll head back to the truck. Damn. *Latin* again."

And of course this always gets better. Stomach pumps, charts, magni-fying glasses. Waterproof insect identification charts. Little jars of killing compounds for knocking off the harmless bugs for future Mengeleseian examinations. No thanks. Muddling along trying to find a fly from among the four or five patterns, and during rare times of ostentation, in two or three sizes, something that approximates what is flitting about me is more than enough. When in doubt "Bugger" is my elaborate dictum. Saves time and self-generated frustration. Energy better spent enjoying my friend's spontaneous behavior, which at this moment features her well-tanned, finely-featured body swimming with grace and stealth amid a school of the sun-blasted trout. The fish do not seem to mind Ginny's presence in their midst. They'd be fools, cads, if they did. Cutthroat of a foot, perhaps a little more, coast in lazy serpentine patterns within inches of her. Perfectly formed bars of vibrating gold ghosting around her legs, arms, stomach. Thin lips take insects mere inches from her delightful lips. Smaller fish tug at the ends of her long hair as it waves casually back and forth like burnished, very finely drawn, burnished copper wire. The water can't be more than forty-five degrees, but Ginny just sails on. I look forward to her exit from the lake, water sparkling from her browned skin, goose bumps everywhere, grey-blue eyes flashing, but I digress here beneath truly hammered, weather-blasted peaks. Snowfields with glacial pretensions crack imperceptibly, soundlessly, into the turquoise water generating minor waves. Eagles, a few of them, work the thermals over the sharp ridges. Bear grass, electric green, bursts through the crusty snow. Some kind of yellow flowers glow in the light nearby. The dog is asleep on a shrinking snow drift that hangs, barely, from a ledge above me, his legs kicked out behind him frog style, large head, tongue lolling to one side, draped over the edge. Far above, just below the sun, a spout of ice-melt soars far out over the lake eventually spattering the surface in a rainbow mixture of mist and droplets that sounds like delicate glass wind chimes playing in a soft breeze.

"Gosh, John. What's with this sweet-dream, idyllic, hippy jive? Get your mind back on its cynical, acerbic, predestined track. The one we all know and love. Lose that other nonsense. Good God. We're becoming ill," or thoughts along that line rattle up upstairs. I look up to see Ginny standing next to me in wild silhouette, the light blazing around her features like an aura.

"Gone again. Some people and acid. Not a productive combination is it or is it?" and she pulled on her cutoffs and bikini top. She was still driving me nuts. "Is it after five?"

"Closer to three, Ginny."

"Just the right time," and she filled a couple of tin cups with bourbon retrieved from the day pack and added a splash of snow-cold water from the Stillwater. She handed me mine and sipped hers with exaggerated grace, little finger extended. "Quite good. Ready for more yet? No? Well, there's plenty of time." Give me a break, girl. I'd already forgotten about casting to the cutthroat and she was laughing at everything around her, head thrown back, arms spread wide. So much for finishing college or my childish dreams of being a writer. Take me now, Lord. My life, such as it had been to this point, is fulfilled. My brief spate of work here is finished.

We lingered over another drink and Ginny decided that we should eat freshly-caught cutthroat grilled over a fire tonight for dinner along with some Idaho bakers and a salad made from fern heads, wild onions and wild flowers she'd foraged earlier in the day, plus some mushrooms she'd spotted along the horse trail far below early this morning. I was hoping for morels. So she picked up the slender seven-foot, three-weight that was leaning on a wind-blown pine by the lake, snapped off my Adams and attached a #8 Olive Woolly Worm with a tuft of red for a tail. She'd tied the thing herself a few nights back and was convinced that the trout up here would love her creation. I didn't tell her that this was the pattern's basic style, though I'd not seen many palmered with cree hackle before or with the tail made with a tuft of feathers plucked from the flaming crimson plume of a stuffed Pileated woodpecker she'd spotted hanging out in a display case in an obscure fly shop up around Wolf Creek sometime last winter. Nice touches with a hint of outlaw exotic to them. She was pleased with the effort and was now casually working fifty feet or so of line out over the water, then she let the fly drop in front of some cruising cutts allowing it to sink slowly, unimpeded, down below the surface for a few feet before giving the thing an enticing twitch. Three trout stopped in their tracks, dropped what they were doing and raced for Ginny's offering. I knew how they felt. Helpless. A trout of thirteen or fourteen inches, big for here, scored first, slamming the pattern with a slash of its head and then it raced for deeper doings at the stab of the hook's point. Ginny let the fish swim around in frantic circles for a minute, then stripped the line in, bent down and grabbed the fish mid-body and whacked its head on a rock. She pulled a knife from a skin-tight pocket, opened the blade and then the trout from one end to the other, tearing out the trout's guts and gills, throwing them behind her into some subalpine fir. Next she lofted the clean, just dead trout in my direction.

"Three more, John. Two for each of us. Tonight's dinner."

Three more casts. Three more trout. Apparently her work was done here, too, except for the salad. The potatoes were half-baked. Appropriate, all things considered. The small fire, now burned down to hot coals, was ready for the fish, that were lightly salt-and-peppered. Ginny worked on the salad. Those mushrooms looked vaguely familiar and not in a morel kind of way. She made a dressing of lime juice, honey and olive oil with a touch of garlic. Life was tough up here.

"I'll open those two bottles of Soave. They should be cold by now, and I'll serve the salad when all else is ready." Or should I say fails? No. Not tonight, I think. "We've got that cognac, too. Remember?"

"Think we'll get through the night, Ginny? Pretty Spartan provisions on the substance end of the equation."

"We'll make it. I promise. Don't panic on me now. Geez. Kids. Some of you are hopeless."

Ginny was in her 50s, closing in on 10,000 or perhaps 7 in an insanely pleasant way. Met her while over for dinner at a friend's house in Whitefish. Well, she liked the same things I did, loud music, strong drinks, photography, late nights, camping, solitude, benign madness, fly fishing, driving way too fast, smoking lots of cigarettes, raising hell. So we were soon living together—within a couple of years, time being relative. Ginny is a woman of quality in my eyes and those of any other male passing within hailing distance, as I frequently noticed. A lady who had so many things spinning around and through her, that just sitting by a fire late at night next to her bordered on an alien experience in the most esoteric, tangential ways. But, as usual, and I admit, unfairly, this is one of those deals where you truly had to be there. (Imagination run riot and bizarre on the reader's part is considered acceptable in this situation, though.)

The cutthroat were excellent, a little like brook trout but even more delicate in flavor with a slight taste of winter. The potatoes were filling and the salad was, well, I guess you could say another one of Ginny's salads, something she was quite famous for within our circle of twisted friends. We worked over the wine. The sun was behind the mountains, the sky a bright white fading to darkening silver then light blue and finally deep blue. Stars were coming on here and there all along the eastern horizon above the serrated ridge tops of the Beartooth Mountains, crowding the sky up the canyon. A chorus of frogs battled their way upstream against the rushing call of the river. The air smelled coolly of distant snow and ice mixed with lodgepole and the wood smoke. The only sounds were those of running water, the curling flames and a touch of breeze pushing softly through the trees.

"Good dinner, huh?" and Ginny shot a fierce grin in my direction. "Seems we have plenty of wood for the evening and I see you found the cognac and glasses. All set. What shall we talk about, not that it matters in cases like this?" I could live this way with her for a long time, a very long time, but money was always going to be an issue. Sometimes a lot of work for little money, but my time was my own. Over the decades I've discovered that all of this, the writing con, really is quite easy, a lot more so than staggering out of bed at dawn, five-six days a week, every week, year after year and wandering mindlessly into some real job overseen by some ego-crazed jerk in search of his mind.

"Ginny, how do you feel about handguns and 7-Elevens?"

"Don't worry about money. It always takes care of itself. Hasn't it so far? I can work as a substitute at the Middle School while you write. No problem. Piece of cake. No robberies just yet. You think you're kidding about that stuff, but I know you better than you do yourself on some things. Don't dwell on the guns. Please? Let it slide for a while. Okay."

When Ginny said "Please" that way, I was through, and besides, at this point, blowing off any concept or potential problem was brain-dead simple. My head was not rolling along with straight-line thinking at the moment. Figuring a way to keep earning a living, of manufacturing more cash, that could wait 'til tomorrow. A meteor sizzled directly overhead leaving a trail of sparkling exhaust in its wake. A natural sign to forget the real world. I opened the cognac.

♦ ♦ ♦

One of Montana's smallest amphibians, the boreal chorus frog grows to only one or, perhaps in a trophy-sized individual, two inches in length. The first time I encountered these diminutive, yet extremely vocal individuals, was on a long ago trip around the northern high plains with my dear friends John Talia and the late Robert F. Jones. The last time I experienced the frogs' amazing sounding abilities was when Talia and I scattered our friends ashes in some of his favorite country.

The memory of that din remains undiminished despite the expanding distance of sometimes-rough years. I wonder if my friend John Talia and I have figured things right this year. Timing, while not everything in this case, is of some import. Is this last week in April when we need to be here or are we already late? Maybe even a little early? Would we hear that insane noise again after all this time? What a dilemma. What inane and manufactured drama for an audience of nobody. Questions of no importance when I think about them a bit. The point is that we're here, back in the Breaks and it's spring.

We lurch along in Talia's '84 Suburban, The Great White as we did ten years ago. The land moves upon us in leaps and jerks. Grassy swales grow large through the windshield then slide past us to be replaced by eroded rips in the land that drop for a hundred feet or deeper. Then these too are overtaken by still another emerald green wave of grass mixed with blue-green clumps of sage. Deep blue, crimson, yellow, pure white throughout. Wildflowers. Sage grouse burst up with loud clucks and the hammering sound of wings beating frantically in escape. The air smells sweet, rich and pungent—of life. Small grasshoppers of early season bounce off the rig by the hundreds. All of this is exactly as I remember it from the first trip. No *déjà vu* jive. Only flat-out, reconstructed exactitude.

And now that raucous spring of our past with its roar of millions of the boreal chorus frogs screaming their little lungs out in full-tilt, mating frenzy and sounding like countless fingers running over the teeth of an infinite number of combs, that experience is plugged into this present. The moment is fresh in my mind. It is part of right now. Maybe it always will be, like the first time with a woman or the first hit of some psychedelic drug I did long ago. These crazed amphibians had one thing on their collective mind and that was sex. Reproduction. Preserve the species. And they were damn loud about it. The sound would drop down a few decibels to the roar of a mid-sized commercial jet and then began rising in intensity and pitch until the air hummed and vibrated with a high-pitched scream like a tree-top level squadron of F16s flashing directly overhead, the air crackling and vibrating. Unbelievable. A bald eagle takes flight, working enormous wings as it leaps from a weathered, solitary fence post draped with gnarled strands of rusted barbed wire that drop in a tangle, the ends disappearing in the dead, matted grass of last year. For some reason the sight of this huge bird lends certainty to the idea that all those whacked-out frogs are down along the muddy, willow-choked river bottom raising their raucous brand of procreational nirvana once again, even as we cruise along this rutted two-track slowly closing in on the secluded breeding grounds. I imagine that I can hear the wild noise drifting up from the river, over the tops of the dusty bluffs, down along the dirt path we're on and through the window opening. I glance at Talia. He's focused on the road just as I remember him looking back when he, Bob Jones and I were doing this. And I think about the sound all those frogs were making back then and how I yelled "Unreal," Talia just throwing up his hands and laughing. Bob puffing on his smoke and staring at the river. Neither one of them could hear me from a distance of ten feet.

The frogs rocked on unabated. The cacophony jumped, twisted and soared on the spirited, warm spring breeze. The truest song of being alive I'd ever heard ricocheted back and forth among the limestone cliffs, tore through the pines and sizzled across the already tall grass flanking the river. The frogs' frenzy gathered in intensity. The air became charged as what must have been a group orgasm within the Montana contingent of the species became so loud I could not sense anything but this sound. Forget millions. Try billions of these little one-inch animals. Grey-green with three dark stripes. The landscape rippled with their movement like a surreal snake. The land was seething with life.

We looked at each other and laughed, and I must admit to a slight sense of fear mixed with awe and wonder at this natural outburst. This land is magic. The kind of country the three of us have lived for all our lives. The day before, on that trip, we'd spotted an elk the size of a rhinoceros with a five-point companion that seemed a dwarf in juxtaposition.

We're in the best of good country way out here on the high plains. Wild. Mind blowing. Dangerous in the quickest and subtlest of ways— muddy roads dropping off into space, lightning storms with hundreds of strikes a minute, rattlesnakes and their enemies the milk snakes. And a decade ago this country provided the clearest vision I've ever seen of spring exploded to full-scale riot. I remember looking up and watching flights of ducks and geese coming down from the north—Canada's, mallards, a few teal. Farther out and way over by a serrated series of salmon, ochre and charcoal ridges and gullies, hawks and eagles circled in easy truce with each other as the large raptors scoured the grassland below for jack rabbits, prairie dogs and, for all I know, small deer. Coyotes dashed along ahead of the Suburban, often turning back to face us, barking and yipping at the large rig before resuming their dog trot as though they were employed as our guides.

Rebirth after weathering the illusion of a slow-motioned, dark death of winter. The three of us doing whatever we pleased from floating the Bighorn to fishing the small ponds here for rainbows and bass to eating way too much Talia-grilled meat to drinking a lot of whiskey and brandy. Bob called the whole, self-absorbed fiasco our Spring Breaks Trip.

All of that seems like a very long time ago. I glance at Talia and he nods, no doubt thinking along similar lines. Bob died the previous December. When I told John, he suggested scattering some of our friend's ashes in this country. Bob's wife, Louise, agreed and sent us some. That's why we're here this spring. To say goodbye in a way we understand and Bob would appreciate. Unspoiled land. Late night fires. Talk. Freedom.

We eventually reach a dry camp that John's used for years, dropping down from a brief rise and then moving along a expansive bench covered with prickly pear and clumps of native grass. A coulee looking like a serrated wound made in the land with a dull knife runs north-south not far from camp. A cluster of pines whose tops are bent from the constant harsh winds of the area dominate the site. A small rise provides shelter from the western gales. Setting up camp doesn't take long. We've done it before. I look over and see a fire is already burned down to coals. Several thick, stuffed pork chops are sizzling on a grill. Ten years ago we had the same thing. The smell of cooking meat mixes with the scents of grass, sage and pine.

"Hey Holt. Anything look familiar?"

"We're missing your Avon raft," and we both laugh.

On the first trip in, we'd dragged along John's Avon after fishing the madhouse that is the Bighorn for three days. We'd had uncommon luck. By that poor over-worked river's standards, the floating was relatively uncrowded, perhaps only 150 drift boats and rafts per day. The browns were active, hammering a variety of nymphs we dredged down deep in front of them. Lots of trout over twenty inches, a number over two-feet. Bob connected with one that was past twenty-seven inches. That fish tore line off as it fled downriver. Talia rowed in pursuit. The brown won the race when it snapped the tippet.

And I remember taking photos of Talia sitting in the raft as it rested on the trailer in camp here with Bob casting artfully to several prairie dogs. None of them took, but we've learned to take fishing as it presents itself. And I recall a biologist rolling past at sunrise on her way to study the ghost prairie dog town that had been wiped out by the Bubonic Plague. She roared by but caught site of the raft, slammed on the brakes, skidding with a cloud of red dust. She looked through the cab's rear window, started to drive away, hit the brakes again and looked back one more time before accelerating down the two-track and away from what was clearly an ugly situation waiting to happen.

I reminded John of this. We both laughed, then were silent, thinking about our departed friend. Bob and I had known each other for years. We'd met in the Paradise Valley at Chico one stormy early May night. Since that time we'd visited each other in Montana or Bob's home in Vermont with a frequency that frightened our editors, family and one or two friends. Fly fishing, gunplay, late nights around fires, a bit of booze and many road miles in the process. Over the years we killed trout, bass, sharp-tailed grouse, woodcock, antelope and bar whiskey. Talia had been along for a number of these excursions. All through the years Bob, who was one of this country's finest writers with novels like *Blood Sport*, *The Diamond Bogo* and *The Run to Gitche Gumee*, had been a staunch supporter of mine, both through good times and uncommonly bad ones. He'd connected me with writer friends of his like Howard Frank Mosher and Annie Proulx, and always had time to edit and critique my book manuscripts. We both grew up in southern Wisconsin, loved sports, the outdoors and were outspoken in our opinions on a few things. We'd made a pact on the first trip in here that the last one standing would drink a bottle of whiskey in memory of all of it. I kept my word on the Jim Beam end of things. As for Talia, it was his slightly sodden suggestion that I write a collection of short stories about my experiences with fly fishing guides and that I should call it *Guide Wars*. This idea was offered with one of his characteristic wise-ass grins and a bunch of enthusiasm late one night in the middle of everywhere. I wrote and sold the book. His fault, not mine.

We talk about all of this as we eat our meal. Then the two of us walk away from camp and look out over the vast, ranging, rough cut country that seems to stretch out from us for eternity. The land is turning sunset pink, orange and soft gold. Thick indigo shadows move across the grass, sage and small pines. We raise our glasses in remembrance of Bob and take long drinks.

"Tomorrow we go out to the overlook above those frogs and scatter Bob's ashes," said Talia. "He'll have a good view of things from there. It's only a couple of hours. Maybe we'll fish one of the ponds along the way."

We walk back to the fire beneath a moonless sky that is going black in a hurry and filling up with maybe too many bright stars and galaxies— the stuff of serious brain fade.

Late afternoon. High overcast. The sun glowing behind high cloud cover casts a metallic glow across the land. Cool southwest breeze. We stand on the edge of the bluffs. The river flows steel grey hundreds of feet below. Rafts of ducks hold tight to shoreline reed beds. Strings of geese tack across the wind. The grasses ripple like waves.

Earlier we'd cruised along these bluffs farther downstream. We passed reservoirs and ponds. Fish rose in some of them. We didn't cast to them. We dropped down a crumbling, narrow cut through blond then tan then ochre then grey rock, down to a path that twisted along the river. As we came around a turn that hugged a limestone outcrop the blast of the chorus frogs nailed us. John stopped the Great White. We got out and walked closer to the water, pushing through what seemed to be palpable waves of amphibian racket. The frogs were everywhere. So much so that they appeared to be a moving extension of the earth. I started to miss Bob and wish that he were here to experience this madness again, but stopped. Hell, I could hear his gruff but patient voice in my head and I could smell the smoke from the Merits he liked to puff on. He was with us. Good friends never leave. Not really.

I walked a hundred yards through a storm-battered stand of Ponderosa pine. I approached the grave site of a long-ago homesteader. The weathered headstone was guarded by a small rectangle of wire fence. This man had lived more than a hundred years and died nearly as long ago. Years ago, when we first stood here, Bob had removed his ball cap, stepped between the strands of wire and placed it on the marker. The hat was gone now. We returned to the Suburban. We turned around and began the slow climb that twisted along the face of the bluffs. The river was soon well below us. Dry balls of tumble weeds or Russian thistle rolled across our path bound for who knows where. The sun broke through briefly. Shafts of light cut across the water, through the pines and down brightly on the grave site. We rolled on.

On the bluff I unscrewed the lid of the jar that held Bob's ashes. I handed them to Talia who moved downwind of me and spread half of them along the ground at the edge of the precipice. John was right. Bob could keep an eye on things from here. The weather couldn't sneak up on him. He returned and passed me the ashes. I raised the jar and shook the rest of the remains into the wind. The light grey ash dispersed across the land blowing to the northeast.

I don't know how Talia felt about all of this, but I believe that we both knew that we'd done the right thing. That our friend would have approved, nodding with a wry smile. We were alive. Bob's spirit rode along with us as it always would. And death had come full circle once more.

♦ ♦ ♦

Billings is the largest city in Montana, located in the south-central portion of the state. And along with Great Falls, Missoula and Helena one of my least favorite places in the state. All of them are too busy, too obsessed with growth and, for a loner like myself, they all have far too many people. It's nickname is the Magic City because of its rapid growth from its founding as a railroad town in 1882. It was said that Billings "grew like magic." Billings is named for Frederick H. Billings, president of the Northern Pacific Railroad. Billings is the largest city in a 500 mile radius (south-central and eastern Montana and northern Wyoming).

Before the Europeans came, the Crow People lived in the Yellowstone River valleys and the surrounding areas. Their true name is the Apsáalooke, which means "people of the large-beaked bird."

In 1806, William Clark traveled through the region with the Corps of Discovery. He signed his name twenty-five miles northeast of Billings. The inscription consists of his signature and the date July 25, 1806. The whole scene strikes me as a bit odd because this signature is hiding behind a glass case that is viewed from a seriously sturdy wooden platform. Necessary for preservation I suppose, but also plastic in feeling. Clark claimed he climbed the sandstone pillar and "had a most extensive view in every direction on the Northerly Side of the river." The pillar was named by Clark after the son of Sacajawea, the Shoshone woman who helped to guide the expedition and had acted as an interpreter. Clark had called Sacajawea's son "Pompy" and his original name for the outcropping was "Pompys Tower." It was later changed, in 1814, to the current title, Pompy's Pillar. Clark's inscription is the only remaining physical evidence to be found along the route that was followed by the expedition.

The growth of Billings is a good example of the overall growth in the West. In 1870, the city's population was 145 intrepid souls. By 1900, it was 3,211. In 1950, it was 31,834 and, in 2006, it was around 102,000. Lord only knows what the number will be in 2525 that fateful year delineated in the long-ago Zager and Evans song "In the Year 2525."

♦ ♦ ♦

While drifting the river from below the Huntley Diversion we glided past large fields of sugar beats and corn, mainly along the southern side of the Yellowstone. Along the flats and bluffs to the north are miles and miles of sagebrush. Looking at this open, sere landscape reminds me of a hunt for sage grouse that some friends and I had a couple of years ago…

…the rancher, a tall lean man with skin that is permanently browned from years in the sun and wind, tells us with a easy pointing of his long index finger to head across the creek, that, "By the way, that has some damn nice browns in it." Then we are to follow the gravel road that winds up and through gentle draws full of wild raspberry, chokecherry, alder, matted grass and Lord only knows what else. Finally he says we'll strike a two-track up on top that ran the length of the crest of a broad bluff. "Haven't been over that way in a few years, but they're always birds hiding in the sage along the top," the rancher said. "They like the water in the stock ponds."

We follow his instructions and in no time reach the flat that gives way to sweeping views of the Big Horn Mountains shining lavender and snowy below the state line in Wyoming and beyond this further west the northern half of the Pryors peek around the top of the Big Horns showing themselves as rounded distinct silhouettes. The Wolf Mountains hold in the east. We'd hunted Sharp-tailed grouse there yesterday with plenty of birds and a few good shots. And we watched as perhaps a ton of turkeys lumbered into the air in front of us and, with deceptive grace, disappeared into a stand of Ponderosa. They did this with only the sound of their large wings whipping the air as they gradually gained height above us. North towards Billings hills of dry buff and tan grass roll off into the distance. Still-life waves cresting against an ultramarine sky, a sky without clouds. The air smells of the dry grass and dust and the distant snows of the Big Horns.

Early October. Near eighty. Warm breeze. Not ideal conditions for upland bird hunting. We lean back against the Blazer and savor the view, one as fine as it gets in a land somewhat famous for its landscapes. The only sounds are those of the wind sifting through the grass and the ticking of the cooling motor.

Eventually we uncase our shotguns and begin walking through the clumps of sage, kicking up white clouds of alkali as we go. Soil not good for anything, really. Wildly eroded sandstone formations resembling mushrooms, addled giants and abandoned battlements rise up here and there among the pines. Working beside and beneath these natural sculptures is like wandering through an open-air museum of mysterious Cretaceous art. Side-hilling our way up one sage-clogged draw we jump not a single bird, and by the time we reach the top we are all hot and thirsty. One of us fetches four beers from the cooler in the back of the Blazer. We down them quickly while silently wondering if there are any grouse out this way, then we crumple and place the cans in a neat pile for retrieval on our return.

We slog off once again through the heat and bugs and sage that smells perfumey in a strong—almost choking—way. When, suddenly, not one or two but perhaps thirty sage grouse explode into the air with surprising quickness for such large birds—five to eight pounds. They move downwind in a hurry and we're pressed to draw a bead on these guys.

I remember my shots clearly. Two from a Berretta over-and-under 20-gauge. I saw one bird clearly among the many and swing through its arcing rise to my right and fired, marking where it fell, and then a late riser burst in front of me and I caught this one before he was twenty yards away and well above me, framed against the blue of the sky and the flickering motion of the other grouse. He fell, too. A rare double for me.

I hear my companions shooting around me as I retrieve the grouse. The first one is heavy and warm in my hand with one drop of crimson blood in the corner of its beak. I find the other without trouble and push it into the pouch in the back of my vest with the other one.

Shooting is exciting. A rush. I love it, but the shading that outlines all of this is the feeling of remorse, even the responsibility for the lives I just took. I can't nor do I ever intend to justify any of this to anyone, even my bird-hunting friends. This part of hunting, the killing, is private, internal and the feelings subtly unique for each of us.

I reach the top and the dusty two-track. Among us we've dropped seven grouse. Two each for three of us and one for our other companion. We leave the nearly forty pounds of birds in a pile on a couple of bales of hay and walk back to the Blazer. A good deal is said between us with few words, lots of smiles and a shared vibe of how good it feels to be out in this country at this time of the year. Paradise, simply paradise. We enjoy our success in silence sipping, beers and watching the sun begin to dip and the light turn golden.

We drive the rig back to where the grouse are piled and after taking some photographs of the birds and gun on a bale of hay, drop the birds in a mesh bag and place them on a sheet of canvass in the shade behind the bench seat. As we sip our beers in the breezy peacefulness, the day turns more intense. Blues, golds, oranges, greens of juniper, all of these and more, intensify to a depth of color that appeared to glow softly in the late afternoon light.

None of us wants this timelessness to end. Good cigars, Cuban Quinteros from an unnamed Florida source, are produced. Superb coronas to finish off a great day. We turn silent enjoying our smokes and some beers before breaking our guns, climbing in the Blazer and beginning the long drive back to hotel rooms waiting in Billings. Finally we head back down to the ranch house. We stop and speak with the rancher telling him of our successes and thanking him for his generosity. One of us produces a bottle of Lagavulin single-malt Scotch from his duffel and presents it to the rancher from all of us along with the sage grouse.

"Have to soak these bastards overnight to get the taste of sage out of them," he says with a grin. Then we shake hands and drive out towards the highway.

A full moon rises brightly above the Wolf Mountains as our designated driver plays it straight, something of a stretch, while the rest of us work on another bottle of the Lagavulin, the whiskey tasting of peat and smoke. We cruise within the night beneath the moon and the stars back to the city. A perfect day concluding a fine trip.

◆ ◆ ◆

After running a shuttle from the East Side Bridge in town to below the Huntley Diversion Dam, about nine river miles, we drove back to Billings and replenished our supplies and topped off the Suburban. The day was blisteringly hot so we decided to kill a few hours, in time-honored fashion, at a couple of bars in town after completing the hellacious run down from Columbus to Laurel. I can't remember what the places names were, but we passed an early afternoon in what may have been the Rainbow or the Reno Club, perhaps the Tap Inn or Buck's Bar—all establishments designed with the drinker in mind. Later that day, at camp on an island some miles upstream of Pompey's Pillar, I verbally sketched in my impressions of the murky time mainly because the experience entails so much of what generates my ambivalence about cities and being around people in numbers of more than two or three.

I push in to the cool dark. The white-hot blasted light drops away behind with the whoosh of the door closing. I sit next to a group of guys having a few and order a bourbon ditch. I'm soon drawn into the mix, the conversation, like my canoe, being sucked into standing waves.

One of the patrons, a person possibly once raised around sports and the trappings of a privileged birth, remembers the days of *American Sportsman* on television showcasing cape buffalo in Africa, trout in Ketchum, partridge and pheasants far out on the Dakotas. Those were the old days on ABC-TV, back when networks championed quality instead of marketing scams devised by young punk ad execs with no life skills or talent in anything but mediocrity. With Bing Crosby and Phil Harris holding forth and another batch of men—hunting, fishing, drinking buddies—similar in many oblique ways to the boys sitting in this bar today.

Raising hell all around the place: fishing for sea run browns in Tierra del Fuego, lion hunting in Kenya, dove shooting in Mexico, tarpon fishing off of Boca Grande, tracking Faro sheep in the Yukon, ancient lake trout in Great Slave, and at the end of every day, as a wild landscape sun touched down, there were the drinks and Phil Harris raising his tumbler high saying "post time" with the joy of a real drinker. The boys in this bar did the same thing only it was mule deer and chukars in the Pryors, browns and rainbows on the Yellowstone and Big Horn, elk in the Beartooths and sharptails in the Bull Mountains.

The one who remembers tells his tales to the others. They all nod and think that this is one hell of a way to travel. So they sally forth to another bar down the street and I tag along, a welcome outsider. We stroll in with great aplomb, panache, a certain air most commonly associated with those of regal birth rights. After all, we have sixty-eight bucks and change between us. A twenty found along the curb hiding among the litter of cigarette butts, gum wrappers, hand bills for strip shows, brings the total to eighty-eight. Enough for the afternoon and some of us have credit cards if things get moving pretty good.

We pull into the next stop—maybe the Elusive Trout or the Tap Inn. Doesn't matter. We order as one entity, "Double bar whiskey on the rocks for each of us." The bartender looks at us with weary curiosity, but we seem assured, happy, confident so he doesn't say much as he slides the drinks across the cigarette burned mahogany bar to us. This may be an unusual occurrence along this hard-time part of town where the cool wind blowing down from the high country is normally knocked senseless by desert-like furnace temperatures this time of year. This breeze, gale, tornadic gust shoots down streets, around corners, whips up dirt, dust, paper, making life a little tougher than it needs to be.

"And one for yourself good man."

We all raise our glasses high, the bartender getting right with this as soon as he finished slamming a man's face onto the bar. Business is business. A bit scary, expected, depressing. We laugh and smile at each other and at the grinning bartender and then with the best of Phil Harris in a neighborhood he'd never visit, we say firmly with the rare power of recognition that they too are hunters of a peculiar sort, and more importantly, men who stay with it hard times or not:

So they say as one, "Post Time."

We continue this way for some time and I learn some about all of them except one guy who smiles slightly but is largely silent. Not much known about the tallest and maybe oldest of them. Quiet, stare down eyes, he sits dead still, motionless. Keeps to himself and is called Ed. Maybe fifty-five, maybe thirty. Who the hell knows. The years make liars of all of us as they allow persona shifts largely undetectable even by stone cold wolves.

And I find myself inside my head as I watch these guys and myself in the smoky mirror behind the bar, even while talking with them and working on my drink. Spinning around like listening over and over to a bad advertising jingle or maybe John Dean's *"At this point in time"* doublespeak. Always the damn images of what might have been. Still there's this easy life in the mountains away from the BS, fishing for cutthroat, floating the Yellowstone, working the ridges for spruce and blues, playing tag with grizzlies, walking with elk, moose.

I can see clearly from sea to shining sea. Thank any God for these guys this afternoon. They don't ask and I don't tell. We drink away the hours, the days. Taking certain roads sometimes hurts hard, but there's a little peace now and then, more so as years wander by. Enough so I can catch my breath and these guys are friends for now and that's long enough. And really none of us are hip to all that much about any of our past lives, which don't matter. Who cares. All of it is dead and gone. Worthless, blown away like that gun smoke after a gone-wrong liquor store robbery. This afternoon, such as it is, adds a little to the river of white light we ride each day.

Maybe the one the others know so little about was a big deal back when, back where none of us are interested. As we sit here taking it all in, as nothing at all keeps on happening.

Yeah that's it and why I prefer being out on the river by myself or with Ginny taking all of the natural ride in and actually feeling pretty damn good about life.

◆ ◆ ◆

While drifting the river from below the Huntley Diversion we glide past large fields of sugar beets and corn, mainly along the southern side of the Yellowstone. Along the flats and bluffs to the north miles and miles of sagebrush and tumbleweed hold the day.

Artemisia tridentata (Sagebrush, Big sagebrush, Common sagebrush, Blue sagebrush or Black sagebrush) is a shrub or small tree from the family *Asteraceae*. Some botanists treat it in the segregate genus *Seriphidium*, as *S. tridentatum* (Nutt.) W. A. Weber, but this is not widely followed. The name sagebrush is also used for several related members of the genus *Artemisia*, such as California sagebrush (*Artemisia californica*).

It is a coarse, hardy silvery-grey bush with yellow flowers and grows in arid sections of the western U.S. It is the primary vegetation across vast areas of the Great Basin desert. Along rivers or in other relatively wet areas, sagebrush can grow as tall as three meters (ten feet), but is more typically one or two meters tall.

Sagebrush has a strong pungent fragrance, especially when wet, which is not unlike common sage. It is, however, unrelated to common sage and has a bitter taste. It is thought that this odor serves to discourage browsing. Sagebrush leaves are wedge-shaped 1–4 cm long and 0.3–1 cm broad, and are attached to the branch by the narrow end. The outer and wider end is generally divided into three lobes (although leaves with two or four lobes are not uncommon), hence the scientific name *tridentata*. The leaves are covered with fine silvery hairs, which are thought to keep the leaf cool and minimize water loss. Most of the leaves are carried year-round, as sagebrush tends to grow in areas where winter precipitation is greater than summer precipitation.

Sagebrush leaves compare favorably to alfalfa for livestock nutrition value. However, they also contain oils that are toxic to the symbiotic bacteria in the rumen of most ruminants. These oils have the greatest effect on cattle. Cattle that resort to sagebrush due to the lack of other fodder in the winter often freeze to death before starving, as they rely in large part on the heat of their digestive action for warmth. Ranchers call this condition "hollow belly." Sheep can tolerate moderate consumption of sagebrush leaves, especially the fresh spring buds. Pronghorn are the only large herbivore to browse sagebrush extensively.

As pronghorn are the only remaining large herbivore that evolved along with sagebrush (deer are a more recent arrival from Asia), this is not surprising. There is speculation that some of the herbivores that went extinct in North America at the end of the Pleistocene such as the Ground sloth or the American camel were also capable of browsing sagebrush.

Sagebrush is not fire-tolerant and relies on wind-blown seeds from outside burned areas for re-establishment. This is in contrast to many of the other plants of the High Desert, such as Rabbit brush, Ephedra and bunchgrasses, which can root-sprout after a fire. Cheatgrass has invaded much of the sagebrush habitat, and if left unchecked could possibly create a fire cycle that is too frequent to allow sagebrush to re-establish itself.

In the Great Basin, sagebrush is the dominant plant life in the Upper Sonoran and boreal life zones, and is the primary understory species in the Transitional zone between them. Prior to heavy grazing by cattle and sheep of these areas, sagebrush is thought to have been less dominant, and perennial grasses more common. In the Lower Sonoran life zone, sagebrush is generally replaced by shadescale or greasewood.

The Greater Sage grouse, *Centrocercus urophasianus*, is a large grouse. Adults have a long, pointed tail and legs with feathers to the toes. Adult males have a yellow patch over the eye, are greyish on top with a white breast, a dark brown throat and a black belly; two yellowish sacs on the neck inflate during courtship display. Adult females are mottled grey-brown with a light brown throat and dark belly.

The breeding habitat for the Sage grouse is sagebrush country in the western U.S. and southern Alberta and Saskatchewan in Canada. They nest on the ground under sagebrush or grass patches.

Sage grouse are notable for their elaborate courtship rituals. Each spring, males congregate on leks and perform a "strutting display." Groups of females observe these displays and select the most attractive males to mate with. Only a few males do most of the breeding. Males perform on leks for several hours in the early morning and evening during the spring months. Leks are generally open areas adjacent to dense sagebrush stands, and the same lek may be used by grouse for decades. Many biologists consider the sage grouse a threatened species.

The U.S. Geological Survey National Wildlife Health Center has reported that the West Nile virus continues to spread into previously unaffected populations of Greater sage grouse across the West. The disease has now been detected in sage grouse in California, Colorado, Idaho, Montana, Nevada, Oregon, North Dakota, South Dakota, Utah and Wyoming, as well as Alberta. Experimental studies at have shown that West Nile virus is usually fatal to sage grouse, resulting in death within six days of infection.

West Nile virus represents the latest factor in the decline of Greater sage grouse populations. The species already suffers from habitat loss. Livestock grazing, oil and gas drilling, off-road vehicle use, the spread of invasive species, and the placement and construction of roads, fences and utility corridors continues to fragment and degrade what remains.

"The evidence that supports listing Greater sage grouse under the Endangered Species Act is mounting," said Mark Salvo, Director of the Sagebrush Sea Campaign.

The historic range of Greater sage grouse closely conformed to the distribution of sagebrush-steppe in what became twelve western states and three Canadian provinces. But, since 1900, sage grouse populations have declined. Greater sage grouse distribution has decreased by at least 44 percent, while overall abundance has been reduced by as much as 93 percent from historic levels.

◆ ◆ ◆

Eventually, after drifting below miles of ochre and grey cliffs and bluffs with lengths of emerald fields of corn, sugar beets and hay, we come to a wooded island where camp is made. The place is perhaps a half-mile above the outcrop of rock known as Pompey's Pillar. The rock is visible rising above the cottonwoods.

Across the river on the north side I see a lone buck mule deer peering at me from behind a weathered barbed wire fence. The animal probably doesn't see all that many people in a canoe, so I'm of at least marginal interest to him. We hold each other's gaze for an indefinable period, the only sounds are those of the river burbling over and around rocks and gravel shelves, a gentle wind moving through the leaves and a magpie talking away to itself about who knows what. Then we resuming our business, the deer grazing and me attending to camp.

Yellowstone Drift

We're beat from the long float, so we build a quick fire, make soup, eat some cashews and a Mounds Bar and wash all of this down with a cup of green tea. The night is clear and mild. Stars everywhere. We forgo a tent and spread our sleeping bags on top of a tarp and cushion. We're asleep in seconds. Tomorrow will have to wait.

Chapter 5

Back Into The Sun
Pompey's Pillar to Howrey Island—54 miles

I HAVE COMPLETED THE STRETCH BETWEEN HUNTLEY AND HYSHAM that moves quickly but relatively smoothly past Pompey's Pillar, a large elongated chunk of 200-foot-high sandstone that towers above the river. I shoved off a little after the brilliantly red and orange sunrise. A herd of perhaps forty pronghorn was standing, feeding and resting in a large field on the north side of the river when I struck out. Their dark eyes followed my quiet passage, heads rotating smoothly to track my course, tails flicking now and then in some form of pronghorn communication. I beach, tie off the canoe and stroll up the paved sidewalk to the stairs leading to the top of the rock. I spot a rattlesnake sunning itself on an exposed patch of adjacent walkway that leads off into sandstone and cottonwoods. Hopefully the snake will remain undisturbed and not panic too many visitors.

It was here that William Clark carved his name in 1806. I've been here before but make the obligatory pause to stare like a drooling imbecile at the signature preserved under a large frame of glass for all to see as they trudge up a boardwalk series of steps to the pillar's summit, where a park employee greets everyone with "I see you made it," then shoves a replica of an ancient compass in their shaking hands so that the visitors can feel like they are actually experiencing the real Lewis and Clark extravaganza. All of this is quite exciting and after six seconds I race back to the canoe secure in the knowledge that I'm a snob traveler who is much better off (for all concerned) out on the river, away from the state-promoted expedition bicentennial lunacy.

Pompey's Pillar was part of the original 1803 Louisiana Purchase. It was in the public domain until the mid-1800s when a treaty made it part of the Crow Indian Reservation. A later action removed the area from the reservation but gave Crow tribal members the first right to homestead the lands.

♦ ♦ ♦

Many people dislike snakes, in general, and poisonous ones like the rattlesnake, in particular. I've had my moments with the reptiles. Bending over a bank only to see a coiled snake rattling a dry leaves sound, slitted eyes boring into me as I begin my panicked spastic ballet back to safety. Or I've watched them sunning supinely on flat shelves of rock, comatose, storing heat for the cold night. And I've seen their smashed carcasses all over the roads of Montana or their bodies roped over barbed wire, heads shot off by morons. Their reputation for danger, though not deserved, has resulted in needless killing of these mostly shy creatures.

Some years ago, on one of Ginny's first trips to a camp on the bluffs above the Tongue River, a major tributary of the Yellowstone, the following encounter with a rattlesnake occurred. One of the most intense experiences out in wild country we've ever had and there have been plenty over the years. It is as vivid in my mind today as it no doubt was back then. The fact that she still returns with me to this country says a lot about her inner strength. Following the incident and several drinks to calm our nerves I wrote down what happened as accurately as I could in a weathered reporter's notebook that survived from my inglorious newspaper days. I will admit to a small touch of literary artifice. Sometimes artifice is all we have. I stumbled across the notebook recently while organizing my desk. Sometimes I'll do damn near anything to avoid writing.

♦ ♦ ♦

The rattlesnake's scales are hot, but being cold-blooded, it didn't notice. The snake lay stretched out like a piece of well-used and now discarded hemp rope, all five feet of its dusty yellow and leathery-brown body extended to absorb as much of the day's heat as possible. Its sharp tongue flicks languidly, tasting the still, dry air. The sun is directly overhead. The open stands of Ponderosa forest cast stunted shadows in the harsh light, an unrelenting radiance that burned the color from the land. Green, blue, orange, red—all are fried into shades of dusty white. A few deerflies and gnats buzz among the parched grasses. The only sounds here. A slow undulation, the slightest of ripples works its way down the length of the snake's body as it unconsciously adjusts itself to the movement of the sun. Other than the soft burbling of a nearby spring there is no other motion anywhere.

We wander down a dry, ephemeral creek bed of water-smoothed limestone stairs that cascades in sedimentary still-life through the trees, winding around weather-worn formations of rock that were once ancient sea beds. Thin seams of soft, pure black coal define several geological epochs. Fossils of long-gone animals that neither of us have the slightest inclination or chance of identifying lie in bleached piles on top of mounds of pink, grey and yellow-green soil. Curled-up shells. Spiral ones. Those that look like waterbugs. Millions of them. Juniper bushes grow tight to the ground in areas that received at least infrequent shade. Small cactus clumps here and there. The land appears dead, motionless, already baking. The sky has lost its blue and is now fried to a white-silver severity. One-hundred degrees-plus easy by noon. Nothing moves. The coyotes are silent, perhaps gone forever. Turkeys being turkeys, they could be anywhere or nowhere or loafing in the shade, invisible a few feet away. Brown recluse spiders hide under those same rocks and the millions of mindless ants retreat to the depths of their nests. The streamcourse pours out into an open valley that gradually widens and eventually drains, mostly in the spring when there is snowmelt and rain water, into a muddy stock pond. A few cows, open-range-lean Simbrah, lay in the mud, flies buzzing around them, the dumb animals' tails and ears lazily twitching.

"I've never seen such a stocky, muscular breed and with that deep brown coat, almost like the soil here when it rains," said Ginny. "What are they?"

I turned, laugh and ask, "Are you ready? I did a story for a cattle magazine years ago on these guys."

"Sure, John, but let me have a hit of the gin and tonic from the Jinny flask," said Ginny referring to a battered pint silver flask that has a quote from Hemingway's novel *True at First Light* engraved on it that reads:

> In Africa a thing is true at first light and a lie by noon and you have no more respect for it than the lovely, perfect weed-fringed lake you see across the sun-baked salt plain. You have walked across that plain in the morning and know that no such lake is there. But now it is absolutely true, beautiful and believable.

I hand her the cherished flask, one much like the one described by Hemingway in that book, which we both read not so long ago at this very camp, the summer when we drove into Sheridan to a jewelry store and purchased the flask and had the words cut into the then-perfect, shiny metal along with the date *June 21, 2000* and each of our names. Since that time the flask, like the two of us, has endured many good and many hard times. It goes where we go together. Ginny takes a long swallow, hands it back to me and I do the same before tucking it away in my jeans hip pocket.

"Hang on girl. Here we go," I said. "The breed is a hybrid and quite rare. An experiment combining Simmental with Brahman that began in the pastures of a few dedicated and quite possibly slightly-crazed cattle-men in the late 1960s has evolved more or less logically into the breed called Simbrah. The Brahman or Zebu, the most numerous cattle type on earth, contributes heat and insect tolerance, hardiness and excellent foraging ability, as well as maternal calving ease and longevity.

"The Simmental complements these worthwhile traits with early sexual maturity, fertility, milking ability, rapid growth and good beef characteristics. The very docile disposition of most Simmental is also a plus for those who work with the creatures everyday. Anyone who's dealt with Texas Longhorns, like our old friend Elmer Yoter over in Otter Creek coulee, can tell you how much fun it is to try and handle unruly cattle, especially the bulls. Wonder how his hip's doing since that Longhorn smashed into him and his horse? Anyway, Simbrah has been described as 'The All-Purpose American Breed.' Developed in America,

Simbrah genetics may be called on to infuse superior maternal traits into a herd."

"I need another hit from the flask, John, this is getting tough, but do continue," and Ginny does and I resume my monologue.

"Or, due to their rapid growth, vigor, and heat tolerance, Simbrah may be the answer in a terminal cross program. In the final analysis, Simbrah will produce a lean, high quality beef product that in this health-conscious, fat-conscious climate is a definite plus for market-ability. Originally developed in the hot, humid areas of the Gulf Coast, Simbrah have shown they can thrive in the northwest and northeast regions of this country where temperatures may range from 115 degrees in the summer to 25 degrees below zero in the winter. That's it, Ginny."

"Are you sure? Did you memorize that for a school play or what? Boy, I should know better than to ask you a question like that by now," Ginny said.

"Pedantic is my middle name, girl."

We resume our walk in the gathering heat, the air feeling good and yet close at the same time.

In the pond, algae has turned to a green-brown scum coating the surface of the water. Dragonflies track down the few gnats and mosqui-toes that whir above the scant moisture. They work towards a timbered slope that eventually gives way to an expanse of open bench where they will be able to see the Bighorn Mountains shimmering purple seventy-five miles away in Wyoming. Echoing cries of red-tailed hawks sounds far above them, then the buzz and hum of the predators diving, scream-ing down through the thick air, the noise increasing in pitch, before the hawks break off, first parallel with the ground then swooping steeply back into the sky. The birds are hunting us. Not trying to drive us off, but instead intent on knocking us down, killing us.

This is the hawks' territory. Ginny looks up and sees the pair, black silhouettes against the blazing sky, hundreds of feet above us, soaring in large circles, then she watches as they fold their wings and drop down on us again.

"Damn, John. Into the pines." We both run for shelter as the birds break off at tree-top level this time, followed by fierce screeches of anger and defiance, not warning. Death is the raptors' intent. "Let's get the hell out of here. Over that hill. Enough of this. I don't want my neck broken."

We quick-step up a dusty cattle trail and over into the next parched drainage, only a few hundred yards, but we are breathing hard and sweating.

"Want a Camel, John?" Ginny huffs. "We really need to get our wind back."

"Yes we do, but let me have one anyway. I see we spaced the water. I'll hold off on the gin for now. Drinking agrees with me down here. It doesn't become a preoccupation, more like recreation or something. I'll have some drinks with you tonight at camp."

Ginny smiles in agreement. She knows that I'm at peace here, truly happy. We drink to enjoy life, not turn it off.

"Maybe that spring up by those rocks is still running," I say. "Looks green enough that way. It's never been dry in the past."

Thirst in parched country has a special intensity. Water here tastes better than any other liquid you can imagine. Cold and wet. Just wet will actually do the trick. Pretty damn basic. We push through the piles of rock, wiry undergrowth and sharp cactus to the spring that was bubbling from a cut in the limestone. We drink until our stomachs ache, soaking ourselves in the process.

"Best damn water this side of Stanford," I say and swallow a touch more. "A bit of natural carbonation or as a friend of mine said just before he enlisted in Warm Springs for the duration, it has a little bit of Christmas in it."

"John, where in the hell do you find them? You're a magnet for lunatics. They don't just cross the street to get you. They run full speed. They walk right up to you at Wal-Marts, trout streams, call you on the phone at 3 A.M., write you letters in crayon on legal paper. Hell, that one from Kansas even sent you 50 bucks in 20s rolled up in a tin cup. Are they all nuts in Wichita?

"I still can't figure that young manic depressive, though. Jeff was his name, I think. The kid who used to play his Fender Stratocaster in the shower with the water running without getting a shock. Damned good and never missed a lick. And how 'bout that old woman you let sleep on the porch a few summers back, the one who wandered in from the highway wearing eighteen layers of clothes, a Cleveland Indians baseball cap and clutching all those dirty Styrofoam cups. I'll never forget the night she tried to signal Venus by turning the truck radio on and off. And of course there's Ollie. Boy, he used to get high on prolyxine for the fun of it. It was like he was in a cerebral straightjacket six days out of seven and he loved it."

"They're my people," I say with a smile. "They ask nothing of me except to pay them a little attention. Some of them even spend their own money on my books. I owe them something. We're just trying to get by. So are you. That's about it for a lot of us anymore."

"Sometimes I almost believe you. Scares me, but you never do anything just to get by. If I ever figure out what you're really up to...what difference would it make? No one would get it anyway. Here's that smoke you wanted."

The day grows still hotter and we keep splashing the forty-some-degree water on each other, content to be well out of sight, out of touch with things, working over the cigarettes and enjoying the companion-ship of our silence. We each sip from the flask that seems to be bottom-less, a small bit of magic that we've marveled at and been grateful for over the countless road miles we've traveled. A chunk of rock breaks loose across the way, clattering and bouncing down a cliff before explod-ing into sedimentary shrapnel on impact with the valley floor. Then the silence again. Eternal. Time stops dead. Everything, including both of us, sizzle unconsciously beneath the sun. We turned into lizards, not even bothering with the Camels now. Just lying on our backs blinking in the razor-sharp light.

Finally the sun begins dropping down to the horizon, its light slant-ing through the trees in subdued hues of orange, yellow and the vaguest suggestion of soft pine green. The temperature also drops, from well over one-hundred down to the nineties and then the upper eighties. Comfortable in a dry way. The night would be cool, in the fifties or even the forties. A fire. Some coffee, with a splash of whiskey, a couple of cigars and a little rambling conversation. I come to first, recovered from my reptilian reverie. I glance at Ginny. Then glance again in disbelief. A rattlesnake has slithered onto the rock shelf we're resting on and coiled up near Ginny. Fortunately her body heat is less than that of the rock's surface or maybe the snake would be resting on here. She opens her eyes. I raise my hand, palm out, facing towards her and whisper "Don't move." She looks over at the snake, its tongue flicks out rapidly tasting the air. She doesn't move. She couldn't even if she wanted to. Ginny's petrified, frozen in place.

She is terrified, but her look says, "Yes. Do it. Now." I slowly move my hand just above the rock until I feel a large stick with my fingers. I grab it gently and slide my hand back to my legs, again low to the ground to avoid casting a shadow on the snake. In what seems like hours I finally position the rough point of the stick a half-foot or so from just behind the snake's head. I look at Ginny.

"NOW!" her eyes yell.

I focus on a spot behind and below the rattler's head and jab the point. I feel the stick push into the soft resistance of the snake and clash against the rock even as I lift up with the snake, that is flipped by the force of the action head-first over the edge of the rock.

"Thank the Lord. Damn," Ginny yells as she rolls hard into me. "Damn. Oh Boy, John."

"Easy. Come here," I say, as I draw her to me shaking like mad from the release of stress and fear. She's shivering like she's cold. I hold her until she relaxes some, then push her away to look at her chest. There are no signs of bite marks on her. Another disaster avoided.

"It didn't get me, John. I'm all right. Thank you doesn't get it, but thanks. God, I bet that's a first. 'Woman Wakes Up To Find Venom-Spitting Viper Sleeping Next To Her," she said. "Hand me the flask, please."

She takes a big hit and then another before screwing the small top back on, but she doesn't let go of it. I smile and finally she does, too.

"Actually, according to Bob Jones, his brother-in-law had something similar happen to him while fishing for stripers along the American River near Sacramento a few years ago. According to him, the fishing was slow and his relation fell asleep around midday only to wake to the same scene. Luckily the snake was out of it like yours and he managed to knock it away from him."

"You take all of the sport out of my little adventures, John" and she gives me a quick kiss on the lips before drinking some more from the flask then some cold spring water and splashes still more of the cool liquid on her face.

We start back to camp.

♦ ♦ ♦

Well, that's our snake story and I won't bother anyone with our bear, wolf, man-eating arachnid or alien spacecraft masquerading as Jupiter rising stories. Snakes are powerful animals and what seems abnormal or bizarre when we are not around them turns into just another reptilian day at the office when a rattlesnake makes the scene.

♦ ♦ ♦

Years ago, when I first began to explore the coulees, bluffs and sage flats of the northern high plains during an initial turkey hunting trip, I stopped into a grocery store in Ashland in the Tongue River drainage. I needed some beer (Pabst), steak and eggs. As I approached the checkout counter I passed one of the most impressive humans I've ever seen—tall, muscles like iron, dark, dark-weathered face, coal black eyes that saw right through me like I was transparent and long jet black shining hair that passed his beaded belt. Northern Cheyenne. Magnificent. Fearsome. I'll never lose that image so burned into my mind.

The name Cheyenne is derived from the Lakota name *Sha-hi'yena*, *Shai-ena*, or Teton *Shai-ela*, "people of alien speech," from *sha'ia*, "to speak a strange language."

Spring turkey hunting near the Northern Cheyenne Reservation is: wind. The only truth is wind. Cold. Chinook warm. Strong. Blustery. Often from the north. Always.

The turkeys are big. The turkeys are not around. Hard to find. Easy to find. Grouped in roost trees. Around everywhere. Loafing in the dust. Trotting through Ponderosa needles in the shade. Then gone again. Nowhere to be seen.

The weather always wins. The landscape is staggering. Surreal. Lonesome. It will snow. It will rain. The sun will blast down. Ashland is depressing.

After twenty years of doing this early-season stuff I've learned that I know next to nothing about the hunting, the turkeys, the country or the people that live here. I've always been an outsider despite childish pretensions otherwise, thinking I was a friend while being pimped for PR. That's how it goes. No big deal. The return my way has been fair. Money for stories or book chapters. Wild country. Huge birds. A touch of freedom. Unexplained visuals that spin around bluffs or race along ridges. Blue-light-glows arcing from the tops of buttes. Extraordinary howlings. Unusual footprints. The usual suspects.

When I used to hunt the turkeys, I killed some well over twenty pounds with beards protruding from their necks of seven or eight inches.

But I don't know anything up this alien way. Alien to my soft, white mind. Rhythms, techniques, dictions all beyond me.

Summer. Autumn. A bit calmer, vaguely familiar, feeling safer.

Spring means hardball. All the juice turned loose after a dark winter's frozen dormancy. Moving along muddy two-tracks up onto windy bluffs. Opening, closing rusting barbed wire gates. Spending a ghostly night in an abandoned radar base barracks eating canned beef stew. Drinking whiskey. Smoking a lot of Camel straights. Listening to my fear creaking through twisted, corroded beams and rotted window frames. Even the pigeons don't spend the night in this place. Coyotes howl near daybreak, saying "Thank god" to the sunrise. Mule deer running at my motion. Crop duster landing his beater biplane just over my head on a red dust road in front of me. Eagles soaring with more grace higher up the sky. Looking for rabbits, mice, voles.

Vicious winds tear down from the Bighorns in Wyoming blowing everything ahead of their course. Russian thistle, clumps of sage brush, license plates, cigarette packs, beer cans, crop land, ball caps, large rips of plastic that used to masquerade as storm windows, all of this sucked along in a swirling wake of confused detritus.

The Northern Cheyenne.

Yeah I know them. Quite well. You bet. Not at all. Never will. How could I?

Lame Deer, Busby. Government housing. Abject poverty. A sense of humor that mocks me with no hope of entrance. Long-time tribal acquaintances seeing me as a means to an end. In the schools, on the streets, riding in cars—too much booze, too many drugs, just like everywhere, but way different on the Rez—poison taken to a bad land nomadic death trip. High-plains wanderers fenced in by the inevitability of modern change. Happens to all of us, but true murder for these people.

The great American pastime crashing head on where the front is obvious. Not running down buffalo and not looking for images in ice water or wandering after scapegoat seasons. Not a hack movie-actor's wannabe film trip. A lot of green thunderbirds discarded and smashed along dusty roadsides. Dead men gasping with whitewashed education draining from torn ears that could not bank on truth. Reservations not honored around Chinookville. Sliding along on fusel oil and ancient dreams. Kicked aside by forgotten collisions with rotted pickups. The breeze drinks it all bone dry.

And even with all these imagined memories and images rattling around in my head, I've always come back here in the spring. Hot-cold April. Paradise May. Wet June. Northern high plains energy running madly. Green grasses waving ocean visions. Wildflowers exploding. Rafts of cloud racing the sky.

Magnificent in its isolation despite its desolation.

I haven't been over to the Rez in a few years. I want to give the place one more shot to see if the good memories, those twisted high times remain. Does any of the crazed, somewhat demoralized magic still hold or have I hammered through too many years and too many arcane mistakes to see anything up this way?

Was any of the illusion left?

Rolling magically upwards with my foot off the accelerator on a stretch of road that seems to defy gravity. Illusion in country driven by tilted horizon. I marvel at a ridge of cloud that probably stretches far into Canada. The wall of moisture spins back on itself as it is torn between an updraft caused by the distant Pryor Mountains and I have a desire to roll on eastward across the high plains towards the Dakotas. I watch all this while keeping an eye on the highway largely empty of traffic today except for a random semi or pickup. I turn left on a lesser paved road, then right on another. Within a few miles I cut left on a dirt road that winds up into the foothills and mountains. A beautiful, familiar and sometimes-fished stream sparkles alongside the serpentine, now rutted road as I drift through aspen only beginning to leaf out and through stately stands of old Ponderosa that are intense green with a new year's exuberance. Eagles, Roosevelt elk, mule and whitetail deer, coyote, chickadees, swallowtail butterflies and a few turkeys that live in this blasted country that seems to be little changed over the past fifty years. A perfect place, or nearly so, and that's enough these days.

I get out and begin to walk down a steep coulee. In a little while I look and see that I'm well below table top bluffs that tower above the drainage. The sky is blue shading to silver-white in the hot light. A pair of red-tails works a ridge on my right. Sharp cries slice the stillness and mix with the talking water. Bending down on my knees, I drop my mouth to the surface of a small spring and drink the water that tastes of snow, gravel and tannin. The walk back takes awhile but seems like nothing. Tossing daypack in the back of the Suburban, I open the cooler, grab a beer, light a cigar and enjoy what's left of the light. I'll find a motel room in Hardin about two hours away to the west: TV, lousy pizza, neon, slamming car doors, whiskey, little sleep. Later.

This day's been good. Tomorrow. Who knows? A couple more days alone. Ideal after a bad trip earlier this month, one riddled with commercialism and too much booze and melancholy. All this will be pleasant, peaceful, but honestly now after a couple of decades of lying to myself, despite the fantastic country and the turkeys and all of this, tribal reservations are mainly sad experiences. That's my problem, but a real one. Poverty. Hopelessness. Future oil and coal bed methane development. As a late friend used to say "It's all going or gone." Feels that way here. Hopefully I'm wrong. The gut says I'm not. But then…

…out where it's empty, wind talks. Rain is an uncommon friend. There are some strange people blown away by the electric hum of nothing, running small stores, growing weeds in the dust. Real drunk. Linked together by the white light express that ties all of us in a twisted knot. Bighorns blast out of nowhere screaming in the sky. Large creatures wander fearless disrupting the current with their curious buzz. Snow and hail sweep down. Cattle freeze. Minds vanish. The beating moves in constant time and is hard to disguise, but the trick to this is to skip off to oblivion and enjoy the view.

Yeah, it's weird and sad down here, and I'll always feel like a stranger, but the land is beyond believing and the solitude is restorative, so when I'm perhaps into my sixties, I'll more than likely wander back here in the spring.

That's Northern Cheyenne country for me. A slightly twisted variation on the Yellowstone drainage two-step.

♦ ♦ ♦

After spending too much time at Pompey's Pillar staring off into the distance at the top on a large wooden platform and listening as visitors appeared and were issued the standing "Glad you made it" greeting before turning around and walking back down the stairs, I head downriver bound for the campground next to Meyer's Bridge at Howrey Island about forty-five miles away. This normally would be a two-day float, but because of three diversion dams—Waco, Rancher and YID—the section took two long, hard days. I can't figure out how government flacks are comfortable touting the Yellowstone as the longest undammed river in the lower 48 in light of the numerous diversion dams, some of them over six feet high and all of them potential death traps. The BLM maps of the river (they only go as far as Bonfield so far) have photographs showing what the approaches to the dams look like and the dams themselves. It is a good idea to check locally on each dam concerning where to portage and what to sight in on concerning the approach.

Portaging around these obstructions by myself (oh, how I miss Ginny's help on this section, but she'll be back home in a few weeks) is tough, often brutal in the heat as mosquitoes and flies bite exposed skin, worry eyes, nostrils and ears, while I punch the canoe through thick brush along dusty, uneven, sometimes rocky, portages. I miss Ginny but am glad she's somewhere else right now spending time with her family. This bit of furnace heat bushwhacking is not fun. Each portage takes four or more roundtrips for the canoe, cooler, water-tight bags, and so on. At the end of each detour I'm beat, so I have a sandwich, lots of water, an apple and a short rest before heading on once more. The landscape is a long-running reel of stark bluffs, ridges, prairie, arroyos and buttes punctuated with riotously-colored tended fields flashing every shade of green—alfalfa, the ubiquitous sugar beets, corn and wheat.

I stopped on a sandy bank, rigged an eight-weight rod with a large chartreuse barracuda fly that always seems to trigger a killing response from northern pike. I cast out into deep runs, along gravel shelves and close to bankside obstructions near where a small spring poured in. I was about to quit when I saw a large vee-shaped bulge in the water closing very fast on the streamer. The pike slammed the thing with wide-open jaws, white mouth visible and whirled in an explosion of watery spray.

The northern pike headed back towards the security of the tangle of limbs and brush, but I managed to check the fish and weather several strong runs out into the current. When the fish tired I brought it to me, twisted the hook from its up jaw while carefully avoiding the rows of wicked, razor-sharp teeth, lifted the northern with both hands to admire its brown-green muscular sleekness—a true freshwater predator—then returned it to the water. The fish, maybe eight pounds, sped off to the dark depths out in the middle of the Yellowstone. I returned to the canoe and my downriver doings.

The days begin to slip along seamlessly one into another, logically building into a limitless mosaic of timeless natural world images. Even when doing shorter sections of forty or fifty miles, the rhythm and pace of the river takes over within a few hundred yards of paddling. All of the motion and effort is natural, as it should be. I'm enjoying myself, but look forward to reaching the pleasant campground at Howrey Island. My rig is parked there and I'll spend the night organizing and packing gear before running back to Livingston, a four-hour drive.

Chapter 6

Prairie, Coulee And Bluff
Howrey Island to Tongue River—90 miles

T HE YELLOWSTONE HAS MANY MOODS, SOPHISTICATED FACETS
of an elaborate personality that flickers regally down through
time and is influenced by the changing seasons and the vagaries
of shifting landscape. Within autumn, working the upper reaches of this
tributary, out here alone, just the two of us, all of it combines to form
an atmosphere of total aloneness. This is not a mood of loneliness or a
desire to seek out the comradeship of my fellow humans. Nothing that
drastic or even morose. Only the feeling of being totally by ourselves on
one last float before the severe weather clamps down on the land, with no
one else around or even to consider for these few days of dwindling bril-
liance. A casual run from just below Amelia Island near Hysham down
to the Highway 12 Bridge above the dangerous Cartersville Diversion
Dam at Forsyth.

We work our way along the river past open prairie, corn fields and
sage flats. Yellow-tan bluffs and buttes rise in the distance against a
cloudless horizon. Canada geese by the thousands honk and frantically
flap their wings as they reach for the sky at our approach. Mule deer,
whitetails, ravens, crows, a pair of Great Grey owls, pheasants, bald and
golden eagles, Great blue herons, grebes, and coyotes on the prowl are
common, wonderful sights. Fish jump. Smallmouth bass, catfish, goldeye.
Life everywhere.

I rig my fly rod with a small woolly bugger and take one silvery fish
after another, eager goldeyes. I release them and they vanish in bursts of
silver. In the riffles I catch some smallmouths of a pound or so. Ginny
maintains course up front while I screw around with the fish in back like

a mindless little kid, which I truly am at this moment. I keep three of them for dinner tonight to go along with some baked beans, rice, canned peaches and coffee.

Up ahead I see the gravel and stone beach of the island where we'll spend the night. On the north side of the river, sheer cliffs of yellow and soft orange stone rise one-hundred feet or more above us. We are far away from anyone else.

Along this stretch of river between Amelia Island and the Tongue River are a number a small towns that give the Yellowstone much of its current personality. Places like Hysham named after the late Charles Hysham, owner of the Flying E brand, whose cattle once grazed more than seventy miles across the countryside. The town is now a small but bustling ranching town of several hundred residents. And there's Forsyth with several motels, restaurants, a movie theater, and everything else a person would need from a smaller community, a place that is something of a railroad ranching community of about 2,000.

Miles City is not so small any more, at least by eastern Montana standards. There are over 8,300 residents in this ranching community that is famous for its annual Bucking Horse Sale in May where much of the national rodeo stock for the upcoming year is selected. This is a blow-out of major bacchanalian proportions attracting cowboys, cowgirls, ranchers and wannabes from all over the hemisphere. The town is named after Gen. Nelson A. Miles, commander of the Fifth U.S. Infantry at now-gone Fort Keogh about two miles downriver during the time of Custer's rampages in the region. The town was in the 1870s in its wild west heyday boasted a solid block of saloons, gambling houses and brothels on the south side of Main Street. The "decent" folk (buffalo buyers, bankers and pawnshop keepers) held forth on the north side.

According to the 1939 WPA Guide for the state, "On one occasion, it is said, a member of the respectable group hit a gambler on the head with a singletree (swinging bar from a harness), and killed him. To save the good man embarrassment, his friends hastily hanged the dead man as a dangerous character." Saved the guy from public embarrassment while apparently being tried for murder was of no concern. Ah, for the good old days.

Colstrip is about forty miles south of Forsyth on state Highway 39. Colstrip, lovely name, is a town of around 2,300 and is dominated by the enormous coal-fired generation plant. Stacks tower hundreds of feet of the prairie floor disgorging a steady plume of steam from the plant. The town is new with a new school, new fast food joints, new trailer parks, manicured public parks and greenways. New, clean, sterile everything. The coal arrives on long trains ripped from the ground at enormous strip mines southeast by Decker and the Wyoming line. The place is depressing, grim to both of us. A sign of corporate and local greed, a chase for the quick buck at the expense of the land's spirit.

Farther down the highway, which parallels brush-choked Rosebud Creek that winds like a demented serpent beneath buttes and hills covered with Ponderosa pine, is Lame Deer. It is located at the center of the Northern Cheyenne Indian Reservation and serves as the tribal headquarters and the site for the offices of the Bureau of Indian Affairs. Lame Deer was named for Chief Lame Deer, of the Lakota, who was killed in a battle with the U.S. Calvary in May of 1877.

We've come here to visit the graves of Dull Knife and Lone Wolf in a cemetery located on a grassy knoll behind Dull Knife Memorial College. The two chiefs led their people on what is considered the greatest forced march in history from the Oklahoma Territory back to this land during the dead of winter, while thousands of soldiers and citizens attempted to trap them in canyons, hunt them down and extirpate the people. We've come to pay our respects. I've not been here since the spring of 1993 when Bob Jones, John Talia and I visited quietly and briefly.

We drive through the college parking lot filled with Cheyenne students engaged in what seems to be both earnest and happy conversation. They pay no attention to us as we slowly enter the cemetery grounds in the suburban on a narrow dirt road that winds up and around gravesites that are decorated in an abundance of color with both plastic and real flowers, flags that flutter in the cool breeze, spinning miniature windmills in chromium and reds and blues, signs with blessings in both English and Cheyenne, and new and eroded grave markers. Lots of fresh mounds of earth and unblemished white gravestones. Drugs, alcohol, fights leading to murder. A high plains people more or less imprisoned on this modern-day reservation—a prison without walls, only razor wire of lost souls with tough hopes of reclaiming their past freedoms while trying desperately and heroically to adjust to the modern insanity that is the white world.

We park below the gravesite and walk up to an area of maybe twenty by twenty feet enclosed with brown fence. Dull Knife and Lone Wolf lie here marked only by weathered headstones. The place is full of power, long-ago warrior vibes, loss and honor. I've heard that the graves are always watched by members of the Northern Cheyenne. The pressure of eyes on the back of my head is strong. I say to Ginny that it's time to leave. I silently pay my respects. We drive out, past the students, through town and north past Colstrip, still powering away beneath a cloud of generated steam and on up to our waiting motel room in Forsyth.

♦ ♦ ♦

There's a small stop just off of Highway 12 about a half mile south. The place is called Ingomar. Friends of mine used come here often to hunt large antelope that wander about in healthy numbers. They camped near a pair of abandoned wooden boxcars.

Ginny and I drive up through rounded hills and dull-colored bluffs and then through rising sage flats from our motel in Forsyth. We have a day before we hit the river again and decide to make the run here to check out a bar and restaurant called the Jersey Lilly. The Jersey Lilly Bar & Café had its beginnings as a bank in 1914. The place is famous for its ambience and bean soup served in a small pot. The Jersey Lilly is also renowned for its steaks. The cherry wood, back bar of the Jersey Lilly is one of two which were transported from St. Louis by boat up the Missouri and Yellowstone rivers and installed at Forsyth in the early 1900s. This bar was stored at Forsyth during Prohibition, sold to Bob Seward, and installed here in 1933. The other back bar was destroyed in 1912, when the American Hotel burned in Forsyth.

In the early days Ingomar and Sumatra were the chief trading towns for the homesteaders in western Garfield County. Freight wagons were often caught in the Gumbo Flats—a wide strip of land south of Sand Springs that can't be crossed when it's wet.

Today everyone we meet here is friendly. The cook puffs away on a cigarette while on break after making cheeseburgers and ladling out the soup. A mailman running a very long circular route from Billings to Roundup and back talks to me about how Ted Turner is buying up all the ranchland in the vicinity and won't let anyone on the place even though he rarely visits. The steaming beans arrive hot and backed with Tabasco sauce. Ginny and I finish them off, pay our bill, walk out into the sunlight, enjoy the view—wide-open land stretching down to the Yellowstone many miles in the south—and then decide to take a leisurely back road drive back to our room. The cottonwoods are their standard outrageous flaming yellow-orange. Wind plays a rustling tune through the leaves. The river is sweet blue. Geese and ducks are all over the water or working nearby grain fields. Clouds glide by headed towards Glendive. As Buffet said, "Just another shitty day in Paradise."

♦ ♦ ♦

October. Everything about the day looks as Montana in October often does this sunny, blue sky afternoon. The aforementioned blue is deep. The light breeze with its swirling mixture of warm and cool is familiar. The scent of dried-out sage, lightly pungent and earthy is intoxicating. The shades of dead grass rocking easily on the wind like an old man sitting on his front porch remembering years past while sipping coffee grown cool with the driftings of memory. The colors range from flat tan through silvery yellow and on into a wind-polished golden patina the finish of well-used metal. A Western meadowlark calls out, not with the exuberance of spring and the promise of warm months, but with the voice of a creature that knows hard times are coming and that a day like this one is money in the bank. A pair of antelope work across a rising fold in this flat, maybe a mile away. They winded me as soon as I topped the slope, maybe earlier, and are working without nervousness away and soon over the rise. Several ravens follow the river's course as it flows north towards Northern Cheyenne country. Light glistens off black, moving wings. They squawk and caw among themselves, but the distance mutes the conversation.

Camp is a few miles behind, tucked next to a group of bushy juniper. Small fire ring out of the wind. Expansive view stretching far to the southwest and the Big Horn Mountains forty-some miles away in Wyoming. I'm walking along this bench looking for a couple of sharp-tails that maybe I can drop for dinner. Whether I'm successful or not doesn't matter. The walking with my late step-father's twenty-gauge Beretta is what counts. Whenever I do this, all of the fine times he and I had together chasing fish and birds return. I relive these without any awareness of specific moments, only an overall awareness of days well spent with a good friend.

That's all this afternoon spent pushing across this bench is about. I don't expect to kick up anything. The simplicity of the colors is good. The blue, gold, browns, buff, ochre, charcoal and salmon in the cliffs rising above me on the east, the different blue of the river far away and below, the fading green clinging to life along the stream's banks, all of this makes sense because it doesn't have to. I like that.

Twenty feet in front, from out of a tall bunch of grass, four of large grouse lumbers up about six feet then starts to beat down with the wind. I see tan, grey, buff and yellow feathers. Sage grouse. Wings beat rapidly as the birds shout "*kuk kuk kuk kuk.*" Then they glide swooping near ground level before the beating begins again. The gun is at my shoulder reflexively. I see clearly a bird ahead of the bead at the end of the barrels, dark brown spikes of its tail feathers aimed at me. An easy shot as images from past autumns merge with the fleeing bird…

…past 8,000 feet, many miles above the primitive campground at less than 6,000, hanging out beneath a battered group of storm-blown pine trees. The river I want to fish is 1,000 feet below, the trail slippery, vertiginous, deadly. Lightning, wind, rain, hail blow all over the place. I think that I should have stayed at my dry camp in the Tongue instead of running down the Interstate into Wyoming and up into the climbing tilted slabs of country that are the Middle Fork of the Powder River, yet another Yellowstone River tributary that is part of an intricate system that drains and nourishes tens of thousands of square miles in Montana, Wyoming and western North Dakota.

There are fish way down there—browns and rainbows that maybe are fished over once every couple of years in this remote stretch. Difficult to fathom that this water will eventually pour into the Yellowstone more than one-hundred miles to the northeast, not all that far from Terry. And that if the trout were so inclined they could travel downstream to hang out with channel cats and burbot in the slightly turbid waters of the big river. Not likely, but an intriguing thought. For now there's no safe way to reach the trout far below me. As I check the trailhead, three mule deer slip and clatter passed me, making remarkable four-hooved-off-the-ground-at-once leaps to the side to avoid running into me. I inch down the path on my butt in the slop. Everything seems to drop away hundreds of feet down to broken rock, sage, tangled brush, matted grass and cactus. In less than one-hundred yards of slipping on the greasy surface I come to where the deer stopped and made their turn around. If they won't go further, I won't either. The view slanting down across sere though damp grasslands gives way to the walls of the opposite side of the canyon. Red, ochre, bluish-grey, pink, the black of a coal seam spin in and out of view as the weather hammers the high country with what will surely be the first snowstorm of the year. What was seventy degrees at noon is freezing now.

Back at camp I touch off some charcoal in my Little Smoky grill, open a modest bottle of Merlot (I've brought several), pull on a sweater, then a waxed cotton poncho and wool hat. The grill is positioned on the lee side of the Suburban. So is my chair. The small blaze casts sufficient warmth. The wine tastes okay. Hell, it comes with a cork. I've wrapped a sliced potato with onions, butter, salt and coarse black pepper in foil and buried it in the coals. A rib-eye will follow soon. I'll survive.

A Cuban cigar from a friend savored after dinner with some more wine sounds reasonable.

Dark, rolling clouds, lots of lightning and thunder that crashes like it's right behind me. Close enough that when the wind is down I can feel the compression of the air caused by the detonation push on my eardrums and brush my cheeks. The land way up this way is wild—no people, buildings, lights—made even crazier by the weather. Snow is falling as the thunderstorm plays on. This is great. The steak sizzles. Then I eat before putting things in order. I open some more wine, light the cigar and enjoy the evening by myself, surrounded by so much of what's kept me alive all this time. Eventually I crawl into my sleeping bag resting on top of a foam pad covered with a quilt in the back of the rig. True luxury that would be considered ostentatious by my years-ago persona.

In the morning I rise. Under a foot of snow the landscape has a blinding intensity in brightness of the sunrise. Orange blinding wandering to blaze yellow into silver and then just white-hot blinding. I snack on some fruit and bagels, load my gear and prepare to head back down in four-wheel-drive—slippery but doable. I check around for anything left behind as always and realize that the Little Smoky grill is not around. The wind swiped my friend of hundreds of fires in the dead of night. Scatters of ash from last night's fire mark the snow to the cliff's edge. I grab my binoculars and follow the awful trail. Easing to the precipice I lie down in the snow and scan the terrain below me.

There.

Down on a ledge several hundred feet is the Little Smoky. In the glasses I can see that the handle is mashed into the lid's surface. The main part of the grill is mangled, twisted, bent beyond recognition.

Lord, life is hell sometimes. I say a prayer, walk back to the Suburban and drive somberly back down to the low country that is shadow-flashing red sand and yellow dirt, no snow, beneath the partly cloudy sunlight way off by Kaycee…

…crawling up the narrow two-track just this side of the North Dakota border I pause in front of a rusting barbed wire gate. I unlatch the thing and pull it across the road so that I may pass. The wire and tree limb posts make a muffled scratching noise on the ground. Even in the silvery light of a full-moon night I can see that the tall dying grasses appear flaxen, a slight silvery blond like Harry Morgan's wife's hair after she had it dyed in a Havana beauty parlor to please her husband in *To Have and Have Not*. After driving through the gate I close it and walk back to the Suburban. The dust puffs around my moccasins along the path. The powder feels soft, giving.

Climbing and coming around a sharp, Ponderosa-lined bend, the sandstone rock formation that I've come to see rises starkly against the sky like some ancient monument with a large bell-shaped crow capping the structure nearly dead center. The rock that was forced up by unimaginable pressure millions of years ago is eroding from wind and rain. Crenellations, holes, spires and parapets stand out in moonlight relief, the features growing more distinct as I come closer and the moon rises higher in the sky.

I stop on a gentle rise that looks across a broad depression to the natural sculpture, from what appears to be equal footing. This is an illusion created by distance and the night, but I feel like I am standing level with the bell. The air is warm and moves through the grass and trees with a faint hiss. Nighthawks boom above me. A bird I don't know makes a persistent cry that sounds like a phonograph needle riding on vinyl that goes around and around at the end of a record, perhaps the Stones' "Let It Bleed." The land grows brighter as does this formation beneath the persistent moon. Most of the stars are overcome, made invisible by this radiance. Coyotes howl to the south in the direction of not-so-distant Wyoming. In the morning I'll be able to see the northwestern edge of the South Dakota Black Hills one-hundred miles away. For now I sit on a smooth boulder and enjoy the fall night…

…and I see the image of sliding across high plains that used to be always dark out at night. The roads are still straight at one hundred miles an hour and in some circles running this quickly is even accepted behavior. What better way to chase down a starlight mystery within wild emptiness that never needs filling, but is being smothered in a neon avalanche, a vastness that now glows bleakly in gathering locations like a prairie Vegas full of losers crapped out on dead dreams. A certain dirt road is hard to find, but cautious navigation scares up friendly desolation—rare places unseen, connected by undefined space. Standing up here on this old eroded rock dome looking down I can see that there's still spaced out darkness, quiet, sanity…

…now the sage grouse is moving away from me but remaining the same size in my vision. I swing the Beretta with and slightly ahead of the bird and squeeze the trigger. The golden grass ripples in sharp focus against the blue horizon.

◆ ◆ ◆

If you do the road long enough you'll eventually find yourself wandering around in circles seeing the same old stretch of highway on a regular basis. With this curious shortcoming in mind, I offer a looping cruise through some of the finest country Wyoming has to offer. There are even some trout along the way. Sometimes the fishing can be quite good for moderately-sized fish, but this angling will never be confused with the action found in Yellowstone or the Wind River Range. The intrigue in this cruise is the variety of country, elevation changes and the relatively pristine fishing. And this is truly a trip where those who like to camp will enjoy the best of this good country.

This slightly haphazard adventure begins in Sheridan, Wyoming by running briefly north on I-90 then heading west on U.S. 14 into the Big Horn Mountains, cutting off on Hwy 14 to Greybull, on down U.S. 20 to Worland, back east and way up and over the Big Horns before finally coursing north from Buffalo back to Sheridan. Along the way desert flats, alpine country, steep descents through ragged mountain canyons and the sage flat vastness that is truly Wyoming is encountered. The circuit is about 270 miles with possibly another couple of hundred thrown in for exploration purposes.

The following are a few Wyoming Yellowstone River tributaries I've fished over the years and have had some good times on.

The South Tongue River is a delightful stream that flows through pine forest. Perhaps forty feet wide at its largest, this little river features pocket water, pools, riffles and shallow glides where rainbow, brown and brook trout hang out. The fish average about a foot, but there are some larger surprises lurking here and there that are susceptible to elk hair caddis, attractors like Humpies, Wulffs and soft hackle patterns that are cast slightly upstream, allowed to drift below the angler and then swing out with the current. This is often when a good trout will hit. The South Tongue has been managed as a wild trout fishery with no stocking since 1991. The water is open all year (as are the remainder of the streams I'll mention), and the ice normally clears around mid-April. Access is gained from Highway 14 to Prune Creek Campground and south on

Forestry Development Road (FDR) 193; and also from 14 to FDR 26. Campgrounds are abundant, and as with most Wyoming National Forest waters, camping is allowed outside of the riparian zone.

The North Tongue River is similar to the South in many ways but differs in that it often flows through wide open, high country meadows where elk, deer and even moose can be seen. There are also fair numbers of Snake River cutthroat. The water also is usually clear by mid-April. Special regulations for the North Tongue stipulate that upstream from the mouth of Bull Creek in Sheridan County all trout, except brookies, are to be released immediately. Only artificial flies and lures are allowed. The river parallels Highway 14 to 14A. The Snake River cutts are stocked annually in the restricted area.

The Little Bighorn River reminds me of a combination of both the South and North Tongue Rivers—forested, open and flowing through classic mountain scenery. Yellowstone cutthroat, brook, brown and rainbow swim here, some over fifteen inches. In addition to patterns mentioned for the South Tongue, nymphs like Prince and Hare's ear work well as do streamers in sizes 6–8. Access is from Highway 14A to FDR 11 to FDR 125—four-wheel drive is needed here to the end of the road. Fish habitat structures have been in place since 1996, the Yellowstone Cutt are stocked and the brook trout are wild.

From this point, all the way to Greybull then Worland and finally Ten Sleep you are out in the desert, sage flat coulee and bluff country. What fish there are have names like sauger and catfish. One river I've never fished but looks great is the Norwood. Turning off Highway 36 at Manderson and running along Highway 31 to Ten Sleep this river looks like designer trout water with deep blue runs and pools filled with gently waving aquatic plants. I'm told that the water is too warm for trout and that only sauger, catfish and sturgeon swim here. A gentleman (and aren't we being polite here) told me in a bar in Worland that there are also some "damn big browns" in the river. Perhaps bar talk. Perhaps not. I've not checked this out, but if anyone does, please let me know what you find.

The quality trout fishery of the Bighorn River flows north through Greybull and several days can be spent exploring this water that rolls and swirls deeply in shades of dark green beneath sheer canyon walls.

Now heading back east into the spectacular canyon country that, while not part of the Yellowstone drainage, is in terms of geology and, more importantly, spirit and rhythm a close relation to the river. This all begins with Ten Sleep Creek as the road begins to climb back up into the Big Horn Mountains and up and over the divide back into Yellowstone country. Campgrounds are located up and down the stream, with sheer rock walls plunging hundreds of feet directly behind your campsite. I've caught numerous rainbows, brookies and browns to fourteen inches here on almost any pattern. The wading is a scramble over boulders and through dense bankside brush. On one late-July outing I was in a twelve-inch trout groove and cast a Woolly Bugger to the head of a large, sapphire plunge pool. I let the streamer sink for several seconds and began to strip in the line when a very healthy rainbow hammered the Bugger, shot to the surface, tail walked across the surface of the pool away from me and snapped my tippet. Maybe eighteen or twenty inches. A true eye opener. Highway 16 parallels the stream and access is straightforward.

The last stream of the five is Crazy Woman Creek with its rainbows, brookies and browns. This little wonder flows through more canyon country with rock walls pinching in on the angler. Access is from Highway 16 to FDR 470 to Crazy Woman Campground. There is a trail at the dead end that leads to the best water. This is truly pocket water with trout, sometimes several holding behind mid-stream rocks and boulders and tiny pools along the banks. Attractor patterns work well on Crazy Woman.

As with any road trip, maps are crucial. All of the roads I've mentioned here are on these maps, so for twenty bucks you can't go wrong. Hip waders cover most water, but chest waders come in handy on Ten Sleep Creek. Two- to four-weight rods under eight feet are ideal. Tippets of 4x or 5x are sufficient.

So, don't expect to catch a twenty-four-incher on this drive, but do count on connecting with plenty of wild fish in some of the finest country anywhere.

♦ ♦ ♦

Like anyone who's lived here for more than a couple of years, I've spilled a lot of blood in Montana—physically, emotionally and spiritually. So when I become angry and call out those who are destroying Montana for a quick buck or their own personal uses I do so with a clear conscience. What follows is an abridged laundry list of bad things that are happening in Yellowstone country and other places around the state.

One spring Ginny and I headed down to our dry camp in Tongue River country. The one of rattlesnake mayhem infamy. This has always been a place where we could go and disappear. We'd eat and drink well. Take long walks. Lounge around in the heat of the day. Lie in our sleeping bags late at night and watch the stars and northern lights come out while the moon rose and the coyotes howled.

Not any more. The oil industry has bought out most of the mineral rights from area ranchers and is tearing up the sage flats and hills laying thousands of miles of pipeline for coal bed methane extraction. This is going on right up to the borders of the Custer National Forest. It was bad enough the enormous coal strip mines not so far away around Decker were doing a permanent deadly number on the land, but now these venal cretins are ripping up some of the finest country in the Yellowstone drainage—not to mention the lower 48.

This rapacious activity is clawing the soul out of the land and to what good? A quick fix to our energy needs? Maybe. You and I won't save a dime. Prices for energy will continue to climb while our tax dollars subsidize an industry that posts record profits quarter after quarter. Nothing can be done. The land is hammered. Go see for yourself. Elvis has left the building, man.

And to make matters worse, in the Custer National Forest the Montana Department of Fish, Wildlife and Parks (MDFWP) in what now seems to be state-agency infinitely greedy, dollar-generating wisdom that has, among other atrocities, extended the turkey season in spring from a sensible two weeks to more than six weeks. This deranged extension is being promoted nationwide in hook-and-bullet rags, web sites and such. Gun toting lunatics (true turkey hunters, though few in number are good guys, sportsmen) from as far away as Marco Island, Florida, dressed in full camo, are marauding through the Ponderosa groves. Motorhomes and campers are everywhere, as is random gunfire. Over a period of thirty-five years, I only had one person come into my/our dry camp. This last visit we encountered six intruders, fully armed, fully camouflaged and arriving motorized on ATVs, dirt bikes and pickups. The turkeys, what few remain, are long gone. Litter is everywhere. Black bear and elk are being driven into small little niches of temporary safety.

You've really got to love those fun-loving boys over at Fish, Wildlife and Parks.

And while I'm on the subject of my favorite Montana band of maniacs consider the following:

Imagine a grassy field along a joyful brown trout stream in the West. The Crazy Mountains rise madly to the south. The Castle, Belt and Little Belt ranges hold the western and northern horizons. Every spring hundreds of sandhill cranes clack and chatter among themselves as they feed in the fields along the river before heading far north into Canada. This place is the Selkirk fishing access along the Musselshell River in central Montana—a pristine stream less than two hours north of the Yellowstone River. This is a place where I've taken friends from places like Seattle, Cocoa Beach, Baton Rouge and Boston. It's the place where I proposed to my wife one gorgeous October day when the cottonwoods were flaming electric gold-orange. This is a place I've been coming to over and over again since 1972. Two weeks ago, Ginny and I decided to stop off here for a few days after an extended road trip around the state— decompressing in familiar surroundings a bit before heading home to Livingston.

We never got there. In its imperious wisdom the FWP installed a chain-padlocked gate across the narrow two-track access to the grassy plain. There was no need to do this. The land was not abused or over-used. Litter was rare and always picked up by others who used the place. The two-track was in good shape and its narrow nature prevented land yachts from accessing the area. We were looking forward to some spring fishing for the trout, watching the Great Grey owls that live along this fecund riparian corridor, as do countless whitetail deer, black bear and kingfishers to name a few.

Of course there was always the option of going over the slight ridge half a mile away and camping amidst a herd of motor homes, perhaps even the maintained site alongside the two outhouses the FWP has installed, perched atop six-foot earthen mounds, would be available. High rise outhouses. Great idea I guess, almost as great as taking out the spigot that used to pour out cold, clear water.

More and more when we travel around Montana we see signs of the FWP run riot.

The first time I observed this departmental chaos was in 1984 when the Kokanee salmon population crashed in Flathead Lake in the northwest corner of the state. The reason for this turned out to be an inspired decision by those fun-loving boys at the venerable department. Flathead Lake is 28 miles by 15 miles with 185 miles of shoreline. It is pristine and one of the largest natural freshwater lakes west of the Mississippi River. Up until about 1984 it had annual runs of Kokanee salmon of several hundred thousand fish that would migrate and spawn up the Flathead River, which feeds into the lake. The runs of fourteen- to twenty-inch fish would literally blacken the river. The salmon provided a quality fishery and a necessary food source for local people. The salmon runs crashed in a very small way from over-fishing but mainly due to MDFWP planting mysis shrimp in the ecosystem. Mysis compete for plankton that the salmon feed on. Lake trout numbers and size in the lake has dwindled because of the loss of the Kokanee food source. Since the loss of the Kokanee the Lake trout have turned to aggressively feeding on juvenile bull trout and westslope cutthroat trout, both endangered species.

A direct result of this misguided move is that the annual bald eagle migration that used to number in the hundreds no longer exists. The glorious birds used to feast on the Kokanee, diving and swooping along the creek, tagging a salmon with their talons then gliding up to a tree limb to enjoy their prey. We used to watch this spectacle for hours. When the salmon population ceased to exist, the eagles went elsewhere.

Another example occurred last year when we drove down to the Tongue River to camp along the river at a very rough and rustic state campground, another place we had stayed at for years. In one year the MDFWP had turned the place into a zoo, replete with manicured lawns and smoothed gravel parking spots that were inhabited by a flock of motor homes—loud generators, TVs, radios and such tearing up the air. A manicured row of dwarf willows impeded the view of the river.

Needless to say, Ginny and I drove off for more isolated doings.

A side note here: FWP claims that they do not stock any rivers in the state with trout, that the populations are self-sustaining. There are hundreds of rainbow trout in this stretch of the river that are cookie cutter replications of each other. This in a system that is well outside of trout country and more commonly associated with small mouth bass, carp and channel catfish. Those were clearly hatchery fish and unless the almonds made a break for freedom, absconding with a FWP tank truck, they were clearly planted.

With few exceptions, telling the truth to the public and media goes against company policy. One biologist in the Deer Lodge area was so well-known for his deviations from the truth, that any of us who interviewed the fellow assumed that the actual situation was 180 degrees counter to what he said.

The list of atrocities to Montana's natural resources is lengthy. The FWP, when it isn't busy gating off good country, is busy turning state lands into a ghastly Disneyland clone. An agency that is sworn to preserve the state's wonders and provide access for recreation to the public has become an isolated, self-serving monster—a paradigm for everything that is wrong with government.

When I wrote an opinion piece for *CounterPunch* on the subject, I received the following letter from former Montana state representative George Ochenski that says it all.

"NOTHING has changed in FWP as far as I can tell from Schwinden (a former Montana Governor) on through Schweitzer. The head of the Parks Division now who is responsible for stuff like gating off the little road to the field at Selkirk (one of my favorite places, too), is none other than Joe Maurier. Don't know him? No surprise. He's one of Brian Schweitzer's college roommates who in-migrated from Colorado parks division to Montana after BS took office. How handy. Now we have someone from a state with developed, expensive, parks running ours.

"Luckily we passed the Primitive Parks Act in '93 and put about half the parks into non-development status. Did the same for Fishing Access Sites via the administrative rules after FWP told the legislature we didn't need to do it in law. And then made all state-owned islands 'island parks' in '97 or '99 (can't remember exactly which year) and made them all primitive, too. It's the only way we could keep the agency under any semblance of control. Selkirk, by the way, is a primitive park and I'm not sure they can even get away with gating it unless they're calling it 'maintenance.' But as you wrote, there was virtually no damage caused by that two-track except for the out-of-state hunters who burned the picnic table a couple years back and the fact that FWP wouldn't dump a load or two of gravel into the rutted area in the willows—you know it because you've been there—just beyond the new gate.

"I've written about virtually all the stuff you covered before and am so glad to see someone else doing it, too. Quite frankly, the so-called 'conservation' organizations, Trout Unlimited included, kiss FWP's ass and won't hold them accountable for the transgressions like those you've elucidated. Too bad. Those organizations are supposed to be advocating for the wildlife, the fish, and the resources—not a corrupt, authoritarian, and arrogant agency.

"Let me know if there's anything I can help you with and I'll see what I can do.

"Well, I'll add this caveat—we went looking for the fish planting records where FWP bought the trout from Colorado while Colorado's policy was to plant hatchery fish with whirling disease because their biologists thought it wouldn't flourish in the wild. So, Colorado stocked the rivers with diseased fish there for years and Montana, believe it or not, bought eggs from Colorado hatcheries. We found the records of the buy—but I think they destroyed the records of where they planted those fish. I'm saying they planted them in Hebgen (as they do by the hundreds of thousands every year) and they went through the dam (no power plant), into the river, and suddenly 'WHIRLING DISEASE IS DECIMATING THE MADISON!!' they yelled.

"Some outfit, let me tell you. And the grim thing is, under Schweitzer the Future Fisheries money [names deleted] fought so hard to get under Republican administrations has now been reduced to a quarter or less. We had $1.75 million a year—Schweitzer's administration now has it cut down to $500,000—and that's Resource Indemnity Trust Fund money that only goes to mine damaged lands first.

"So, Brian Schweitzer, in my book, is exactly his initials—B.S."

What all of this says to me is that FWP has been systematically closing off public lands for its own self-absorbed purposes, and that nepotism in the form of Schweitzer appointing his old friend Maurier to the head of the agency reigns supreme as usual in Montana. More importantly all of the responses I received indicate that large numbers of citizens, taxpayers who pay FWP bureaucrats' salaries, are fed up with this self-aggrandizing and non-responsive behavior. I would like to add that I can think of numerous fisheries and wildlife biologists who are doing excellent work to preserve various wild species in the state. They are not the problem. They are part of the solution. The career bureaucrats are the problem. Period. And they don't like their shortcomings exposed to the light of public scrutiny. I've received enough obscenity-laden emails, letters and phonecalls from FWP employees over the years regarding theses issues to confirm this assessment of their thin skins.

Well it would seem that I am incapable of writing a book, or even a modest-length article, without at least a few pages of red-faced ranting and raving. Fourteen previous titles are testament to this inescapable fact. If no one yells about the indecencies being perpetrated against Montana, "The Last Best Place" may soon become "The Lost Best Place."

◆ ◆ ◆

Emmylou is riffing with gentle energy about Halley's Comet as a Ginny and I roll down a red dusty road that cuts through early-May, thigh-high emerald grass on the Tongue River plateau. All of this magnificent country is part of the Yellowstone River drainage. That river flows west-northwest about a hundred miles north of where we are right now. Wyoming's substantial Bighorn Mountains and Montana's lesser Pryors show silvery purple and snow-crested white far to the west under a plain old high plains blue sky. Not a vault of impossibly perfect blue, whatever that is and certainly not cerulean or indigo. Just common blue. A few puffy clouds drift overhead, no doubt on contract with the powers that be for this daytime shift. But the main player is the grass flowing along beside us. When we stop here and there to enjoy this spring afternoon, the motion of all the green makes us think that we are moving, that the old Suburban is still rolling along. The only proof that we are somewhat motionless is the absence of a salmon-colored dust cloud trailing behind in a diminishing stream.

Halley's Comet is coming around again through the speakers after an 84-year absence and we negotiate a 120-degree corner that rises gradually all the way. I glance to my right out the passenger window. A bunch of antelope (pronghorns if you must) is keeping pace with the rig, 30–35 mph, white bellies and tan legs invisible in the grass. The animals seem to be floating on the surface of the tall stems like miniature sloops working downwind on the sea. Ginny punches replay, she likes Emmylou, this celestial tune. The antelope never even glance in our direction but move in synch about twenty feet away. When the road sweeps left, so do they. And when we roll along a casual stretch of straight flat road, so do they. These pronghorns are along for the ride—theirs and ours. The song lasts a bit over three minutes, the volume is up and they must hear it, because when it ends they ease off away from the Suburban, eventually vanishing beyond a far swale. Here then gone.

We stop in the middle of what is now a dirt two-track, work our way to the back of the car, open the doors, lift the cooler lid, grab a couple of cans of beer, open them, take long pulls and enjoy the low-eighties madness of putting another winter behind us. The only sound is the wind pushing through the grass in a steady, rasping rush. So much green that even the air around us seems slightly tinted, glowing with the softest of green hue.

We say nothing about the antelope. No need to. A coyote emerges from the needlegrass (I think that's what this is, but I'm still working on the difference between bull trout and Dolly Vardon not to mention the various species of fir trees) about one-hundred yards ahead, begins crossing the road, looks at us, barks a couple of brief, laughing notes with a head shake then wanders out of sight in the greenness on the far side. The grass shifts from emerald to dark green to almost quicksilver as it plays with the wind and the sun. This colorful motion is hypnotic, intoxicating. Thirty minutes pass before we climb back in the old rig and continue towards the drop that winds like a sunning rattlesnake to the Tongue River. There are carp to catch and maybe a rogue rainbow or two, and possibly, just possibly—and I realize that the limits of credulity are being stretched to the limits here—a brown trout. But remember, spring is a time of infinite possibility, even miracles.

◆ ◆ ◆

We make an early morning start from our island camp across from the rock cliffs guarding the north bank of the river. All through the rapidly warming day we spot wildlife on the river, along shore, working the prairies or soaring above us. During our lunch break on an island by Arnells Creek we look for agates. The light is intense and we find several of them, stones that betray their presence with a subtle orange internal fire and a potato-like surface. Looking down for the agates for an hour and eventually every rock looks like what we are seeking. Time to return to the canoe and the river.

The lower river from Forsyth to its confluence with the Missouri at Fort Buford, North Dakota is an easier time, a more genteel cruise, when compared with the free-form, chaotic, whitewater staircase tumble of the upper river from Yankee Jim Canyon in the Paradise Valley down through the standing-wave insanity below Columbus and on to Riverside Park in scenic, downtown Laurel.

Below Columbus to Laurel the river is brutal, and I feel fortunate and very lucky to have survived the stretch alone in my cedar-strip canoe.

The stretch of river we're on now, with few obvious and clearly visible exceptions, is a casual float where the main obstacle is bucking an afternoon, upstream wind. No big deal. Too strong a blow leads to an early camp on the nearest island. Soon we are drifting lazily along broad, smooth stretches of water that glides beneath sere badland shapes of cones, pyramids, buttes and deep ravines layered in the colors salmon, ochre, soft grey, charcoal black, faded green and other earthly shades not named by humans. Our paddles dip into the lazy current and provide a slight boost in our speed as we skim over the mirrored surface of the river that reflects the blue sky, white cumulous clouds and the tan-yellow bluffs in colors gentled by their contact with the dark water. We spot more mule deer, white tails, cranes and golden eagles. We also far above soaring on gyrating thermals vultures. Along some muddy banks there are beaver. Western meadowlarks are everywhere thick in numbers. This abundance of wildlife is unknown to the more obviously spectacular mountain ranges far to the west.

The day warms into the upper seventies and we are down to t-shirts as we push hard through the seams of fast current and work hard to fight the upstream headwind on the slower flats. We are getting tired as we always do near the end of a trip and wonder where the bridge at Forsyth is. When rounding a left-to-right bend we see the structure rising above the river.

Unloading the canoe, loading the Suburban that Joe Wilson, owner of a motel in Forsyth that we stay at when in town, shuttled for us a few days earlier. Joe is an agate collector, a rock hound who showed us many of his stones including some reddish jasper. And he filled us in on what to expect from the stretch of the river we've just completed. During our conversation, Sheriff Jay Paff comes in with a younger man in tow who is here to pick up a Western Union money order for $300 from his family so he can return to wherever home is. Joe and Jay discussed where they thought the best put-in would be for our float. Amelia Island won out in a close battle with a spot on a rancher's place along Sarpy Creek.

"If you have any trouble, I'll be the one in the boat to help you out," said Joe as he gave Ginny his phone. The beauty of her cell phone vaguely surfacing with uncommon servitude this bright morning.

Good people, as everyone we met in Forsyth was, from Dave who worked for Joe and exclaimed "You two are a couple of old hippies," while giving us each bear hugs (actually we're crazed hipsters, but why argue?) to our waitress at the Hong Kong later that evening, where we dined graciously and drank a couple of Chinese beers each. A fine time.

When we headed out well-rested the next morning, we realized that we could live here with all of the great, open country and the decent people. One more home on the road. You can never have too many.

Chapter 7

High Plains Badlands
Rauche Juan to Glendive—92 miles

WE BACK THE SUBURBAN DOWN THE CEMENT BOAT RAMP
at the put-in about a mile above where the Rosebud joins the
Yellowstone and about thirty-seven river miles upstream of
Miles City. We plan four days and three nights of leisurely paddling past
down to the take-out at Far West, a landing that also sports a cement
ramp. The stretch is sixty-three miles, so sixteen per day is nothing but
a stroll down the road walking on water in the White Guide that by now
has become an old friend, a trusted member of our little crew.

We slide the wooden canoe (every time I think of the canoe as being
constructed of wood Jefferson Airplane's eerie cover of "Wooden Ships"
drifts through my mind. The words written by David Crosby, Stephen
Stills and Paul Kanter make an ethereal appearance—*Wooden ships on
the water, very free, and easy, easy, you know the way it's supposed to be…*
—from the roof rack and set it in the shallow water. Loading the gear in
the craft is habit, routine by now, and takes fifteen minutes even with
securing all of the water-proof bags and cases with straps, just in case
we should founder after striking an unseen deadhead or rock or perhaps
capsizing through some unimaginable error on my part.

The country is open range to the north, sere, sage land that rolls up
to rough coulees and dusty bluffs. On the south shore, the one we're
skirting right now, Burlington Northern-Sante Fe tracks hug the base
of sharp cliffs and more coulee country. Long trains of four, five Dash 9
engines thunder past us in each direction, on a regular every half-hour
or so basis, pulling heavily laden coal cars or strings of boxcars, con-
tainers, autoracks and reefers. The engines are the classic Sante Fe red

and silver or the dark green BN, all of them smudged with soot from the hard-charging diesels, finishes dulled from the grime of thousands of miles pounding over the rails. The power of the engines rumbles through us deep in the pits of our stomachs. Railroads—still the life line of the West.

In years gone by, Buffalo Rapids (a dozen miles below the Tongue River) and Wolf Rapids (just below the mouth of the Powder) proved to be serious obstacles for steamer traffic. Perhaps because I always did these stretches during relatively low water they were not much of a problem, more a quickening diversion in an otherwise smooth paddle.

As we move down to our camping site on an island sixteen miles away, we spot a herd of mule deer with their big ears set on high alert, coyotes ghosting through the brush and ducking beneath sagging strands of rusty barbed-wire. I wonder if we've passed over any paddlefish or perhaps a pallid sturgeon trapped in this section above the Intake Diversion dam that was built decades ago. The fish are long-lived but the state Dept. of Fish, Wildlife and Parks predicts that the wild population will go extinct by 2018. What a lovely promise for the future. Yucca cactus is all along the slopes, narrow-pointed leaves and spiked stems holding open seed pods that still have remnants of the cottony seed carriers caught on the rough edges of the openings.

The sun is warm, no hot, and we ritually douse ourselves with river water or pull over and soak ourselves before letting the heat of the day dry us in minutes and then apply another coat of sunscreen.

The island in question glides into view on the north side of the river, several acres of cottonwoods, willow, alder, wild rose and grapes, clumps of grass. We slide in, set up camp and I rig a spinning rod with a treble hook, a sinker that could do double duty as a doorknob and a glob of chicken livers. I fling the sophisticated mess far out in a deep run, prop the rod between a forked stick I've wedged into the moist bank and sit back leaning against a smooth boulder. Ginny and I are here at this out-of-the-way location a little more than 200 years after William Clark passed through here and noted in his diary:

> Set out this morning at day light and proceeded on gliding down this
> smooth Stream (the Yellowstone) passing maney Islad. And Several
> Creeks and brooks… The cliffs on the South Side of the Rochejhone
> are Generally compd. Of a yellowish Gritty Soft rock, whilst those
> of the N. is light Coloured and much harder. Straters of coal in the
> banks on either Side those on the Stard. Bluffs was about 30 feet
> above the water and in two vanes from 4 to 8 feet thick, in a horizon-
> tal position…

♦ ♦ ♦

The endangered pallid sturgeon and the warm water fish in the
Yellowstone River system have an unlikely ally: irrigator Roger Muggli.
I discovered this fact by roaming the Montana Chapter of the Nature
Conservancy's website. According to a story titled "Friend of Fish—
Eastern Montana Irrigator Spurs Yellowstone Conservation Efforts," the
Nature Conservancy, the Tongue and Yellowstone Irrigation District,
several state and federal agencies, and this third-generation, eastern
Montana farmer are making an effort to revive the warm water fishery of
the Tongue and Yellowstone Rivers.

The coalition's first task is the 12-Mile Dam on the Tongue River.
This dam, operated by the irrigation district which Roger heads, diverts
irrigation water from the Tongue to about 300 farm families and 9,400
acres of crop land. The 12-Mile, like several other diversion dams on the
Tongue and Yellowstone, prevents fish from reaching their traditional
spawning and rearing habitat. The group plans to build a fish-bypass
canal around the 12-Mile Dam, which will allow about thirty species of
fish to access fifty miles of their native spawning habitat for the first time
since the dam was built in 1885.

"None of us were around when these things were built, but that doesn't
take us off the hook for doing something to fix them," says Muggli.

Lack of access to spawning habitat has led to a major decline in
several warm water fish species, including pallid sturgeon. These mysterious relics of the Cretaceous period have not spawned in the lower
Yellowstone River system in about fifty years and are facing extinction in
the entire upper Missouri/Yellowstone system.

"If we could remove the barriers to fish at just five of these irrigation dams, we could increase fish access to spawning and rearing habitat on more than 415 channel miles of the Yellowstone and Tongue rivers," says Burt Williams, the Conservancy's southeast Montana program manager.

"The great thing about this project," said Williams, "is the enthusiastic leadership of a local ag [agricultural] producer and irrigator to pull together these groups to solve a problem for the fish that also benefits the local irrigators."

All the partners in the 12-Mile project have said they are willing to work together on future conservation projects in the Yellowstone system said Williams.

"I really want to show the world that we can do these things," said Muggli. "I hope I live to see the day when we have a thriving fishery in the Tongue and Yellowstone rivers."

The same coalition working to build the fish-bypass canal is also planning to build a bypass fix at the Intake Dam. Intake is a death trip for boaters who try to go over and through the massive boulders and piles of rock that channel the water in a gothic looking diversion channel fixture on the north side of the river. Going downstream through this is insanity.

Going upstream for the pallid sturgeon is an impossibility. A friend of mine who works as a fisheries biologist for the state has spent considerable time and effort studying and trying to preserve the species that lived when dinosaurs roamed the earth during the late Cretaceous period 70 million years ago. With its flattened shovel-shaped snout, bony plates and long reptile-like tail, the pallid sturgeon looks like an ancient beast trapped in a modern time warp. I think this is the main reason he's so attracted to the pallid sturgeon, the seemingly anomalous fact of its existence in the new millennia. The sturgeon can weigh as much as eighty pounds and reach lengths of six feet. This isn't any sissy rainbow trout of twenty inches we're talking about here. This is serious piscatorial business on the lower Yellowstone.

◆ ◆ ◆

Even during the dried out heat of early September, the wheatgrass ripples in the breeze along the reddish-brown two-track on the backside of these badlands and still retains some of the summer's dense green color. The hills, coulees and bluffs that stretch many miles to the north and rise up all around me are now turned various shades of natural death—light and dark brown, tan, buckskin, ochre, dun. Silvery-green clumps of sagebrush loom just above the grasses and tint the air with an aromatic mixture of sweetness and herbs. The ground cover radiates the colors of autumn in purple, red, oranges and gold, all highlighted by patches of dark green clumps of junipers, the plant's dusty blue berries moving in and out of view on the wind in a strange game of hide-and-seek. The distant sound of a herd of cows bawling drifts by me.

I'm walking along this dusty byway that meanders through a prairie pocket in the middle of the sere tablelands, holding my twenty gauge Beretta in the crook of my right arm while hunting sharp-tailed grouse. I've kicked up several already and dropped two. All of the grouse burst up quickly and raced downwind. Not the best shot. I prefer them crossing to my right and then left. With a little luck, a couple more will make a fine main course for me and Ginny this evening when grilled, lightly seasoned, over our modest fire, along with some grilled corn and zucchini. A little red wine will be okay, too.

We're camped on top of a broad ridge in the austere badlands that look down on the Yellowstone River and the small ranching community of Terry nestled amid irrigated fields on the far bank—a quiet place somewhere between Miles City and Glendive. The community offers a few bars, a small grocery store, hardware store, the Diamond Motel, the Dizzy Diner drive-in with sage growing in cracks of the pavement, a falling down, abandoned Rialto Theater, a Cenex station along with churches, barbershop, high school, well-manicured town park—all of what one would expect from small town, eastern Montana. And there's also Al's Agates, the reason we first stopped here, but that's later in all of this.

Below our camp, fantastic cones, mounds, long slopes, ragged cliffs and mangled arroyos stumble off in ordered chaos down to the river cloaked in every earthly color imaginable. The shapes resemble palaces, pyramids, volcanoes and one looks like a home for dwarves and a princess (remember the red wine). I'm convinced that the little suckers cruise up to the ridge late at night and drag me off my sleeping pad because each morning I wake up at dawn well below the pad, arms stretched out clutching for purchase to no avail. This has happened every night I've slept here and nowhere else in my travels. Perhaps an increase in lithium is in order. Ginny, my companion of many years, merely nods and laughs. She's Irish and believes in many things that I don't even wish to consider.

Right now she is walking the top of this weirdly eroded landscape taking pictures, hundreds of them with her digital camera—petroglyphs, the sky, a distant train pushing its way west—while I play with the birds and the land a couple of hundred feet below. We may be separated by a half-mile, but the strength of this place, and everywhere else for that matter, keeps us connected in ineffable ways we no longer try to explain to anyone. Mad is as mad does. For me, the fall of year is the best of times with its deep blue skies, reasonable temperatures and compressed intensity, brought on by the palpable approach of winter that's lurking somewhere up in the Northwest Territories. The land, the animals, everything senses that time is short. The days last forever but are distilled to their essence like wine into Armagnac.

We found this country a couple of years ago while ghosting eastward towards the confluence of the Yellowstone and Missouri Rivers at Ft. Buford in North Dakota. Running down the Interstate, the crazed forms of these badlands kept drawing our eyes to the north until the pull was too much and we turned off the highway. We followed our eyes and eventually climbed up a rocky road to this ridge, and fell in love with the spot—the isolation, the wildness, the usual stuff a couple of recluses live for—and return every chance we get. We plan to move to the area in the near future, but that's another fantasy not directly related to the one I'm telling now.

◆ ◆ ◆

The first time I spent any time in this land was perhaps twenty years ago when I was on a duck walk—as in "follow me kiddies and look where I point,"—fam (as in "familiarization") trip courtesy of the state of Montana where four of us, all writers to some degree, traveled from the abandoned mining town of Bannock up to Butte over to Yogo sapphire country and then by twin-engine prop to Glendive—a fine flight that soared only a few thousand feet above the orderly erosion of the twisted landscape that led the way to our destination. Landing in a cascade of crimson-yellow-gold, sunset radiance set the tone for our too brief stay. We spent several days there working up the muddy brown river in aluminum boats powered by outboard motors guided by a local businessman looking for moss agates. Eventually, after hours of staring at gravel bars beneath a relentless late-spring sun, we developed agate eyes (much like morel mushroom vision) and were able to discern the faint orange glow coming from the potato-shaped agates, instead of picking up tons of worthless leverites, as in "leave it right there, it's just a rock."

The last night in town, the businessman—a great guy with a wonderful sense of humor and a true knack for finding agates and, as I discovered later from numerous photos held by small magnets on his refrigerator, catching enormous trout—invited us all to his home above the Yellowstone in Glendive for a barbecue and corn boil. Eventually most of us found our way up onto his roof where we worked on pitchers of ice-cold martinis. The roof was covered in a layer of rejected agates that he'd tossed up there over the years. How the house bore up under this strain of rejects, I'll never know. Several other guys were there, too. Sun and wind-burned with distant expressions prowling within their eyes. Dinosaur hunters. One of them said he liked my work in *Fly Fisherman*. Another of them was Jack Horner. The evening sky soon grew dark and filled with stars. We ate tons of beef and several hundred ears of corn. The martinis did the talking for all of us. Then it was morning and I found myself on another small commercial plane, this time aiming west towards Helena.

◆ ◆ ◆

Al Siegle of Al's Agates lives in a comfortable home in the center of town not far from the park. A vintage camper trailer rests in the yard next to the stone drive. We knock and shortly Al opens the door for us. He smiles widely as he greets us and asks us to follow him into his living room. He looks to be in his eighties, and has a ruddy complexion highlighting a cheerful face. Al moves well despite using one of his hand-crafted willow canes. Walking through his home is a geologic wonder with polished globes of agate in display cases along with hundreds of finished flat agates and countless detailed pieces of jewelry. Photos of his family, of remote places in Montana, of long-ago-visited landscapes throughout the West, along with paintings and prints line the walls.

Al directs us to sit. Ginny sets up her camera equipment while Al and I talk or, rather, he mostly talks and I mostly listen as he tells me of the process of turning agates.

"I had always wondered why 'tumbled' agates lost their shine and luster after a year or so. An elderly gentleman who was a chemist for the Holly Sugar Company solved this mystery for me," says Al. "He told me that he had done a lot of experimenting and found that agates have small pores, and that these pores fill up with dirt and dust. The heat and friction, when hand-polishing, seals these pores and you have a lifetime shine.

"Another old gentleman taught me to cab and hand-polish agates. I will never forget his booming voice when he said to me, 'Never do that cheap tumbling. It will ruin your business.' So, that's where I get my slogan … 'Hand-polished agates, like true friends, are precious and everlasting.'"

I walk over to an illuminated display case that holds agates of all sizes and varied shapes. The globes intrigue me, draw me into their shining, almost fluorescent centers. They appear to be the tools of vanished alchemists or perhaps one of them is sitting in the chair right behind me.

"Years ago some lady friends and I would float the river looking for agates after the runoff was over," said Al. "The best years were when we'd had a cold winter and lots of ice. When the ice broke up it would scour the gravel beds and turn up more agates."

Most of the agates have been washed down from ravines, canyons and coulees that flank both sides of the Yellowstone. Some are enormous, the size of footballs, though these are rare.

When I ask him about canoeing the river around here, he says, "You don't have to worry if you pay attention. Even Buffalo Rapids is not a problem if you know what you're doing and it's not high water."

Ginny continues to shoot, and I can see that Al is enjoying all of the attention and our appreciation for his work. We continue to talk about the land around here, a little politics, of course the weather, and he points out the various individuals in the photos and explains their relationship to him with heartfelt friendship and a touch of longing for those departed. In the middle of all of this a woman knocks, comes in and asks Al if he would fix a gold chain for her. He looks at it briefly and then with nimble fingers performs the operation.

"How much do I owe you, Al?" she asks.

"Oh, it's nothing," and they smile and nod and she leaves.

"She has a ranch on the other side of the river and owns most of the land over there," he says.

Ginny finishes up. Before we go Al hands Ginny a handful of polished agates and one of his willow canes. We make polite small talk and Al shows us out. He says as we leave, "You're always welcome here," and his right arm sweeps in an arc that takes in not only his home, but all of Terry. "Please come back soon."

We can see that he means this. We say that we will and we mean it.

Unfortunately we were not to see Al again. I came across this obituary in the *Billings Gazette* in mid August.

> Albert John Siegle, 78, of Terry died Monday, Aug. 14, 2006, at the Billings Clinic Hospital in Billings after a brief battle with pancreatic cancer.
>
> He was born on Easter morning, April 8, 1928, near Marsh to Lydia Schock Siegle. His father, John McCormick Siegle, had died 11 days before his birth. His mother later married Gottlieb Lassle.
>
> Mr. Siegle grew up on the family farm on Bad Route between Fallon and Glendive. He attended school through eighth grade and was confirmed at the area Trinity Lutheran Church. He worked on the family farm, at R.L. Robins Farmers' Union, the Glendive railroad roundhouse, Colgate Sectrum, and Holmes Construction prior to joining the Army in 1950.
>
> He was trained and served as a medic in the Army. Mr. Siegle was assigned to the Russian Border Patrol in Germany. While in the Army

he also served as a German translator for the United States Army hockey team. He divided his time between serving on the Russian border and traveling with the Army hockey team, who played against hockey teams throughout Europe.

While on leave from the Army, he married Lorraine Helen Jones at Terry on May 22, 1951. Following his discharge from the Army in 1952, he worked as a mechanic at the Ford (1952–1956) and Turnbull's Chevrolet (1956–1958) garages in Terry.

He leased a small farm west of Terry for a number of years. In addition to raising sheep and a few cows, he drove the school bus north of Terry (1965–1975) and was a contracted mail carrier for a mail route from Fallon through Marsh (1958–1972). He also spent several years working as a butcher at Reynold's Market in Terry.

He later worked for Pine Hills School, State of Montana Department of Family Services in Miles City for over 10 years. Following his retirement from Pine Hills, he ran a small agate and jewelry shop from his home in Terry.

Mr. Siegle enjoyed picking agates, hunting and fishing. In his later years he enjoyed visiting with friends and playing cards at the Terry Senior Citizens Center. He was a member of Grace Lutheran Church in Fallon, where he served as treasurer and elder for many years. He was a lifelong member of the American Legion, a member of the Prairie County Council on the Aging, and a former member of the Prairie County Museum Board.

His survivors include one son, Delbert Siegle, and his wife, Betsy, of Mansfield, Conn.; one daughter, Debra Siegle of Miles City; and seven brothers, Erwin Lassle of Glendive, Harold Lassle of San Ramon, Calif., Marvin Lassle of Cresent City, Calif., Clarence Lassle of Billings, Donald Lassle of Lyma, Wyo., Eldon Lassle of Pinehurst, Idaho, and Raymond Lassle of Makoti, N.D.

Fairly long and detailed as far as newspaper obits go, but the words give only a shadowy image of a good man, a true Montanan, and sadly, one of the last of his kind. Ginny and I feel blessed to have spent the time we did with Al.

♦ ♦ ♦

The sun's dropping behind a ridge and I turn around to make the climb back to camp. Cool air flows down past me as I near the end of the grassy flat. And then a pair of sharps kick up one flying straight into the wind and the other cutting right and behind me. I fire twice, dropping the straight shot and missing on the swing. The smell of gunsmoke is whisked away on the moving air out into the big open north of here. I pick up the grouse, still warm with just a drop of bright red blood showing in the corner of its beak. I put it in the pouch of my vest with the other two. Three birds will be plenty for the two of us. I'm grateful—for the sharptails, for the day, for people like Al, for this fine country.

As I begin working uphill I spot Ginny in jet black relief walking the ridgeline back to camp, a bundle of wood cradled in her arms.

Again, I'm grateful.

♦ ♦ ♦

If you're of an adventuresome persuasion, pursuing the rainbow and brown trout of northcentral Wyoming's Middle Fork of the Powder River might be something to check out. Some steep up-and-down hiking/scrambling is involved so you need to be in decent shape. This remote, high country tributary of the Yellowstone sees some traffic, but the farther up the rock and dirt two-track you go, the fewer people you encounter until after perhaps twenty miles (about two hours) you'll be all alone in staggeringly beautiful canyon country. Just another personality of the main river hiding out way down in Wyoming. There are ancient petroglyphs scattered here and there among the table top eroded sandstone boulders. One set is marked and has a well-used trail. Others are found during casual wanderings along game trails that skirt the rim of the canyon.

The best water is located approximately thirty miles west of the small town of Kaycee that sits just off of I-25. This is the Hole-in-the-Wall country of Butch Cassidy and the Sundance Kid, and there are plenty of reminders in town and along the way to make sure you don't forget this.

The final few miles of the drive are over a rough rock and dirt two-track and then a final mile to the campground through shelf rock and sand. A good rig is desirable though I did see one guy and his wife drive a late-model Continental with Texas plates up this way. They both took a quick look then headed back to town with martinis on their brains. Along the dusty way there are three state trailhead fishing accesses and another at the primitive campground, meaning a newer outhouse, fire-pots and picnic tables, but no water. The fishing is down in the canyon anywhere from 600 to 900 feet below the rim. The trails are steep, but easy to follow. The climb back up takes about an hour. The season goes from the end of runoff in late June through mid-October, depending upon the arrival of cold weather. Deer, antelope, mountain lion and black bear are present. The weather is normally hot and dry—often above 100 degrees, so bring lots water (at least two gallons per person per day) and food in a daypack. A quality first aid kit is an idea, also. Mosquitoes have never been a problem, and flies only a minor nuisance.

I've caught browns and rainbows from ten inches to over twenty inches using tan Elk Hair Caddis 12–16 and small mayfly ties from 16–20 in the sapphire pools and deeper runs. There are shallow stretches of white marl-like rock here and there along the streambed where using a 14–16 Gold-ribbed Hare's Ear Nymph about two feet below an indicator works wonders. A 3-4 wt. 7'-6" rod is ideal. Wading is relatively easy and straightforward. If you fall you'll get wet but you won't die. Hip waders work, but I wade wet and bring a light-weight pair of wading boots tied to my daypack. There is some scrambling as you work your way upstream over boulders and through pines, willows and brush.

This is fantastic country with a giant scarp of red wall stone running from north to south along the eastern horizon. Altitude varies from about 6,000 feet to nearly 8,000, so evenings can be chilly. And I have seen very few rattlesnakes sunning themselves on the rocks. One of the caves that Butch and Sundance hid out in is just downstream from the trail end from the campground. Outlaw trout I guess.

Getting to the accesses is easy. Take Hwy 191 west from town for a mile, then turn left on 190 for about twenty miles until you reach Arminto Road. Turn left-south and travel another five miles to turn right-west to the final rough pitch that goes past the marked stream access points and on into camp, several miles. The turn onto this road is a mile past the Willow Creek Ranch.

The water looks good and the buildings are well-maintained as far as I can tell from the road.

For those interested in camping, be absolutely sure to bring plenty of water in five gallon jugs, your own food and charcoal. The camping is free, but wood is sparse. In mid-summer, giant airborne beetles come out after dark on some evenings, attracted to body heat and fires. The lumbering beasts dive bomb you as you sit around a fire. I suggest a squash racket for unique after-hours sport.

This is truly spectacular land, offering a uniquely-accessible canyon experience and some fairly good fly fishing.

◆ ◆ ◆

Of all of the animals that live in the Yellowstone drainage, my favorite is the coyote. I love the way they riff, chatter and howl in the night when the moon rises over the horizon or when they smell food cooking over our fire. They always seem to be lurking just barely in sight or hiding in tall grass and brush waiting to complete some nefarious deed.

One time, on a red-dirt two-track, a coyote bounded in front of my rig and ran ahead of me for a mile or more, constantly looking back with bright eyes and an open-mouthed grin. Then it sopped and so did I. He turned and faced me and launched into a series of leaps straight up-and-down with all four legs working as springs. Next the playful guy dropped to the ground and rolled over and over in the dirt before rising and shaking himself releasing a minor blizzard of dust. He looked at me once more, barked several times and trotted off into a hillside stand of Ponderosa, a grey and now light salmon-colored wild canine out for an afternoon stroll. Coyotes are like that in my experience. Life seems to run on another plane or planes than we narrow-minded humans function within.

On August 12, 1804, northwest of what is now Onawa, Iowa, Lewis and Clark first recognized the "Prarie wolf which was barking at us as we passed" like a large "fest." On September 17, one of the expedition's hunters shot "a Small wolf with a large bushey tail," and the next day Clark shot "a Prarie Wollf, about the Size of a gray fox bushey tail head & ear like a wolf." Lewis wrote his description of what proved to be a new species on May 5, 1805, in northeastern Montana.

> The small woolf or burrowing dog of the praries are inhabitants
> almost invariably of the open plains; they usually ascociate in bands
> of ten or twelve sometimes more and burrow near some pass or place

much frequented by game; not being able alone to take deer or goat they are rarely ever found alone but hunt in bands; they frequently watch and seize their prey near their burrows; in these burrows they raise their young and to them they also resort when pursued; when a person approaches them they frequently bark, their note being precisely that of the small dog. they are of an intermediate size between that of the fox and dog, very active fleet and delicately formed; the ears large erect and pointed the head long and pointed more like that of the fox; tale long;...the hair and fur also resembles the fox tho' is much coarser and inferior. they are of a pale redish brown colour. the eye of a deep sea green colour small and piercing. their tallons [claws] are reather longer than those of the ordinary wolf or that common to the atlantic states, none of which are to be found in this quarter, nor I believe above the river Plat.

Most of the coyotes I've seen have been in country, where I used to hunt turkeys and now just camp, walk or sit. I no longer hunt turkeys. I can't bring myself to kill one of these magnificent creatures. Grouse, Huns, pheasants and chukar when I can hit them—shooting these birds is fun. It doesn't bother me. But knocking down a turkey is a different matter. Their call, which sounds ludicrous in captivity, brings home the wild nature of the land I love more than any—the coulees and bluffs of southeastern Montana. That crazy, undisciplined sound, the internal vision it conjures of the turkeys moving secretively and swiftly across exposed sage flats, down eroding sandstone washes and beneath stands of tall Ponderosa, says it all for me. Thirty-pound birds that move with the swiftness of horses and the stealth of the night wind. To me they're special. At my dry camp, one I've been going to since 1973, in the middle of not much at all down on the Custer National Forest in Tongue River country—land that is the essence of the Yellowstone River drainage. When I arrive and after I set up camp, I like to walk to the edge of a bluff and sit on a downed tree trunk. I've done this for years.

From this spot, I can see across miles of broken and twisted landscape, across small valleys filled with pine trees and across rolling hills of native grasses and sage. Within a few minutes I normally hear coyotes barking and chattering away in the distance. They often know I'm back before I do. And then, sometimes, I'll hear a turkey call, the strange sound carrying and softly echoing through the land. And maybe another will answer the first one. I'll keep sitting where I am, smoking a cigar as I enjoy the ensuing silence. I'll watch the stars come out, the moon rise and perhaps the green glow of the northern lights will appear and shade the country in their unique radiance. The coyotes, mule deer and, of course, the turkeys are a part of all of this. But I remember well this hunt in coyote country that was one of my first and took place oh so long ago, maybe thirty years back when I still lived in the northwest corner of Montana about thirteen hours away...

... I had only the vaguest idea what time it was. Very early, for sure. The Ponderosa pines were visible as towering, many-armed demons standing all around me in the dark. The stars were still out, shining intensely. The first suggestions of a false dawn glowed faintly on the edges of the hills and bluffs. Long needles carpeted the ground, covering patches of last year's dry grass. The spring had been unseasonable warm so far and dry. Scant moisture had fallen and the melting snow was long gone, soaked up by the thirsty ground.

My feet crunched on the duff, a brittle, hollow sound. Trying to find the roost tree I'd discovered yesterday was proving troublesome. The thick-trunked pine should be right around here only a few hundred yards from my camp, such as that was. No water, a small fire ring, the back of the truck serving as a kitchen, and my sleeping bag and tarp passing for a bedroom. Austerity has a well-remembered ring, one I'm comfortable with on the road or out in the sticks.

The drive over to this sparsely populated part of southeastern Montana was 600 or 700 miles, 12 hours, but this was one of the best places in the West for hunting the large birds. Back home in the Flathead you had to put in for a permit to hunt turkeys. There were less than 200 openings available and the odds were long. Out this way all you needed to do was walk into a sporting goods store in Billings or down in Sheridan and pay for the various permits and a conservation license, a total of less than 15 bucks this year (approximately $70 if you were from out-of-state) and an additional few dollars for an autumn license.

I first came to this place years ago in what proved to be a hunt of heroic and slightly mad proportions. Now I come back every opportunity to spend a little time perched on this pine-forested bluff that looks out over miles of rolling hills and eroded coulees. The varying shades of green displayed by the native grasses, small cactus. Conifers and sage blended easily with the ochre, buff and subtle pink of the rock formations and exposed earth. Mule deer, rusting barbed wire and prickly pear cactus all over the place. I'd stepped on enough of the cactus to become almost comfortable with the tiny, sharp bites of the needles in my feet. Almost but not quite. This was wild, unspoiled country and I'd never seen another hunter in all these years, not even at the small store some miles distant that served as a post office and gas station. One pickup truck was the extent of human visitation during my undisciplined forays.

That was the main reason I drove all this way. To be alone, by myself. The turkeys were just an excuse, though a damn good one in my mind. I've not shot many Merriam's in this span of years, but I know where they are, to some extent. The trick is in the timing. Too early and the birds are scattered all over hell and back. Show up after the spring breeding soiree has completed its bizarre dance and the situation is similar. The turkeys have dispersed and even if they are trotting around in the trees or strutting in the grassy meadows, they are more than a shade reluctant to come to my calls, amateur efforts at best, but productive during the peak of the breeding season. In truth, when the birds are in full rut, so to speak, discordant notes bombed away from the belly of a tuba would work. Neophyte scratchings on a hollow cedar box sound like a symphony to the love-struck turkeys. At the first annoying notes, again if the timing is right, gobblings emanate from the hills in all directions. Pure lunacy. Lovely sounds singing through the air.

The roost tree I was trying to find right now was one of several I'd discovered in the area. Arriving in the afternoon, I set up camp, grilled a burger and sipped a few gin and tonics (no limes, Spartan trip). Around the time the sun started fading over the horizon, casting the countryside in an eerie orange-gold light, a series of "gobbles," "putts" and assorted other forms of turkey madness issued from the coulee behind me. The cacophony advanced nearer, finally culminating in thwacking sounds of wings beating and some disgruntled utterings from the birds as they settled into their perches for the night. What a crew. I was sure I knew which tree they'd pulled into. The other three roost trees were growing on a gentle slope a couple of miles away. Too far for the birds' racket to have sounded so close to camp. Tomorrow I'd shoot my turkey and then head to a small river running freely even farther in the middle of nothing where I'd try my hand at some untamed rainbows that ran to good size. Killing a couple of weeks in these parts was almost too easy.

Standing well alone in this landscape, looking away towards Wyoming in the south and then in the direction of Billings many miles north, the familiar feeling of loneliness descended. Not unwelcome, another reason to be out here and away from the smothering security of civilization where it seems I never have the chance to feel anything but what I'm told or programmed to feel. Do this. Think that. Buy into another administration con. Don't step out of line. That's where the loneliness comes in handy. The feeling is a means to connect with life, to turn briefly humble without being publicly humiliated. We all get enough of that trying to earn a living.

That's the power of this country, a place so foreign to most of us, alien to me at times, that we don't have a natural clue about what's taking place. Lightning strikes an exposed seam of coal and a smoldering fire starts, watched by no one. The coal makes smoke and flares into flames, sizzling for centuries, until it is doused by heavy rain and runoff or burns its way through to the other side of the hill or runs out of fuel. The fire is so hot that mud and sandstone is baked rock-hard and kiln-cured to the color of dried blood. A 50-foot seam of coal may cook 200 feet of rock lying above. What do the mule deer and the coyotes and the turkeys think about all this? Probably nothing at all. There's too much thinking going on as it is. Confused brain noise that is detectable, faintly, in the distant glow of Billings late at night. City rap. Disgusting stuff. The clinker eventually builds up into huge beds of porous rubble storing billions of gallons of water that seeps down from the contributions of wicked storms raging on up above. Artificial wells naturally made. Trees and brush grow best in these spots and wild animals know them for their water. There are several such places near camp, wild drawing cards for the Merriam's.

I built up the fire and fried a fat pork chop and some onions in butter and garlic, threw together some salad that was dressed with olive oil and vinegar. It was all I could find at a store some hours up the road. I was hungry and finished off the meal in minutes, then re-stoked the dwindling fire, ignited a cheap cigar from Connecticut, built a tall drink and enjoyed the night. Coyotes howled away from the surrounding ridges, talking to each other. They knew the turkeys were here, too. Earlier, I'd heard a few calls from the packs, then some miles off, as the turkeys began to roost. I'd have some competition, but hopefully the boys weren't armed. After climbing into the sleeping bag, I tried to make sense out of the sky, but my mind faded to black and I was out until maybe four. Now I was trying to find that damn roost tree and then a place to hide.

The stars were disappearing and the sky on the east was actually turning to soft blue when I found the tree. The ancient pine, several feet thick at its base, gnarled and twisted from its long life, hundreds of years to be sure, loomed above me, its thick roots clinging to thin soil and crumbling sandstone ledges. Dark, lumpy objects, a lot of them, were hunkered down on limbs twenty and more feet up. As quietly as possible I crept toward a downed pine, its black bark and the exposed wood weathered grey. The cover was less than forty yards from the birds. Crouching down, I crawled back into an opening in the branches and situated myself so that I had a shot through a man-sized window in the limbs. Sitting on my butt, knees drawn to my chest, I rested the shotgun, an old Savage .22-twenty-gauge, in the nook made by my knees. I was afraid to move or make any noise, but cautiously practiced sighting in on where I thought the turkeys would land, hopefully in just a few minutes. They are notorious early risers.

Long moments passed and my mind wandered far into the coulees. I wondered what it must have been like living out here all year as a homesteader. The climate was extreme, fluctuating crazily between searing heat and teeth-cracking cold. Little wind in summer and fierce gales in winter. Sleet and dust choking the periods in-between. What a way to go. What drove men to leave the perceived safety of towns and cities to risk starting a new life out in this desolation? I knew the answer, for me, at least.

There was freedom in this frightening vastness. A chance to do what I wanted by myself with no one looking over my shoulder. Knowing that what happened, happened and the consequences be damned, was intoxicating. Yes, I knew why I would have taken a chance on this country and I could understand the unexplained drive in others a hundred years ago.

The sky was now a washed-out robin's egg blue across the horizon. The lumps in the old tree were stirring, making small sounds. Not clucks or purts or anything like that, more like the first sounds a person makes when he rides up out of a deep sleep.

I readied the gun and breathed shallowly. Then the turkeys started dropping out of the tree in the growing light. They sounded like sacks of cement hitting the ground and it was not a vision blessed with gracefulness. The birds didn't bounce, rather they went "thump," then tried standing on stiff legs, shaking their feathers and tentatively working big wings. I was reminded of a game where I saw a former Chicago Cubs' player, Dave Kingman, rounding second base, arms windmilling, long legs pumping as he gallantly tried to stretch a double into a very leggy triple. He slid and never reached third, tagged dead out by the length of a Rolls-Royce.

The crowd howled, then cheered at the unconscious audacity of the effort. A Chicago sports writer once described Kingman running the bases to the effect that he looked like an empty paint can being tossed from the window of a speeding car, as it raced along a bumpy road. I stifled a laugh. That's how these turkeys looked. Ungainly, not really with the program.

I sighted in on two males and tried to determine the largest. They were both huge, well over twenty-five pounds, with long beards, blue-white heads giving way to dusty-red wattles hanging from their chins and necks.

I knew the .22 would kill either bird with a head shot, but I was unsure of my ability to hit what I aimed at. I was excited and shaky. I flipped the selector to the lower barrel, loaded with a three-inch ("Magnooms" as a friend calls them) twenty-gauge filled with copper-plated No. 2s. Upland birds, yes, but more like big game. A lot of energy was needed to drop a Merriam's with a flank shot. The turkey on my left walked a few yards closer and gave me an angled profile. A regal bird now standing dead still. I sighted at an area just below the base of the neck and fired.

Boom! The concussion rocked through the coulees and over the bluffs. The turkeys ran, leaped for the air and made sounds I'd never heard out of a bird before. Yelps, gagging gobbles and strained clucks. An avian Chinese fire drill. On the ground was my turkey, on its side, one wing beating a dying tune. I crawled out of my cover, stood up, almost falling back down, legs gone dead with waiting. I was wired, high on adrenaline and weaved my way the short distance to the fallen creature. The others in the flock were gone. Out of sight and sound. I'd hit this one with a number of pellets in the neck making a ragged, bloody mess. The shoulder and wing were damaged as well, though I doubted these wounds did the bird in. I set the gun in the grass and lifted the Merriam by the legs. It felt heavy, like a brace of very big channel catfish.

I let out a scream that had atavism written all over it and then just looked at the bird. That yell. All I could think was, "What a huge god-damned turkey." One of the highest things I'd ever done outdoors and all I could think of was, "What a huge, god-damned turkey." Moments of such profundity are stark, raving amazing, aren't they?

Walking back to camp with the bird slung over my shoulders, wings extended, I could feel the waning heat of the animal through my vest and shirt. Field dressing it was anti-climatic. I left both feet and legs attached for purposes of sex identification in case I happened upon a game warden. Fat chance. The tail feathers, large, mottled bronze, black and tan with a few hints of grey, were stowed carefully in a large freezer bag. Souvenirs for my children and potential wings for grasshopper pattern I would tie for late-summer fly fishing. I hung the bird so that it cooled quickly in the morning air, then wrapped it in a couple of thick garbage bags before storing it in a cooler filled with block and cubed ice.

I made some dense black coffee, Golden Sumatran, added a dash or two of Jim Beam and toasted the turkey, the country, the day, and my good fortune. If only all hunts were like this one. Again, fat chance, but I was a happy boy at the moment. Coyotes were barking on the ridges. They must have winded the turkeys and I heard a lone gobble way off to the west of the pack. Three mule deer worked a nearby ridge where clumps of prickly pear were group, hiding beneath the tall bunch grass.

I'd take a nap and then break camp. The rainbows of a nearby ranch pond were calling me now.

◆ ◆ ◆

Fences, particularly the barbed wire variety, are part of the modern west and they do complicate my life at times with their cagey traps. My difficulties with fences began some years ago, a delicate transmutation arising from problems I had and still have with gates. Either my hands get scratched from trying to latch the ragged compilations of weathered tree limbs and barbed wire that block passage to some exotic fishing water or I pinch my fingers in the workings of the newer hook-type mechanism or I become inextricably tangled in the wire while crossing through. And with the certainty of an eastern-horizon sunrise, I find myself on the wrong sides of these gates after closing them. Coming or going, it doesn't matter. The Suburban is always beyond the gate waiting for me to figure things out.

When I turned fifty, crossing fences turned into a struggle. I'm in fairly good shape, not too much overweight, and manage to totter around with a modest degree of authority, but now I cannot get over, under or through a fence, particularly barbed wire ones, without some sort of mishap. All of the shirts I wear fishing or bird hunting are torn along the shoulders and back. My sweaters have loops pulled from their tight knitting large enough to hold ice axes, and my waders leak, doing little more now than visually announcing that I'm about to chase some fish.

One time along the Shields River I became entangled while stooping and grunting through some wire that silently guarded a delightful stretch of prime water. Frustrated—I could hear trout splashing after caddis less than thirty feet away—I jerked free only to have the tip guide of my fly rod hook on a rusty barb. Jerking the rod sharply I lost my footing, the rod separating at mid-section. I slid to the bottom of the embankment with line humming off the reel as though I'd hooked a five-pound brown. Nothing serious came of this calamity. I lost a few minutes of my life during regrouping. The tip guide was bent into a narrow oval and my torn shirt was now shredded. I was dusty and bedraggled, but that's how I wind up looking after fishing anyway. I went on to have a pleasant day catching a few browns, but that incident was the beginning of my firm dislike for fences and the beginning of an awareness concerning our obsession with closing land in, delineating, and not so tacitly stating that a given piece of property that is owned is no longer a part of what's left of free range in the West.

We're all obsessed with possession. Relationships between the sexes are often defined by the scars of these emotional turf wars. That's to be expected. We're a flawed species. And purchasing a piece of land is overt possession, but controlling this land is absurd. Yeah, I understand that if someone pays the bucks they can do what they want with the acreage. Cattle must be managed. And riffraff such as myself needs to be kept at bay. A dwindling few ranchers still allow access to their land if a person politely asks and remembers to thank them with a Christmas bottle of rye whiskey or such. But the whole ownership thing is out of control on the high plains. Orange spray-painted fence posts by the millions, "Keep Out" signs swaying in the wind and "No hunting or fishing. No trespassing" warnings. How a person can do the former two without committing the latter is a mystery. This variation seems a case of restating the obvious. If you can't pass, you logically can't fish or hunt.

And I loathe the entrances to many of the newer ranches or ranchettes, the ones marked by a pair of enormous Ponderosa pine trunks topped by an equally large trunk across the top. And dangling below the top brace in clear examples of human hauteur are signs that dance to the tune of "Smith's Ponderosa" or "Jones's Wild West Hacienda" or, my personal favorite, "Wall Street Retreat." Thankfully the plains Indians never adopted this insecure form of territorialism. Visions of "Plenty Coups' Palace" or "Dull Knife's Estancia" come shakily to mind.

All of this makes sense to me. Let's all hem in the land and its spirit with miles of barbed wire, and then announce to the world who exactly is responsible for this self-absorbed mayhem. Like we own the good country in the long term. Recent wildfires in Montana and now California say otherwise, as do drought, earthquake and the inevitable ice age. I've never been a wannabe Indian. Not my style, and quite sensibly on the tribes' part, they don't want me, but whatever happened to respecting the land that can never be truly owned? What about honoring and submitting to the long-running buzz that is the electric spirit of the West?

Sure, fencing one's property ensures at least the illusion of privacy and security. We can all drive down our private, dusty lanes, sit on the front porch and arrogantly say, while sipping some expensive single malt, "I've got mine. You can't have it. I'm really living now." The mentality that made us great hideously guts the essence of open space.

Up until a few years ago I couldn't imagine what Montana or the Dakotas would have been like 150 years ago. A land of no fences, few people and a vastness filled with wild animals that rivaled Africa's now ravaged Serengeti. For the past several years I've been drifting up to the far north of the Yukon and Northwest Territories with increasing frequency while researching a book. When I first drove through the hundreds of miles of uncut boreal forest and crossed rivers like the Mackenzie that are more than a mile wide and forty feet deep, when I saw thousands of woodland bison grazing by the dirt roads that are called highways up there, I was blown away. To finally experience such an immense wealth of wilderness, an area many times the size of Montana, with so few signs of people was staggering. To catch countless grayling of several pounds from one small stretch of river was stunning. One June day, as I cruised up to the First Nations Dene De Cho settlement of Pedzah Ki, I watched the Mackenzie flow, not flow, but power its way north to above the Arctic Circle and finally into the Beaufort Sea. The Canyon Range, then the Mackenzie Range, then other mountains rolled away to the west for hundreds of miles. Moose ghosted through stands of dwarf birch. Black bears were all over the place feeding on the green, rich grasses of a short, intense summer. Through binoculars I sighted grizzlies wandering the slopes of the McConnell Range. Fifty miles to the south, Nahanni Butte shimmered silvery blue. For days I saw only a few settlements of maybe one-hundred people each. No phone or electric lines. No fences. The difference in the energy, in the feel of this land was palpable. The countryside sizzled and seemed to flicker with a light that is not seen by the eyes. This must have been what the Big Sky felt like a couple of centuries past. Montana is home in my heart, but the North in its—for now—untamed radiance owns my soul.

Experiencing all of this up north made me see that we don't improve things for ourselves or, more importantly, for the good country when we attempt to stamp our designs of control on the landscape. Instead we cut out the heart of the place and, in the process, slice away chunks of ourselves. In a few years my children will be off to college, and I'm going to move out of Livingston and back into the empty, open spaces. I'd like to believe that I'll tear down all of the fences on whatever place I find, but knowing myself, I doubt it. I want my own piece of paradise just like anyone else.

Last October, while returning from another day fishing on the Shields, I crossed several fences on the way back to the Suburban. Angus cattle were casually grazing on the last of the year's good grass. As is normal these days, I fought with a fence near the highway. When I finally passed through I looked up and saw a lone cow standing on the road-side of the fence. Cattle do this. They always want what they see on the other side, then decide that they really need to return to their original side of the obstruction. The animal was pushing against the barbed wire trying to rejoin its herd. The cow bawled in frustration. A large gash ran along its flank. Blood from the wound glistened in the sunlight. I turned away, unlocked the back doors of the rig and started to put away my gear. I looked down at my right hand. A long scratch ran from the base of the little finger to the wrist. There was a good deal of blood that also glistened in the light.

♦ ♦ ♦

...I turn away from my fruitless catfishing and watch as Ginny prepares our dinner—acorn squash wrapped in foil and baked in the coals, grilled zucchini and catfish fillets I'd prepared this afternoon after taking a ten-pound channel cat right off the bat during our lunch break today. The fish was holding at the bottom of a swift depression in the stream bottom just below a deadfall. The bait hit the bottom and seconds later the rod jerked in a determined take, and ten minutes later the cat was at hand. The best eating fish on the river, bar none, including sauger and walleye and their inbred cousin the saugeye.

The sun is almost an hour or so from the horizon and sunset will be interesting with the buildup of cumulous in the West. I come to camp. Ginny hands me a plate and smiles. A nice breeze knocks down the small bugs and flies, and we eat with quiet contentment. Things are perfect as we wait for the sundown pyrotechnics that have no equal on this part of northern high plains.

Chapter 8

Getting To This
Glendive to Fort Buford at Missouri River
North Dakota—77 miles

W E PUT IN AT THE HIGHWAY 23 BRIDGE SOUTH OF SIDNEY. The road leads into North Dakota and wanders up and down over an immense seep of grasslands that Teddy Roosevelt loved so much for the vistas, the big game—including grizzlies way back then—and the enormous solitude. Oil fields are everywhere. We know. We saw them with their drill rig lights blinking on and off, red and white yesterday as we drove the route in severe wind, followed by a raucous rainstorm that piled in from the northwest with rolling, deep purple vengeance flinging hail, rain, sleet, snow and the occasional cow and lots of shredded pieces of plastic from drill sites.

The weather is supposed to turn really ugly in a few days so we push on as hard as we can, planning to make a long day of it and a shorter one to Fort Buford tomorrow. A strong headwind makes things difficult, unpleasant. It's cold, gloomy and we aren't having all that much fun, but we're determined to complete this last leg of the adventure. One we haven't done yet, even though we've paddled stretches upriver two or three times at least. For some reason we put this part of the Yellowstone onto the backburner.

Ginny paddles determinedly, taking breaks to extricate her camera from its waterproof pouch and compose some shots of the land. I keep up a steady rhythm with my paddling and drift off to the towns we visited while doing a motorized check of the region from Glendive to the confluence.

There's Glendive that, according to the 1939 *WPA Guide to Montana*, boasted a population of 4,269. Today that number has skyrocketed to nearly 4,700, though the place seems much larger with all of the fast food outlets, discount chains and major brand stop-and-goes strangling the original town center in a growing perimeter death grip. Oil, gas, coal, cattle, grain, sugar beets and the railroad keep things hopping today along with paddlefishers, agate hunters and fossil seekers. And there's Sidney farther north and east, a town where we always stay when we are in this distant corner of Montana. According to the WPA Guide, the population of Sidney was 2,010 in 1939 compared to a present-day number of 4,774. The place is oil-boom crazy with roughnecks, company rigs and semis hauling drilling machinery and miles of pipe everywhere. There's a sugar refinery, power generation plant and plenty of bars, casinos and restaurants that grow in number each time we come here, no doubt to unburden the roughnecks of some of their cash. Weirdly eroded buttes, in a range of earthy coals from charcoal to off-yellow to salmon, surround the town. Pheasants, mule deer and rattlesnakes do well in this country.

♦ ♦ ♦

The wind picks up and the day turns dark and cold. Both of us bitch a bit then put our backs into the long slog downriver against the wind. We were on the water by 7:30 and have been making steady progress at over three-miles-per-hour.

"Ginny, let's go for it," I yell through the near gale. "We can make the confluence by 4:30 or 5."

She turns around and flashes a thumbs up. Enough of this madness, so away we go…

♦ ♦ ♦

Two of the most unique man-made structures anywhere in the West are situated on the Yellowstone and Missouri Rivers, less than an hour from town: the Fairview and Snowden Lift Bridges. Tomorrow, with luck, we'll be paddling beneath the Fairview bridge.

The Fairview Lift Bridge is located across the North Dakota border three and a half miles east of Fairview and two miles west of Cartwright, North Dakota. This bridge, along with its sister bridge at Snowden, Montana, was constructed as part of a plan by Great Northern Railroad for its never-completed Montana Eastern Railway between New Rockford, North Dakota, and Lewistown, Montana. About the time World War I began, an economic downturn of the Montana Eastern Railway brought construction to a halt. According to Mark Hufstetler, a historian with Renewable Technologies Inc. of Butte, the Fairview Lift Bridge served as a little-used branch line. He stated, "At its peak, the line probably saw no more than one passenger and one freight train each way per day."

The Fairview Lift Bridge runs 1,320 feet across the Yellowstone River. In earlier times, the bridge not only handled rail traffic, but also vehicular traffic. Planking was placed between and outside the rails to handle automobiles. According to Hufstetler, a watchman was stationed at the bridge to prevent trains and automobiles from smashing into each other.

While now closed to both rail and vehicular traffic, the Fairview Lift Bridge adjoins the only tunnel in North Dakota. The 1,458-foot long tunnel was built in 1912 and 1913.

The Snowden Lift Bridge, crossing the Missouri River ten miles north of Fairview, is a twin to the Fairview Lift Bridge. It, like the Fairview Lift Bridge, was constructed as part of the Montana Eastern Railway.

All river traffic ceased on both the Yellowstone and Missouri Rivers in 1913, the only time the lift section on the Fairview Lift Bridge was raised was at the completion of construction in 1913 to test the mechanisms. The last time the Snowden Lift Bridge's lift section was raised was in 1935 to allow the passage of a freight boat carrying materials for the Fort Peck Dam. The cost to build each bridge was $500,000.

◆ ◆ ◆

Here's Teddy Roosevelt writing about this strange terrain in the late 1880s. "The sun was just setting when we crossed the final ridge and came in sight of as singular a bit of country as I have ever seen. Over an irregular tract of gently rolling sandy hills, perhaps about three-quarters of a mile square, were scattered several hundred detached and isolated buttes or cliffs of sandstone… Some of them rose as sharp peaks or ridges, or as connected chains, but much the greater number had flat tops like little table-lands. The sides were perfectly perpendicular, and were cut and channeled by the weather into the most extraordinary forms: caves, columns, battlements, spires, and flying buttresses were mingled in the strangest confusion. On the tops and at the bases of most of the cliffs grew pine trees, some of considerable height, and the sand gave everything a clean, white look. Altogether it was as fantastically beautiful a place as I have ever seen."

Over the years I've become uncommonly familiar with "the strangest confusion," a situation apparently exacerbated by several years of specious over-indulgence and a sometimes road weary, peripatetic existence. Not really along the theme of "If this is Tuesday it must be Rome," but more along the wavering line of "If this is 2001 can it possibly be Dawson City, Yukon?" or in this early October case "Is that really North Dakota over there?"

Ginny and I have wandered the southeastern corner of Montana many times, but we'd never made it to Medicine Rocks State Park located south of Baker and just north of Ekalaka on State Hwy 7. And, yes, that land of so many rude jokes was lying off on the short grass prairie a few air miles east of us—North Dakota, a much-maligned place of damn good country and all of this way-way out there landscape is tied into the Yellowstone drainage system that eventually finds its way to the Missouri after a couple of thousand miles and then another thousand or so to the Gulf of Mexico. Land is land and it is all connected and buzzes as one entity in a well-ordered naturally synchronized rhythm. Lines on our maps mean nothing to the spirit that pervades and drives good country.

We drive in on a dusty, sandy road that was undergoing some serious construction by the boys from Baker. Twisting and turning through spacious stands of old Ponderosa, the curious sandstone formations described by Roosevelt more than a century ago flash into view like large escapees from a twisted carnival traveling show then disappear just as quickly as we drop down an arc dip in the road only, to be replaced by an even more fantastic shape. This geologic contrariness continues for perhaps a healthy mile until we break free of the trees and come upon a vista of dozens of the eroded shapes resting like long-ago wrecked ships on the native grass prairie that is glowing in autumn shades of yellow-gold, tan, purple-grey, still-brilliant green and rust. Beyond the formations the grasslands stretch for miles towards a horizon whose limits are marked by a soft blue sky that shimmers electric-white near the ground. The day is cool, in the forties, and rafts of dark clouds sailed eastward.

We find a nice place to camp near a pair of the medicine rocks that had been heartily defaced with graffiti, such "Jimmy adores Trish—1996" and encircled by a crude heart. Some artiste has taken some serious time to carve a horse head replete with flowing mane, but most of the scars are of the former variety. I wonder how many of these, no doubt, soulful relationships flourish to this day, but quickly turn addled with the enormity of the question, so I opt for a Jim Beam and ice. Coolers are arranged, sleeping gear settled, wood gathered and a fire built. We grill some brats and potatoes, have a few drinks and watch stars show up between the boiling masses of clouds. Despite the cold that threatens winter, both of us feel energized, the lethargy and slight depression of living in town now vanished.

Medicine Rocks is a good, strong place and it's easy to understand high plains warriors and hunters of the Northern Cheyenne gathering here to draw on what this place offers. Hell, I was ready to jump in the Suburban, drive to New York and battle a few editors, but I fell asleep instead.

According to the *Roadside Geology of Montana,* the Medicine Rocks were originally part of a sea of ancient sand dunes. This is indicated by cross beds in the structures and the fact that the sand grains are small and of uniform size. The rocks appear to be the remains left by wind erosion since there are no stream channels in the area, and each of them stands in a small depression much like the hollow left around a tree in heavy, wind-driven snowfall. The area is located on the Ekalaka syncline, which is a trough folded into layered rocks. As with much of this country, gas and oil is prevalent. We catch slight tastes of the stuff on the ever-present wind. Many of the rocks have eroded into a Swiss cheese-like appearance and a number of birds make their homes in these hollows, including a falcon that screeches, threatens with outstretched wings and puffed up breast and before eventually flying off somewhere each time we walk out onto the grasslands to be among the formations.

We had originally planned on heading down south of Ekalaka to explore the Chalk Buttes, but wind up spending five days here. With the weather turned warm, and the sun changing the colors and textures of the countryside as it passed across the sky, we just never move on. The more time we spend here the more the land opens up in subtle shifts of color, light, texture and sound. The basic green of grass becomes multi-hued. Wind moving through pine limbs grows from a single lonely note to chords of song. No one else camps here during our five-day stay. The only people we speak with are the guys from the road crew who come down to check us out, no doubt stunned by the fact that a couple of yahoos from the big city would like their piece of turf so much that they would spend a number of days here doing not much of anything but walking, talking, eating and sleeping. Being an inveterate fisherman, I query the men about fishing in the area and they say that many of the ranch ponds are filled with rainbows. Seeing my eyes light up, they offer to get me on to some of the water. I noticed on the drive in that many of these waters are clear, relatively deep and surrounded with cattails and reeds. Prime stuff. I say I'll take them up on the offer next time we are over this way and they smile, adding that the bird hunting for pheasants and sharptails is "not too shabby" either. Antelope, mule and white-tail deer live here, also.

Coming into Baker the other day we spotted a pair of Zebras, which caused a pair of triple-takes and a near collision with a tractor. We learn from the road crew that the owner of that land has other exotics and the guys refer to it as a "petting zoo." I have a vision of bringing a Vermont friend of mine who'd spent a good deal of time in Africa out this way, but wonder if the anomalous site will give him a stroke. Some year I'll find out.

We spend long hours feeding the fire both during the day and night. We talk about not much of anything or just cruise in place surrounded by the peace and strength of this place. By the end of the third night I've regaled Ginny with enough scintillating anecdotes about my career as a sportswriter for a small-town daily in Wisconsin many years ago that I am forced to hide the Beam for her own well-being. And I never do get to tell her about that one infamous night with the Milwaukee Brewers' slugger Gorman Thomas at a place called the Pieces of Eight in Milwaukee. Next time.

One of my favorite books on the state is *The WPA Guide to 1930s Montana*. I learned that Ekalaka (alt. 3,031) was originally called Puptown and began as a deadfall (saloon) for cowboys. Claude Carter, the town founder, a buffalo hunter and bartender, was on his way to another building site when his horses balked at pulling his load of logs through a mud hole at the current townsite. "Hell," Carter said, "any place in Montana is a good place to build a saloon. He built the Old Stand, which, in a newer incarnation, still stands and now offers good burgers and decent drinks.

Ekalaka was named for a Lakota girl called Ijkalaka (Swift One) who was a niece of Sitting Bull. She was the best at breaking camp and so acquired her name. In 1875, David Harrison Russell, the first white homesteader in the region, married Ijkalaka, and in 1881 brought her to the community that had sprung up around the Old Stand. She lived in Ekalaka until her death in 1901. The town is home to a museum that has on display many remains and fossils of dinosaurs discovered in the region along with samples of a long-gone swampland forest, now preserved in the form of petrified rock.

During the warm, sunny afternoons we wander through the Ponderosa and among the rocks. I climb over a rusty barbed-wire fence and walk across about a half-mile of prairie to a large formation covered in pines. The rock stands by itself on the southern edge of the park. From the top I can see for miles. Ekalaka was visible. Timbered buttes with wide valleys twist away between them, stretching to the south and east. The crests of the Chalk Buttes are visible as muted green and ochre in the haze of distance. Red-tailed hawks and a golden eagle ride the thermals. Black-capped chickadees bounce among the bushes. Wild roses hang with thick clusters of orange-red rosehips. Woodpeckers hammer on nearby trees in search of insects. A few late-season grasshoppers clack as they bound from grassy clumps to sun-exposed rocks. The clouds are gone now, replaced by a soft but deep blue sky. The multi-colored grasses move in the wind in waves of motion that flow eastward or circle along gentle rises that create large eddies of spinning air.

Thirty years ago this place probably would have bored me after a few hours. No classy trout streams. No jagged, snow-capped mountains. Just all of what I've described. Now Medicine Rocks seems like country I'd like to live near. A few good people. Good country. No cities.

Walking out onto the prairie and the isolated formations, we watch as the sunset casts a glow behind the rocks that moves from yellow to orange to blood red then fades to blue going indigo. A thin streamer of clouds reflects the last of the day's light in the same colors only fifteen minutes later.

The final night we grill a couple of rib-eyes and some corn on the cob. Chocolate-chip cookies complete the meal. Then, in the darkness, we rebuild the fire to a decent blaze and sit back. I look at Ginny and begin "Did I ever tell you about the time Gorman…" She jumps up. Grabs both our cups and races to the picnic table. Builds a couple of drinks. Hands me mine. Throws some wood on the fire. Sits down. I don't continue.

Bright white light begins to illuminate the trees behind us. The Ponderosa and the Medicine Rocks cast deep shadows. We walk to the top of a nearby rise and watch as an enormous silver moon climbs above North Dakota. The light is intense, drowning out most of the stars. It climbs quickly above us, seeming to shrink in size but gain in intensity as it does so. The stars come back. A faint, green glow of Northern Lights moves up and down the horizon beyond Baker. Then a brilliant, bright green flickering startles us in the west. We turn and watch as a meteor low in the sky sizzles towards the Borealis. Pieces of the space rock break off in miniature replicas of dazzling green. I imagine the sound of the thing streaking hundreds of miles an hour towards an earthly impact. Then the meteor is gone, leaving behind the moon and the stars. Coyotes break into excited yipping and howling. They liked the show, too.

The Medicine Rocks reveals itself over time. The longer you stay the more you see. A special place in nowhere.

◆ ◆ ◆

On our way to the town of Sidney, in the northeastern corner of the state, we pulled off Highway 16 and rolled down a small paved, curving road that leads to the Yellowstone and the Intake Diversion Dam boat launch, recreation and camping area. Intake Diversion doesn't look like much until you walk along the river to the base of its rock and boulder-strewn face. Water pours through spaces in the stone, creating wicked standing waves and back flows that spell certain death to anyone unfortunate enough to be swept over the obstruction or crazy enough to try and run the rapids.

We encounter a man dressed head-to-toe in full camo insulated gear replete with thick hood. He's sitting on a chair situated about ten feet in the river in six inches of water. His rod is placed between a forked stick. Related angling gear and a bucket are behind him on the sandy, gravel shore. We introduce ourselves and chat about the fish, which our new friend Norm Schluessler of Orofino, Idaho says has been "very good for channel cats [I love catfishing and make a mental note to return here for the hunt], walleye, sauger and saugeye along with a small sturgeon."

He's with friends and family who are out hunting mule deer and upland birds. Norm says that he's "not much for hunting, so we all do our own thing then hang out together at night in camp around a fire." Ginny asks if she can take some pictures and Norm says with a big grin, "Go right ahead. Have a ball." While she's doing this he pulls a stringer from the river and holds up what we both think is the hybrid of the walleye and sauger, the noble saugeye. Silvery white with the slightest suggestions of blue, a firm, healthy fish. We talk some more about the diversion at full runoff—a "death trip" says Norm—the cool but decent weather, paddlefishing in the spring with the banks lined elbow to elbow with anglers trying to snag the fish and so on. They we part company and enjoy the day in our own ways.

The greatest barrier on the Yellowstone is also the biggest straw sucking water from the river. Intake Diversion Dam, located 18 miles downstream from Glendive, draws up to 1,400 cubic feet of water per second. That's more than the average flow of the Big Hole, Beaverhead, and Gallatin rivers combined.

Intake Dam was built in 1911 to divert water from the Yellowstone River to 50,000 acres in eastern Montana and western North Dakota. Made of rocks in timber cribs, the 5-foot-tall structure stretches 700 feet across the river. Depending on the time of year, it pushes up to half the Yellowstone River into Intake Canal and a 225-mile network of lateral canals that move and distribute water to roughly 500 farms.

According to George Jordan, Yellowstone River coordinator for the U.S. Fish and Wildlife Service, Intake Dam is "a known barrier for the upstream migration of pallid sturgeon, paddlefish, and other species in years when water is low." Intake is owned by the Bureau of Reclamation. Because the Endangered Species Act requires that federal projects not harm listed species, Jordan says "the USFWS is helping the BOR evaluate various options that would allow for upstream fish passage and reduce entrainment."

Jordan says he has no doubt the dam will be modified, but it may take several years. The delay, he says, is due, in part, to the lack of a warmwater-fish group to advocate on behalf of sturgeon and other Yellowstone River species. "It's too bad there isn't something like a Sturgeon Unlimited that could turn up the heat in Washington, D.C.," he says.

While the diversion dams are drawing off downstream-swimming fish, they're also blocking those trying to move up the Yellowstone to spawn. Walleye, sauger, and several other species can swim over the dams during high water. But bottom-hugging species find the structures insurmountable.

"Either way, the vast majority of those fish don't make their way back to the Yellowstone," says Brad Schmitz, Montana Fish, Wildlife & Parks regional fisheries manager in Miles City. "To a pallid sturgeon, for example, a diversion dam might as well be Hoover Dam. They don't have the physical form to swim up rapids, much less over an actual barrier."

The pallid's wedge-shaped head has evolved to keep the fish close to the river bottom, where it finds fish, aquatic insects, and other food. Currently only 4,000 or so pallid sturgeon exist in the United States, making the species one of the nation's rarest, and causing it, since 1990, to be listed as federally endangered. In the Yellowstone—which has some of the nation's best remaining pallid sturgeon habitat—numbers are down to fewer than 200.

"There are now so few," says Schmitz, "that it's hard for a mature male and mature female to even find each other, much less spawn successfully." As a result, there has been no documented "recruitment" (new fish being born into the fishery) in the river for more than thirty years.

Since Schmitz's comments, some good news concerning the species has arrived, in the form of the passage of the Water Resources Development Act. As a result of Congressional override of President Bush's veto in November 2007, this passage authorizes federal enhancement of habitat for the endangered pallid sturgeon, which means funding to reconstruct the Intake Diversion Dam. The bill authorizes the Army Corps of Engineers to use a portion of its roughly $50 million in annual Missouri River Fish and Wildlife Recovery funds to address pallid sturgeon recovery in the Yellowstone River system, by working with the Bureau of Reclamation to modify its Intake irrigation diversion to allow for fish passage. Diversion dams aren't the only reason the Yellowstone's pallid sturgeon may become extinct within the next few decades. Another big factor is Yellowtail Dam, built on the Bighorn River in 1966 to create energy and control flooding in the valley below. Behind the dam is 500-foot-deep Bighorn Reservoir, which releases cool, clear water from its depths. The dam has created one of the nation's top trout fisheries downstream in the Bighorn River, a Yellowstone tributary. However, it has also deprived the Yellowstone's warmwater species of yearly floods, which, for millennia, sent sand, woody debris and sediment downstream, producing sturgeon food and creating spawning and rearing sites.

◆ ◆ ◆

The first time I had any contact with paddlefish and people snagging them by flinging large treble hooks heavily weighted with a lead sinker the size of a ping pong ball, was nearly twenty years ago on the Yellowstone, several miles above Glendive. Several of us were walking up and down the gravel and stone bars of the river one hot, sunny spring day, looking for any moss agates that may have been turned up by the scouring action of the retreating winter ice. While doing this, a large boat anchored about twenty feet from us and two men began flinging these heavy outfits far out into the river, then rapidly jerking the hooks back to them, reeling in the slack and repeating the process. Two other individuals were filming the entire deal with what looked to be expensive equipment. We later learned that this crew was filming an episode for a fishing show on the long-gone TNN channel.

About the third time out, one of the anglers connected with something that jerked the thick rod tip into the water and nearly pulled the guy into the river. For the next forty minutes the battle went back and forth—man reels line in, fish pulls line back out and on and on. Finally an exhausted paddlefish was brought to gaff by an even more exhausted fisherman. His assistant hooked the fish with the gaff and hauled it with a grunt into the boat. Everyone on board cheered, smacked hands and sprayed beer on each other. They maneuvered their boat to shore near us, flashing broad smiles while winging ice-cold cans of beer our way. A nice touch, I felt. The hooked paddlefish, unmistakable with his long spoon-billed snout to a French Chatillon scale, weighed seventy-eight pounds. A big paddlefish by any standards, though small compared to the one caught in the Mississippi on the Iowa side that came in at 198 pounds.

Paddlefish are primitive Chondrostian ray-finned fishes. The paddlefish can be distinguished by its large mouth and its elongated snout called a rostrum (bill). These spatula-like snouts comprise half the length of their entire body. There are only two species of these fish: the Chinese and the American paddlefish. These fish are not closely related to sharks, but they do have some body parts that resemble those of sharks, such as their skeletons, primarily composed of cartilage, and deeply forked heterocercal tail fins. Paddlefish are one of the oldest fish known to man. Fossil records show that they first appeared 300 to 400 million years ago (50 million years before dinosaurs).

Paddlefish are one of the largest freshwater fish in North America. They often reach five or more feet in length, and weigh more than sixty pounds.

When cleaned and cut into steaks (they have no bones, only cartilage), the flesh is excellent barbequed over hot cools. I've eaten this fish at several barbecues, either marinated like baby back pork ribs or merely brushed with lemon butter. It has a slightly resistant, flaky texture, and tastes like a cross between walleye and alligator, if that's of any help. Very good eating for such a large fish.

One of these springs I'm going to have to take a swing at these prehistoric animals. Maybe a hundred-pounder will knock some sense into me.

♦ ♦ ♦

Eventually, in proper time dictated by the land's well-rehearsed and ancient pace, we attain the confluence of the Missouri coming in on the Yellowstone from the north. The Missouri rolls in from the westnorthwest. A large cottonwood snag rises a dozen feet above the water and seems to be pointing the way to the landing at Fort Buford across the river. A large, sand-colored, circular visitor center stands on a bank above us. A few local anglers are fishing near the boat launch. The late October afternoon is slightly warm, breezy and partly cloudy. A week on this stretch and we're ready for a motel room in Sidney and a pizza. Simple wants for brain-fade travelers, especially when the travails of the Lewis and Clark Expedition 200 years before are taken into account.

Ascending the turbid Missouri at a rate of up to twenty-five miles on good days, the expedition's journalists remarked on the rolling, treeless Great Plains grasslands, the weather and the river, and always the profusion of game. "We can scarcely cast our eyes in any direction," wrote Lewis," without perceiving deer Elk Buffaloe or Antelopes."

They encountered increasing numbers of aggressive grizzlies that they called "white bears." Bighorn sheep, wolves, coyotes and beaver were abundant, as were geese, ducks, eagles and swans.

"The table land atop the towering bluffs on both sides of the river," they wrote, was "one vast plain, entirely destitute of timber, extending back as far as the eye can reach."

One week after leaving Fort Mandan, they passed the highest point on the Missouri River that any Euro-American had ever reached. Dealing with strong, swirling winds, collapsing riverbanks and wicked currents, they moved on up river.

On April 25, ranging ahead of the rest of the party, Lewis and his Newfoundland, Seaman, along with four of the men, arrived at the mouth of the "Roche Jaune," or Yellowstone River.

On April 26, 1805, Lewis wrote, "The Indians inform [us] that the Yellowstone River is navigable for pirogues [large rowboats] nearly to its source in the Rocky Mountains, and that in its course near these mountains it passes within less than half a day's march of a navigable part of the Missouri."

Fifteen months later, it would take Captain Clark a little over two days to march from the three forks of the Missouri, through the Gallatin Valley, to the Yellowstone River at what is now Livingston. It's fifty-seven miles on I-90, which parallels most of the Indian roads he followed.

Fort Buford, located near present-day Williston, was one of a number of military posts established to protect overland and river routes used by immigrants settling the West. This is where the Hunkpapa Sioux leader, Sitting Bull, surrendered in 1881.

When Ginny and I visited the site on a fine October day, the three original buildings still remaining at the Fort Buford State Historic Site—the stone powder magazine, wood-frame officers' quarters, and a wood-frame officer of the guard building—stood in vivid contrast to the modern, almost Frank Lloyd Wright-style visitor center in what struck me as a clear juxtaposition of the past with the present, a juxtaposition that left me feeling uncomfortable and a bit down. I would prefer arriving at this location to it left in its natural setting and not turned into a modern-day museum/tourist information center. Time and the river flowing, it seems, at the confluence.

Fort Union is located just twenty miles northeast of Sidney and a few miles up the Missouri from Fort Buford. The place is a mini nexus for the history of the first white settlers in the West. In October 1828, construction of the post was underway and it soon became the center of the Northern Rocky Mountain fur trade. At its peak, in the 1830s, the post, along with other American Fur Company forts in the region sent to St. Louis an annual harvest of more than 25,000 beaver skins, 30,000 deer skins and 55,000 buffalo hides.

♦ ♦ ♦

In the past few days on the river we've floated past field after field filled with large trucks and harvesters that dig billions of sugar beets from the dark earth. Enormous mounds of them are piled along railroad sidings from below Sidney to well north of Fairview. We're in the fertile crescent of sugar beet reality. Oil pumpjacks do their pterodactyl dance up and down in the middle of the fields. Million dollar mechanical babies making farmers and ranchers rich with no effort involved—a curious juxtaposition of economies—sugar beets and oil—hard-won income and slick dollars sliding home through pipes sunk deep in the valley.

I'm enthralled, blown away, by the enormity of the sugar beet doings in the region, and learn some of the following from tourist brochures and talking with a woman at the Cenex station in Sidney.

The sugar beet is from the same species that includes Swiss chard, fodder beets and red beets. The crop has an interesting history associated with war, sacrifice and, undoubtedly, romance. The first modern sugar beets originated as selections made in the middle of the 18th century from fodder beets grown in then German Silesia, but food and medicinal uses are much older. A precursor is known to have been used as food as early as ancient Egypt. In 1747, a German chemist, Andreas Marggraf, demonstrated that the crystals formed after a crude extraction from pulverized beet roots were identical, in all properties, with sugarcane crystals, and attempts to derive sugar from beets originate from his work.

In 1917, there were ninety-one factories operating in eighteen states. In 2005, there were 23 operating sugar beet factories in 10 states, processing 30 million tons of sugar beets grown on approximately 1.4 million acres. Over 4.5 million tons of sugar are produced each year in the U.S. from sugar beets, and beet sugar represents 54 percent of domestic sugar production in the U.S. I always figured that the sugar I used came from sugarcane grown way down south in the land of cotton.

In this country, growers started joining together in farmer-owned cooperatives in the mid 1970s to purchase the processing companies. By September 2006, the entire U.S. beet sugar processing industry became grower-owned.

There are large beets lying along roadsides or flattened in the middle of the pavement, lost sweet souls that rolled and bounced over trucks carrying them to their final resting places. We pull over and examine one that weighs as much as a large brown trout. It looks like an enormous rutabaga, dirty white, slightly yellowish and rough-surfaced. Hard to believe sugar comes from this. We replace the beet gently in the dying grass and move on.

♦ ♦ ♦

…Despite the wind we make good time, maybe four miles an hour. By a little bit after noon we pass under the Fairview Lift Bridge, the black iron structure rising like a monstrous iron-age skeleton, its top struts are barely visible through the mist and fog. We stop, and Ginny spends a half hour photographing the near Gothic beast.

Then back in with cold, aching muscles, and we paddle like death was riding down on us until we round a wide bend and see the circular stone building that is the Fort Buford Visitor Center. We come to the end of the Yellowstone, passing a large, grey cottonwood trunk stuck in the river and pointing to the landing at the fort across the Missouri that drifts in quietly from the northwest. The location is nothing special scenery-wise, only the same old, wind-blasted, surreally spectacular vastness of the Yellowstone Valley. The setting is filled with the power of history and of the merging of two rivers that are the life blood of the northern high plains and the Rocky Mountains, hundreds of miles to the west. As we blend into the Missouri, the canoe rocks in the rip of the two flows conjoining. We push carefully through this and aim for shore.

"We made it, John," Ginny says with a quiet yet strong voice and there is a look of relief on her face as I'm sure there is on mine. A warm room, hot shower, food that someone cooks and delivers to us, a couple of drinks. Sounds good to me.

Our river journeys are over for this year. Fall is telling us that winter is coming soon. The cottonwoods, willows and alders have all shed their leaves. The sun never rises far above the horizon as it slips across the sky south of us. The air has a slight chill and the faint scent of Arctic cold that the two of us know and cherish firsthand. We pull up to the well-designed landing, retrieve our Suburban, load the gear in the back, tie down the canoe on the roof, take one last look at the river holding each other arm in arm, smile, climb in the rig and head for Sidney twenty miles away.

Sidney is a small agrarian community of about 4,800 people, resting above both the Yellowstone and Missouri river valleys at an altitude of 1,902 feet. Both the sugar beets and wheat are grown with the aid of irrigation. The area is experiencing a modest oil boom, and rough necks and their pickups line the parking lots at all of the town's motels. Pipe and drilling companies dot the main drag. Outside of town, weirdly eroded badlands play home to a healthy population of rattlesnakes and mule deer. Sidney feels alive, healthy, happy and energetic unlike the tiny town of Fairview a few miles up the state highway to the north.

Straddling the Montana-North Dakota border, Fairview is at 1,909 feet above sea level and boasts a burgeoning population of 663 intrepid souls, down 46 from the turn of the new millennium. One of the town's streets is actually in North Dakota. The place was named for its panorama of the boundless fertile acres of the Yellowstone Valley. In addition to the ubiquitous sugar beet crop and wheat, some lignite coal is also mined. That place looks like the end of the line for all sorts of failed dreams, but I could be wrong here. Someday, perhaps I will perform a thorough examination and even rent a room at the oh-so-rustic Korner Motel that has it all over anything Norman Bate's could have dreamed up. When we drove past in late October, the office and six rooms had their exteriors decorated with weird pumpkin and skeletal visages and some decidedly excited black-cat cutouts. Who knows what really goes on here?

We settle into our room—twin beds, shower, microwave, refrigerator, TV replete with remote control—all of it. Clean up. Head down the strip beneath the gathering neon cloud of gas stations, motels, restaurants, bars and grocery stores. We enjoy our pizza at a chain joint just down the road apiece, as we eavesdrop on a ranching family talking over several pizzas and pitchers of beer about mending busted fence lines, the price of oil and how it will affect their income from the wells on their holdings, buying a new Dodge Ram truck, heading to Costa Rica for the winter and making plans to shoot some mule deer holding along the river behind their barns. Then we watch the White Sox ice the Astros 1-0 for the Series win on TV. This is good because it's Chicago, but it's not my Cubs so the excitement is low key. Then off to sleep.

In the morning we run along Hwy 16, then I-94 next to the Yellowstone, all the way home for 400 miles back to Livingston. We talk all the way of how and when we'll canoe various sections of the river next year. How much fun we'll have alone on the water out here beneath the bluffs and large cottonwoods. The Yellowstone's in our blood now. A part of our lives. The memories of this season's river, of all of the miles we covered the two preceding seasons, all of the people we met, the country we experienced. All of it. The new dreams and the planning will carry us through the dark winter.

Conclusion

Nowhere At All Is Really Everywhere

NOW THAT ALL OF THE RIVER RUNNING, CAMPING, WALKING, searching and researching, and talking with those who make the river their home is complete, only the writing of this final section remains. There is time to look back on all of the adventure, discovery and wonder of the past two years. Before beginning this project I thought that I knew the Yellowstone from many fly fishing trips on the upper river, casting to the Yellowstone cutthroat, rainbows and browns, and from wading stretches by Mayor's Landing in town, or beneath Sheep Mountain or from driving along the river many times on my way to Tongue River country, the Pryors or the remote interior of North Dakota.

I learned that, actually, I knew very little about the river—its personality, secrets, rhythms, abundant natural, geologic patience. I wanted to show as many facets of the Yellowstone drainage as I could, in a flowing manner modeled after my experiences with the dynamics and natural kinetics of the Yellowstone.

The Yellowstone has shown me far more about the natural world and myself than I can ever hope to return to it. But I'll continue learning, always keeping its well-being at heart.

Now that it is winter I finally realize that part of the enjoyment of the Yellowstone for me is cross-country skiing or snowshoeing along the river's snow-covered banks in the dead of winter. These are opportunities to examine another side, another personality of the drainage and to plan another warm season's floats and also to escape the confines of home—as in the following day trip, the first along the river a few years back...

...Prior to reaching this place I'd stopped along side a tributary of the Yellowstone, strapped on the shoes, rigged a light rod and cast a small Hare's ear nymph through runs, riffles and down deep in somber pools. I didn't catch anything. Didn't see a trout or a whitefish, but that was fine. I only wanted to cast a bit and feel the life that moving water possesses. After an hour I returned to the Suburban.

Before this book project I hadn't done this in a long time, not since the chaotic days back in the Flathead in the northwest corner of the state. Back then I used to push along the deep accumulations of snow on the Going-to-the-Sun Road as it bobbed and weaved alongside the south shore of ice-bound Lake McDonald, through tall stands of old-growth pine and ancient cedar. Or I'd work up and down and around the logging roads of the Tally Lake Ranger District northwest of Whitefish, past locked-up Logan, Griffin and Deep Creeks and across gentle ridges that sliced through stands of winter-bare larch. Sometimes the way dropped onto frozen ponds and wetlands where I'd slide through last summer's cattails, standing like wordless signposts guiding me nowhere, which was silent perfection. No people, just me and my now long-gone Australian Shepherd, Rupert. He was a good guy and loved nothing so much as running along in the tracks my skis made, though he often sank chest-deep in the softer snow. This never phased him. He just kept coming, tongue out, full-tilt grin, tail wagging.

For the past few years I've worked along the edges of the partially frozen river a few times each winter. The experiences take me back to the trips down the Yellowstone a few months back. Memories are retrieved and, as I mentally blend into the cold and snow landscape, all of the days and weeks on the river merge into one overall sensation of wonder and peace. Getting back on the river becomes compelling and I can't wait for the seasons to turn to the promise that spring always holds with its new, fresh green optimism.

On clear days, the majestic mountains of the Swans, the aloof Missions in the distant south, the dominant summit of Great Northern Mountain directly to the east and a few peaks hanging out in western Glacier Park were visible, looking like benign sentinels who casually looked out for the welfare of a peripatetic lunatic and his dog. Moose and deer were around in fair numbers. We'd often surprise one or more of the surly moose or skittish deer as we swooshed and padded around a blind bend in the woods. The deer would flee for their very lives, but often the moose would grunt and snort and make threatening gestures with lowered heads and pawing hooves. Fortunately, our direction at the time was mostly aimed downhill so we were quickly out of sight with no damage visited upon our wayward, yet well-intentioned, souls. We'd cruise along as best we could growing hot with the exertion, especially if the sun was out. We'd stop. I'd pull off my daypack and hit a bota filled with cheap red wine, and munch some cheese and sourdough French bread. Rupert would get some water poured from a plastic jug into a small bowl and some dog biscuits. We had fun and we weren't bothering anybody.

Since my flight from Whitefish to Livingston, I'd managed to look at my cross-country skis at least once or twice per winter, but that was as far as the activity progressed until last January, when I decided to give the somewhat masochistic pursuit another shot—this time along the Yellowstone River somewhere east of Big Timber, along a stretch I'd spotted while canoeing the river last August. No canine friend this time around. I wondered at the memories that might ghost upon me.

I pull off I-90 some miles past Big Timber, coast off the exit and down onto a snow-packed, paved road then turn right after a mile onto what, in the summer is more or less a dusty two track that leads to a fishing access site that is located in an open, grassy bluff running along in gentle swales next to the river beneath large cottonwoods. Filled with trailers and drift boats during the height of the summer fishing, the place is empty, somewhat forlorn, even melancholy in its seasonal abandonment.

I'd checked out the skis last night. They seemed to be in workable shape, though I wiped the frames and webbing to satisfy my neurotic sense of cleanliness. I strike off through the foot-deep snow that is changing from yesterdays new-fallen powder into a coarser, denser grade of crystal within the warming day. I'm wearing my old, faded-blue day pack packed with cheese, bread and faithful wineskin, plus a couple of dog biscuits for old-times' sake.

There are no tracks here—tires, skis, snowshoes or otherwise. So I make slow progress as I push my way through the virgin precipitation. The river flows with thin slices of new-formed ice drifting along—uneven-surfaced stuff that makes the slightest of tinkling sounds when the slabs flow into each other. The sun is mostly hidden behind high overcast, though it occasionally shows itself as a dim yellow ball weakly glowing above the burned-over hills in the south. Forest fires did a number here a few years back. Despite this blackened blight and the cloudiness, the day is pleasant, at least that's the vibe I get from ravens holding in bare limbs above me. They seem to be suggesting by their stoic posturing that, all things considered, life could be much worse. Always odd, these birds. They make me feel like I'm being critiqued about the conduct of my life, by extremely cynical, highly-intelligent beings. Such is my paranoia.

For some reason, my thoughts wander back to a day spent skiing below Sylvia Lake on the Tally District, a place where the forest was once thick and filled with old-growth, but now sports a two-lane paved road/highway and acre upon acre of ghastly clearcuts. That was a time when I kicked and glided easily through the dark green trees dripping long strands of faded blue-green moss. At first, I began by contemplating how long it would take me to ski over the mountains to the west to reach Wolf Creek. Perhaps a couple of days was my estimate. Then the line of thought drifted over to a writer who'd told a friend and I, during one autumn's grouse hunt, to please never write about his piece of the Northwest so that it would remain undiscovered. The fact that the land was mostly logged to oblivion and filling up with back-to-the-land yahoos apparently was a minor consideration for this guy. But his heartfelt, impassioned look and plea held the day. My friend and I easily agreed. We had no intention of writing about the location anyway. In the coming years, this duplicitous soul made something of a cottage industry writing magazine articles and several books on his valley-slice of perceived paradise. Careerist lunacy for the sake of turning a buck.

This type of hypocrisy drives me nuts, but today, in present time, as I move downstream in synch with the Yellowstone, I finally realize the real source of my disgust. It's with myself because, in many ways, I've operated down through the years wearing the environmentally self-righteous mask of the true hypocrite. "Damn straight. I know what's right for the land and what not to do or think in this regard. Listen to me, all ye children, if you want to learn the true way, to walk the enlightened path."

What a load of pompous, sanctimonious jive. They make mirrors for a reason.

The past dozen years of mistakes and hard-time experiences have proved humbling in a way the previous forty-some years of lunacy haven't. I don't fall into this trap quite so often and not quite so deeply. More time is spent merely drifting through the days in often vain attempts to avoid conflict and strife. Minor efforts at achieving some sort of inner peace. I guess I have that literary con artist to thank for this slight improvement in character. I'll take the positive shifts in course, however slight, wherever I can find them.

Well la-de-da, hot-zing, back-and-forth and in-and-out of time with nonsensical predictability. Enough.

I focus on moving with the skis, a basic, enjoyable skill that is coming back to me more quickly than I'd expected after such a protracted layoff—a dozen years or so. Forty minutes or so of nothing but back and forth leg motion and gliding through the powder. The skis sink maybe a couple of inches in the light, white crystals. I soon begin to move efficiently through thick snow, crushing through small waves of drifts dispersed like lazy waves on a still-life lake. There's enough illumination for the trees to cast ghostly shadows that are barely dense enough to reveal slight shading from grey to bluish-grey. My head's gone thoughtless, a fine release in my miniature world of cerebral mayhem. I'm sweating and push up the sleeves on the sweater and take off my stocking cap. The air feels chill, refreshing on my bald head. Life is cruel. No hair. Aching joints. No Bentley parked out front of my home. No Cubs' World Series. Plenty of brown trout and good country, though.

A downed cottonwood trunk provides a good seat and a better view of the river. I step out of the skis and open the daypack. The always-cheap red wine tastes as remembered—a bit astringent, a touch cloying, of strong grapes—good. The bread and white Vermont cheddar are good, too. I squeeze some more wine in a long arc into my mouth as I watch the river drift by almost silently, except for the music of the softly-colliding ice cakes. No wind. No bird calls. No sound of traffic. Nothing. The effort of skiing has worked its long-running magic on my head. No internal dialogues. Only an open mind taking in the scene. I'm probably perched on this trunk with mouth agape, drool running down my chin. What the hell. I've been here before. Familiar country. I think of Rupert and wish he were here digging away at the snow making a temporary nest where he could chew his biscuits in safety and splendor. Who knows. The canine mind is a good deal more elaborate than I initially thought decades ago. I imagine him perched on top of the dry sacks in the middle of the canoe with Ginny taking photos up front while I leisurely push the paddle through the water. I would have liked that. So would have Rupert.

After a while, I work downstream some more, enjoying the solitude and the release of house-bound anxiety. Snowshoeing's always done this, and I'm determined to make this type of exercise a regular deal in my life, which means, loosely translated, "It ain't gonna happen." Still Ginny and I make plans to spend a few days working our way into the Crazies up narrow canyons along frozen creeks, beneath pines and blue sky.

I scan the river as I move forward and remember last summer when caddis, mayflies and grasshoppers were all over the water and the grassy banks. Rainbows and brown trout fed eagerly and I caught my share. That seems a long time ago, and ever having done so under a hot sun along thick, rich green grasses seems improbable. Three months may as well be three lifetimes where warm weather fly fishing is concerned right now. Winter is holding serve in an icy grip.

Finally I turn around and start to retrace my way for three or maybe four miles. The sun is now gone below the southwestern ridgeline and the light is fading to a soft dimness with the least hint of deep purple. My tracks mark my earlier passage. Blowing snow has partially filled them in. By tomorrow they'll be gone, vanished like I was never here. I move along at a good clip. There's a cool breeze working down river and into my face. The chill offsets the heat generated by the steady, rhythmic motion of pushing with the skis and poles and then a smooth coasting for several yards. I reach the crest of the small rise that looks down on the fishing access and my Suburban. Glancing around to store one last panoramic image of this fine afternoon, I spot several deer watching at the edge of the trees on the far bank. Ears perked, eyes bright even in the near dusk, tails flicking in a natural Morse code of sorts. I look, smile and head off down the slope. My pace quickens with the advantage of gravity's pull. Soon I'm at my rig.

In several months, the weather will be warm again, the days light, fresh and bright. Ginny and I will be enjoying the river in our canoe once again, but at this moment I'm a captive to natural forces that pull me from this quiet moment back into time spent on the Yellowstone these past years.

Further Reading

Maps and Trip Planning Information

The following is a selection of books related to the Yellowstone River drainage that I've read over the years. And a couple of these are good books to read while hanging out in camp.

Abbey, Edward *The Brave Cowboy* (University of New Mexico Press, Albuquerque, 1956). Tremendous novel about a mythic, ghostly nomad roaming the opens of the southwest, unable to fit into the modern world with all of its strange rules.

Alt, David and Hyndman, David W. *Roadside Geology of Montana* (Mountain Press Publishing Company, Missoula 1986). A highly readable and comprehensive examination and explanation of the varied geologic conditions found throughout Montana, including the entire Yellowstone River drainage within the state.

Alwin, John A. *Eastern Montana: A portrait of the Land and its People* (Helena, MT: Montana Magazine, Inc., Helena 1982). Great descriptions and photographs of the region, including the small towns and the people who make this tough land their home.

Berry, Don *A Majority of Scoundrels* (Comstock Edition, California 1961). An informal history of the glory years of the fur trade, centered on the Rocky Mountain Fur Company and the likes of Jim Bridger, Jedediah Smith and Hugh Glass.

Blevins, Winfred *The Yellowstone: Rivers West Book 1* (Bantam Books, New York 1988). A novel about the early explorers and trappers in the Rocky Mountain West and the Yellowstone region in particular.

Blevins, Winfred *Dictionary of the American West* (Sasquatch Books, Seattle 2001). A comprehensive listing of words, terms, slang and colloquialisms and their evolution as used by Native Americans, trappers, cowboys, miners, loggers and migrant workers from the Rockies north to Alaska and west to California.

Boller, Henry A. *Among the Indians: Eight Years in the Far West, 1858–1866* (The Lakeside Press, Chicago 1959). A tough narrative of one man's experience living with the native peoples of the high plains more than a decade before the Battle of the Little Bighorn.

Bowen, Peter *Specimen Song* (St. Martin's Press, New York 1995). One of the first books in Bowen's Gabriel Dupre Montana mystery series that now numbers around twenty titles. The plots are decidedly Montana-based and overall the author captures the spirit and character of contemporary Montana.

Bowles, Paul *Their Heads Are Green and Their Hands Are Blue* (Random House, New York 1963). Nine travel essays ranging from Morocco to Central America, by one of the finest writers ever to wander the planet.

Bradshaw, Stan *River Safety: A Floater's Guide* (Greycliff Publishing Company, Helena, Montana 2000). An essential book on river floating safety and techniques for beginner and expert alike written by one of Montana's premier paddlers.

Brown, C.J.D., Dr. *Fishes of Montana* (Big Sky Books, Bozeman, Montana 1971). Every species from Westslope cutthroat trout to Arctic grayling to Longnose Dace is covered including life cycles, growth rates, habitat and identifying characteristics.

Brown, Lauren *Grasslands* (Chanticleer Press, New York 1985). A comprehensive field guide, fully illustrated with color photographs, to the birds, wildflowers, trees, grasses, insects, mammals and other life on the prairie.

Brooks, Charles E. *Fishing Yellowstone Waters* (Nick Lyons Books, New York 1984). Every river, creek, lake and pond is covered in this world-famous nexus for some of the finest trout fishing anywhere. More than just a another fishing book, when coupled with Dan Callaghan's fine photographs, the book serves as a wonderful guide to one of the most curious locations on the planet.

Carrington, Margaret I. *Absaraka: Home of the Crows* (The Lakeside Press, Chicago 1950). First person account of the lifestyles of the Crow Indians and their country along the Yellowstone River from valley to rugged mountains a century ago, including battles, retreats and the Fetterman Massacre.

Chapple, Steve *Kayaking the Full Moon: A Journey Down the Yellowstone River to the Soul of Montana* (HarperCollins, New York 1993). A fine book by a Montana native, about floating the Yellowstone. Chapple also spends a good deal of time hanging out in bars and talking with various luminaries, locals and roustabouts.

Crawford, Max *Lords of the Plain* (University of Oklahoma Press, Norman 1997). A graphic, thorough novel about men who roamed and marauded their way through the high plains more than a century ago. *Womba, Eastertown* and *Six Key Cut* aren't bad books to read at camp either.

Colton, Larry *Counting Coup: A True Story of Basketball and Honor on the Little Big Horn* (Warner Books, New York 2000). One of the best books on the subject of the brutal life Indians have on the Rez—the poverty, despair, hopelessness and racism the people face in contemporary America, and the pride, determination and courage displayed by many of the Crow.

Custer, George A., General *My Life on the Plains* (The Lakeside Press, Chicago 1952). Custer's account of his activities during the Indian Wars on the high plains more than a century ago and well before his demise at Little Bighorn.

Custer Battlefield (Division of Publications National Park Service, Washington, D.C. 1988). Official publication of the National Park Service with excellent archival and contemporary photographs, maps, descriptions of the key figures in the battle and of the battle itself.

Ewers, John C. *The Blackfeet: Raiders on the Northwestern Plains* (University of Oklahoma Press, Norman 1958). A fascinating account of the strongest military power on the great plains up through the end of the buffalo hunting days. The few tribes and settlers that crossed the Blackfeet rarely lived to regret their errors in judgment.

Fergus, Charles *Shadow Catcher* (Soho Press Inc., New York 1991). A historical novel that examines the 1913 Wanamaker Expedition and in the process reveals much about the relationships between whites and Indians, and some arcane and esoteric aspects of tribal existence.

Fischer, Hank and Fischer, Carol *Paddling Montana* (Falcon Publishing, Helena, Montana 1999). A sometimes accurate, and sometimes not, guide to thirty-two Montana rivers, including the Yellowstone, with maps, access points and descriptions of the waters. As with any guide, use in conjunction with personal and current local information.

Frazier, Ian *Great Plains* (Picador USA, New York 1989). A journey through the vast and myth-inspiring Great Plains from the site of Sitting Bull's cabin to an abandoned house once terrorized by Bonnie and Clyde to the scene of the murders chronicled in Truman Capote's *In Cold Blood*.

Garcia, Andrew *Tough Trip Through Paradise* (Comstock Editions, San Francisco 1967). One man's memoirs of the vanishing of the buffalo herds of the West and how tough life was in the wilds of Montana more than 125 years ago.

Halfpenny, James and Biesiot, Elizabeth *A Field Guide to Mammal Tracking in North America* (Johnson Books, Boulder, Colorado 1986). Interpreting tracks and scat discovered while coursing down the Yellowstone, or anywhere else for that matter, has provided me with hours of entertainment and many insights into the creatures that live in the country I'm passing through. This book is thorough, with good descriptions of how to differentiate tracks and signs, and includes plenty of drawings, charts and color photographs. Easy to use.

Hanson, Margaret Brock *Frank Grouard, Army Scout* (Frontier Printing, Inc., Cheyenne, Wyoming 1983). Of Polynesian ancestry, Grouard was caught in the middle of the whites' takeover of the West. As Standing Bear, the adopted brother of Sitting Bull, and as a friend to Crazy Horse, he learned the life and plight of the Indians. He later served as the chief guide for General Crook in the Indian campaigns of 1876.

Harrison, Jamie *Blue Deer Thaw* (Hyperion, New York 2000). The last in a series of four books—the others are *The Edge of the Crazies, Going Local* and *An Unfortunate Prairie Occurrence*—about a fictional Montana high plains town (based on Livingston) and its odd assortment of residents, including Sheriff Jules Clement who somehow manages to always solve bizarre murders and deal with arcane and eccentric situations that happen on a daily and random basis. These are excellent books for anyone interested in the true nature of life away from the California newcomer glitz of the mountainous western third of the state.

Heden, Sven *My Life as an Explorer* (Garden City Publishing, New York 1925). Hedin was the first to explore much of the interior of central Asia more than a century ago, including the then vast unmapped central

Tibetan plateau. A great book to read after a long day on the river when you think you had it tough.

Holt, John *Coyote Nowhere: In Search of America's Last Frontier* (The Lyons Press, Guilford, Connecticut 2004). Free-wheeling, free-form road journey across the northern high plains from Montana all the way north to the Northwest Territories.

Holt, John *Knee Deep in Montana's Trout Streams* and *Reel Deep in Montana's Rivers* (Pruett Publishing, Boulder, Colorado 1991 and 1993). Not just some more gonzo fly fishing tomes. These are more like fishing with an opinionated and experienced guide who always keeps a weather eye peeled for crazed adventure.

Holt, John *Hunted: A Novel* (The Lyons Press, Guilford, Connecticut 2003). A story about greed, surviving the hardships of the high plains and the mysticism of some of the last best country in the Yellowstone basin that is all but gone now.

Holt, John *Kicking Up Trouble: Upland Bird Hunted in the West* (Wilderness Adventures Press, Belgrade Montana1994). According to writer John Barsness, this one "...resembles a combination of George Bird Evans and Hunter Thompson. It's all there: the birds and beverages, the highways and the landscape, the strange bird dogs and stranger adventures."

Holt, John *Montana Flyfishing Guide: East* (Greycliff Publishing, Helena, Montana 1996). A comprehensive guide to fishing all of the waters of eastern Montana, including the Yellowstone River drainage.

Hughes, Dave *The Yellowstone River and its Angling* (Frank Amato Publications, Portland, Oregon 1992). Fishing and floating the Yellowstone from the park down to the Bighorn River east of Billings. Excellent color photos. The book reads more like a crazed river adventure than a dry how-to guide book.

Hugo, Richard *The Real West Marginal Way* (W.W. Norton and Company, New York 1986). Wonderful, brilliant poetry by one of America's masters. The late Hugo nails both the West and the soul in this collection.

Krakell II, Dean *Downriver: A Yellowstone Journey* (Sierra Club Books, San Francisco 1987). Krakel's ten-year series of trips blending into one completed in a battered pickup and car, a canoe and kayak and finally a raft through a variety of seasons on the river.

Lang, William I., ed. *Stories From An Open Country: Essays on the Yellowstone River Valley* (Western Heritage Press, Billings, Montana 2000). Essays on the Yellowstone basin by writers that include Mary Clearman Blew, Bill Tallbull and John Peters-Campell.

Lavender, David *The Way to the Western Sea* (Harper & Row, New York 1988). The best narrative examination of the Lewis and Clark Expedition.

Lucey, Donna M. *Photographing Montana 1894–1928: The Life and Work of Evelyn Cameron* (Mountain Press Publishing, Missoula, Montana 2000). Born into English society, Cameron and her husband moved to the badlands of Montana along the Yellowstone River where she devoted herself to photographing the land, the people and the life of the high plains and prairie. Her work is unique, honest and brilliant.

Marcuson, Pat *The Beartooth Fishing Guide* (Falcon Press Publishing Company, Inc. 1985). An excellent guide to high country fishing in many tributary lakes of the Yellowstone River, but also a fine book to plan hikes and extended trips in remote, above-tree line country. Written by someone who invested the time and effort and truly knows the country. With numerous black-and-white photographs.

Malone, Michael P., Roeder, Richard B. and Lang, William L. *Montana: A History of Two Centuries* (University of Washington Press, Seattle

1991). From prehistory up to 1990, with maps and black-and-white photographs.

Marcuson, Pat *The Beartooth Fishing Guide* (Falcon Press, Helena, Montana 1985). In addition to being an excellent guide to some of the finest high-country trout fishing in the world, this book also serves as a guide to exploring some of the most spectacular country anywhere. Black-and-white photographs.

McCarthy, Cormac *The Road* (Alfred A. Knopf, New York 2006). This one with its spare, exquisite language puts all other post-apocalyptic novels to shame. Leaves them in its grey, sooty dust.

McMurtry, Larry *Lonesome Dove* (Random House, New York, 1985). A novel about the Old West and a cattle drive from Texas up to Montana with all the violence, adventure and romance a reader could desire.

McMurtry, Larry *The BerryBender Narratives* (Simon & Schuster, New York). Four novels—*Sin Killer, The Wandering Hill, By Sorrow's River* and *Folly and Glory*—describing a wildly eccentric British family's arcane and chaotic wanderings about the West, including up and down the Yellowstone River.

McGuane, Thomas *Nobody's Angel- A Novel* (Random House, New York 1979). An excellent portrait of late twentieth century Montana where character Patrick Fitzpatrick—an Army tank captain and whiskey addict—returns home and finds his family missing, divorced, dead or trying out for movies, and the ranch is in a shambles.

Milner II, Clyde A., O'Connor, Carol A., and Sandweiss, Martha A., eds. *The Oxford History of the American West* (Oxford University Press, New York 1994). One of the best overall histories of the American West in one volume, with more than 200 illustrations.

Pierce, Steve *The Lakes of Yellowstone: A Guide For Hiking & Exploring* (The Mountaineers, Seattle 1987). As the title says, with maps and black-and-white photographs.

Ray, Robert J. *Murdock Cracks Ice* (Delacorte Press, New York 1992). One of six Murdock murder mysteries written by my creative writing faculty advisor of the early seventies back at Beloit College in southern Wisconsin. Perfect brain candy for a lazy down-time afternoon on an island in the middle of the Yellowstone.

Reese, Rick *Greater Yellowstone: The National Park and Adjacent Wild Lands* (Two Bears Press, Helena, Montana 1991). Soft cover book on the Yellowstone National Park ecosystem with excellent photographs and illustrations.

Sandoz, Mari *Cheyenne Autumn* (Avon Books, New York 1953). A brilliant factual account, written as a historical novel about the brutal, winter-frozen march of a band of Cheyenne who escaped from an Oklahoma Reservation and eluded more than 10,000 soldiers and ranchers for 1,500 miles to their homeland along the Yellowstone River.

Thompson, Curt *Floating and Recreation on Montana Rivers* (Curt Thompson, Lakeside, Montana 1993). Mostly accurate guide to floating, camping and other activities on Montana's rivers, with maps, photographs, listings for river access sites, campgrounds and information sources.

Turner, Jack *Travels in the Greater Yellowstone* (Thomas Dunne Books, New York 2008). An examination, by the author of *Teewinot*, concerning the numerous threats and issues swirling within and without the ecosystem that is the Greater Yellowstone.

Walinchus, Rod and Travis, Tom *Fly Fishing the Yellowstone River* (Pruett Publishing Company, Boulder, Colorado 1995). A fly fishing guide, and by slight extension, a floating guide to the upper river from just below

Yellowstone National Park at Gardiner all the way down to Billings. Black-and-white photographs and tying instructions for effective patterns.

Whithorn, Bill and Whithorn Doris *Photo History of Livingston – Bozeman Coal Country* (Livingston Enterprise, Livingston, Montana 1976). Hard-to-find pamphlet with many black-and-white photos that show the real side of life in long-ago Montana.

Work Projects Administration *The WPA Guide to 1930s Montana* (The University of Arizona Press, Tucson, Arizona 1994). Everything Montana listed town by town with chapters on economics, politics, geography, etc., all written from the perspective of the 1930s. Much of what is described has remained the same. Much hasn't.

Yellowstone to Yosemite: Early Adventures in the Mountain West (Western Eye Press, Telluride, Colorado 1988). Writings and lithographs about the West a century back, including Yellowstone Park.

The Yellowstone River (Montana: The Magazine of Western History, Helena, Montana Autumn 1985). Wonderful collection of essays about the Yellowstone drainage including "The Native Americans of the Yellowstone," "Steamboats on the Yellowstone," and "Main Streets on the Yellowstone: Town-Building along the Northern Pacific in Montana." With archival photographs and period maps.

MAPS

In addition to providing material for planning floats down the Yellowstone, maps provide windows into the country and plenty of information to dream on over a cold, dark winter. The following offer a variety of levels of detail and data. The accuracy of all of these varies, particularly when the moods of the river are factored in. Stream courses change constantly, and during periods of diminishing flows, especially from mid-August through autumn, channels that were passable during high water are often mere trickles or dry later on. It's always best to stay with the main channel to avoid winding up at a dead end when what at first appeared to be a substantial current peters out into a gravel bar and a tangle of downed trees. Dragging a canoe back up one of these cul-de-sacs is not a great deal of fun.

Montana Afloat. Two maps covering the river from Gardiner to Huntley below Billings. Not highly detailed, but accurate all the same with information on the river, its tributaries and some history of the region.

Montana Atlas & Gazetteer (Delorme-Yarmouth, Maine 1997). Topo maps of the entire state that are fairly detailed, including back roads, campsites, fishing access points, state parks and monuments, and historical locations. This is a must for anyone wandering about Montana.

Montana's Best Fishing Waters (Wilderness Adventures Press, Belgrade, Montana 2006). A complete collection of maps covering all of the state's rivers, each with a number of GPS locations along the way.

Treasure of Gold (Montana Department of Fish, Wildlife and Parks, Billings, Montana out of print). This is—or was—the best collection of maps for the Yellowstone. It's out of print and extremely difficult to find. A spokesman for the MDFWP said that the department receives many requests for this one each year. Perhaps they might consider a reprint.

USGS Topographic maps. The most accurate in terms of elevation and overall terrain detail. Covering the entire river requires the purchase of dozens of maps and spending a good deal of cash. Great for planning future floats and related explorations, but cumbersome to carry on the river.

Yellowstone River Floater's Guide (Bureau of Land Management, Billings, Montana 2006). So far, four maps covering the river from Springdale below Livingston to thirty-five miles below Miles City. Durable and accurate with diversion dams and other hazards marked in red. Photographs above and below diversions help the canoeist recognize where to take out and portage. There are plans to map the remainder of the river in the coming years.

Gear

The following is a list of the equipment we used on the river. Some of the listings are brand specific because they are significantly better suited for the conditions we encountered during our trips. For reasons of dependability, durability and aesthetics I always buy the best equipment I can afford (or, in many cases, can't afford). I've never regretted buying top-shelf gear.

The canoe we used was called a White Guide and was made by Newfound Woodworks in Bristol, New Hampshire. It is a cedar strip construction crafted with meticulous attention to detail. In addition to being a work of art, the canoe was a wonder on the river—easy to maneuver and weighing less than 70 pounds even at 18' in length. In rough water, we gave the White Guide its head and it always took the best line through standing waves, swirling holes and other mayhem. This canoe is not cheap—well over five grand, but worth the price. Another option is the Mad River Royalex Explorer 16' for less than a thousand dollars. This weighs more than the White Guide by a few pounds and doesn't have quite the load capacity but it's performed well on many rivers for us.

Many people think little or nothing about selecting canoe paddles. The standard straight-shafted ones are the usual choice. I happened upon a company called Bending Branches Canoe & Kayak Paddles. Their performance bent shaft Viper paddles are several levels above conventional construction, saving effort, back and arm strain and providing more thrust per stroke. Again pricey, but these, too, are works of art made of basswood and black willow and well worth the cost.

We always wear PFDs (lifejackets) on the water. Too many bad things can happen too fast not to wear one. In the past all of the lifejackets we used were bulky and uncomfortable. Then we tumbled upon Float-Tech Inflatable PFDs. They are light-weight and when not inflated they wear like a thin fly fishing vest. The sleeves can be unzipped and stowed away. They are waterproof and breathable. They will automatically inflate via a CO_2 cartridge if you capsize and go under water. This feature can be deactivated for manual use only. And they can be manually inflated with a tube that is easy to reach. They come complete with two manual inflation backups, a hidden brimmed hood, adjustable side-release buckles, reflective fabric throughout, non-corrosive zippers and an adjustable shock cord.

The Yellowstone River offers some of the finest trout fishing in the world all the way to Columbus. From there, the angling gradually shifts over to warmwater species that include catfish, northern pike, smallmouth bass, ling (or burbot), sturgeon, goldeye and paddlefish. The length and weight of a fly rod for this water is largely an individual choice, but one rod that performed wonderfully for me is the Damon 9'-6" seven-weight Pro Staff. Lightweight and a cannon to cast, this is the best rod I've ever used on big water. Sadly, the company is out of business. A true loss. I keep my eyes peeled for these rods. So far no luck. Reels to match are also an individual choice. Danielsson of Sweden makes a superb lightweight reel in the FW 2Six—lightweight, durable, beautiful. Solitudes reels are also quality products—tough and with a smooth action. Other fine ones we used are made by Hardy, Orvis, Ross and Peerless. For the tributaries I prefer the Fenwick Iron Feather 7"-0' four-weight. A beautifully performing rod that sadly is no longer in production. Occasionally one of this line shows up on eBay. Sometimes, on small waters, I use my delightful Damon 5'-0" two-weight. Lots of fun and more backbone than I would have guessed. Sadly the company no longer takes rod orders, so searching eBay and other locales is the only option. Other excellent rods we used were an Elkhorn 8'-6" five-weight, Redington, Ginny's favorite—a Redington CPS Series 7' three-weight and a Lamiglas 6'-6" three-weight Appalachian Series—a great rod for a moderate cost. Nearly broke and down to my last thirty-seven fly rods. Life is a killer at times. As the years pass, I pay more and more attention to what I use for leaders and tippet material. I've lost too many fish in the past from stiff and/or weak materials on this front. Currently my choice is Frog Hair—strong for its diameter, supple and low in visibility.

There are many quality fly lines. A new series I've been using is the Cortland Precision Trout Floating. I particularly liked the 3.5- and 4.5-weight lines. A nice compromise between even weights. Other lines we used were made by Rio and Orvis.

For warmwater species I use a 6'-0" medium weight spinning rod and matching reel with either 6- or 8-pound test line. Snagging paddlefish involves heavy-duty saltwater rods, thick line, treble hooks and sinkers that resemble doorknobs in heft. Local fly shops and sporting goods stores can provide up-to-date fishing conditions and also suggest appropriate fly patterns and spinning lures. Hip and/or chest waders are a good idea. The river runs cold, especially from September on.

Sunglasses are an absolute necessity on the river. The glare of the sun can exhaust and even burn your eyes. When fishing, an errant or windblown cast can destroy an eye. Polarized glasses help cut through the glare and give one a more accurate reading of the river. I have many pairs of glasses. Among my favorites are those made by Serengeti, Ray-Ban's Aviators and Rudy Project. The glasses by the Rudy Project I wear almost exclusively when in the canoe. They're lightweight, comfortable, have great and interchangeable lenses to adapt to varying light conditions, and no matter what angle my head is or how abruptly I move, they won't fall off.

One item of footwear that Ginny and I both appreciate to the point of considering them luxuries are sandals made for wading in the river. We've got pairs from both Teva—Terra-FI 2—and from Sperry Top-Sider—men's Figawi Ultra Thong and women's Figawi2 2-Strap. All of these are perfect for canoeing on hot days when water temperatures are at summer levels, and wading shoes would be uncomfortable to say the least.

One of the major concerns when traveling on the water is keeping everything dry, especially, clothes, sleeping gear and cameras. Ginny uses a seemingly bomb-proof Pelican hard case to carry all of her equipment, and a large, clear plastic case by Aquapac for the camera body and lens she is using at any given time. We also have smaller cases by the company for a GPS and books. For larger gear, the Baja Bags and Zip Duffels are well-constructed, sturdy and water tight. The firm also makes excellent smaller bags suitable for maps, keys, bail bond cards and wallets.

Because space is limited and weight something of an issue, small, lightweight tents and sleeping bags are important. Mountain Hardware's Haven tent weighs less than seven pounds, is roomy and well-designed. Their Phantom down bags are warm to 15 degrees and weigh less than 2 pounds. Ginny purchased the Sub Zero Jacket and has no complaints. A nylon tarp for a ground cloth is an additional moisture barrier and protection from sharp rocks.

Having a stove along for the ride is convenient and sometimes necessary for quickly heating water for coffee, tea, cocoa, etc. A single burner propane stove is compact, lightweight and efficient. The usual suspect, Coleman, makes an item called the Deluxe Perfect that offers push button ignition and puts out 10,000 BTU. A small diameter grill of 14–16 inches wrapped in a plastic bag works fine for grilling over a wood coal fire. A set of nesting pots and pans is essential. GSI Outdoors' Hard Anodized Extreme Cook Sets are rated by most outdoor magazines as among the best. I agree.

I once thought that having a GPS on the river was not usually necessary, but could be useful for determining exactly where one is at a given moment, if this is indeed important. Brunton sent me one of their Atlas MNS Atlas and I've changed my mind. It is truly nice to know where I am on occasion, and the other features like topo maps, weather information, altimeter, and barometer are handy. This one is waterproof.

When it's warm weather I usually were a pair of wading boots or a pair of low cut hiking boots. When the weather and water temperatures drop, I add a pair of lightweight hip waders. In camp, I use a pair of

Russell Moccasin Company's Kalahari. Durable boar hide soles and are comfortable to wear at sandy or grassy campsites. On rocky sites, I use Timberland's Waterproof Winter Park Slip Ons. Comfortable and warm, with a good sole for walking on rocky, cobble beaches, and waterproof.

I seem to be obsessed with collecting knives. They're all over the place—in the glove box of the Suburban, tackle bags, desks, bookcases, daypacks. Three I used a good deal while doing this book were the Buck Folding Hunter, Swiss Army Boy Scout Explorer and a Xikar folding knife. The Buck has been with me for decades and always does the job. The Swiss Army knife has many useful tools, not the least of which are the bottle opener and cork screw. The Xikar is a work of art that is durable, holds an edge and has a good lock.

Water treatment is necessary on the Yellowstone, especially on the lower river due to turbid water conditions. Bringing bottled water adds weight and takes up valuable space. We used the First Need Deluxe water purification system. It's compact, lightweight and filters out minute microbes including giardia. Filtering a gallon of water takes just a few minutes of pumping. Replacement filters are available. We also used the Aquimira Water Bottle while paddling. You just fill the container with water, screw on the filter and cap and squeeze. It holds 22 ounces and the filter is good for 200 loads.

We carry stick matches, a flint, various Zippo and Brunson lighters and regular matches. We have no intention of being without fire at camp.

Flashlights are a necessity and there are countless brands to choose from. Headlamps are great for coming into camp in the dark and for setting up and moving about. The Streamlight Argo HP Luxeon LED Headlamp has two levels of brightness, the batteries last for over four hours at the high level and it is not uncomfortable to wear.

A first aid kit is a necessity. Again, there are many on the market designed for the outdoors. Once purchased, various medications, salves and implements can be added, including prescription painkillers and antibiotics. Tender's Afterburn and Afterbite really work and quickly for problems from sun exposure and insect bites.

Binoculars are useful for viewing wildlife, the moon and the river ahead. I have a pair of Nikon Travelite V zoom binoculars. Compact with good optics, though a bit hard holding a steady image, and reasonably priced.

I've ruined a number of watches that claimed to be "water resistant" over the years while paddling, fishing and so on. The Casio Sea Pathfinder really is water resistant. It's been dunked, submerged and rained on countless times, with no deleterious effects like fogging inside the crystal. The time piece also has a bunch of other features like temperature, stopwatch, moon phase graph and barometer, including a graph that shows weather trends. It also predicts high and low tides, but this feature is not so useful in Montana.

Index

AK Press

Ordering Information

AK Press
674-A 23rd Street
Oakland, CA 94612-1163
U.S.A
(510) 208-1700
www.akpress.org
akpress@akpress.org

AK Press
PO Box 12766
Edinburgh, EH8 9YE
Scotland
(0131) 555-5165
www.akuk.com
ak@akedin.demon.uk

The addresses above would be delighted to provide you with the latest complete AK catalog, featuring several thousand books, pamphlets, zines, audio products, video products, and stylish apparel published & distributed by AK Press. Alternatively, check out our websites for the complete catalog, latest news and updates, events, and secure ordering.

Also Available from AK Press

The first audio collection from Alexander Cockburn on compact disc.

Beating the Devil
Alexander Cockburn, ISBN 13: 9781902593494 • CD • $14.98

In this collection of recent talks, maverick commentator Alexander Cockburn defiles subjects ranging from Colombia to the American presidency to the Missile Defense System. Whether he's skewering the fallacies of the war on drugs or illuminating the dark crevices of secret government, his erudite and extemporaneous style warms the hearts of even the stodgiest cynics of the left.

PRESS
EDINBURGH • OAKLAND • BALTIMORE

Available from CounterPunch/AK Press

Call 1-800-840-3683 or order online from www.counterpunch.org or www.akpress.org

The Case Against Israel
by Michael Neumann

Wielding a buzzsaw of logic, Professor Neumann dismantles plank-by-plank the Zionist rationale for Israel as religious state entitled to trample upon the basic human rights of non-Jews. Along the way, Neumann also offers a passionate amicus brief for the plight of the Palestinian people.

Other Lands Have Dreams: From Baghdad to Pekin Prison
by Kathy Kelly

At a moment when so many despairing peace activists have thrown in the towel, Kathy Kelly, a witness to some of history's worst crimes, never relinquishes hope. Other Lands Have Dreams is literary testimony of the highest order, vividly recording the secret casualties of our era, from the hundreds of thousands of Iraqi children inhumanely denied basic medical care, clean water and food by the US overlords to young mothers sealed inside the sterile dungeons of American prisons in the name of the merciless war on drugs.

Dime's Worth of Difference: Beyond the Lesser of Two Evils
Edited by Alexander Cockburn and Jeffrey St. Clair

Everything you wanted to know about one-party rule in America.

Whiteout: the CIA, Drugs and the Press
by Alexander Cockburn and Jeffrey St. Clair, Verso.

The involvement of the CIA with drug traffickers is a story that has slouched into the limelight every decade or so since the creation of the Agency. In Whiteout, here at last is the full saga.

Been Brown So Long It Looked Like Green to Me: the Politics of Nature
by Jeffrey St. Clair, Common Courage Press.

Covering everything from toxics to electric power plays, St. Clair draws a savage profile of how money and power determine the state of our environment, gives a vivid account of where the environment stands today and what to do about it.

Imperial Crusades: Iraq, Afghanistan and Yugoslavia
by Alexander Cockburn and Jeffrey St. Clair, Verso.

A chronicle of the lies that are now returning each and every day to haunt the deceivers in Washington and London, the secret agendas and the underreported carnage of these wars. We were right and they were wrong, and this book proves the case. Never leave home without it.

Why We Publish CounterPunch

By Alexander Cockburn and Jeffrey St. Clair

TEN YEARS AGO WE FELT UNHAPPY ABOUT THE STATE OF RADICAL JOURN-alism. It didn't have much edge. It didn't have many facts. It was politically timid. It was dull. CounterPunch was founded. We wanted it to be the best muckraking newsletter in the country. We wanted it to take aim at the consensus of received wisdom about what can and cannot be reported. We wanted to give our readers a political roadmap they could trust.

A decade later we stand firm on these same beliefs and hopes. We think we've restored honor to muckraking journalism in the tradition of our favorite radical pamphleteers: Edward Abbey, Peter Maurin and Ammon Hennacy, Appeal to Reason, Jacques René Hébert, Tom Paine and John Lilburne.

Every two weeks CounterPunch gives you jaw-dropping exposés on: Congress and lobbyists; the environment; labor; the National Security State.

"CounterPunch kicks through the floorboards of lies and gets to the founda-tion of what is really going on in this country," says Michael Ratner, attorney at the Center for Constitutional Rights. "At our house, we fight over who gets to read CounterPunch first. Each issue is like spring after a cold, dark winter."

YOU CANNOT MISS ANOTHER ISSUE

The Secret Language of the Crossroads

How the Irish Invented Slang

By Daniel Cassidy

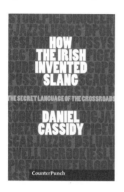

In *How the Irish Invented Slang: The Secret Language of the Crossroad*, Daniel Cassidy co-director and founder of the Irish Studies Program at New College of California cuts through two hundred years worth of Anglo academic "baloney" and reveals the massive, hidden influence of the Irish language on the American language.

Irish words and phrases are scattered all across the American language, regional and class dialects, colloquialism, slang, and specialized jargons like gambling, in the same way Irish-Americans have been scattered across the crossroads of North America for five hundred years.

In a series of essays, including: "Decoding the Gangs of New York," "How the Irish Invented Poker and American Gambling Slang," "The Sanas (Etymology) of Jazz," "Boliver of Brooklyn," and in a *First Dictionary of Irish-American Vernacular*, Cassidy provides the hidden histories and etymologies of hundreds of so-called slang words that have defined the American language and culture like *dude, sucker, swell, poker, faro, cop, scab, fink, moolah, fluke, knack, ballyhoo, baloney,* as well as the hottest word of the 20th century, *jazz.*

Born Under a Bad Sky

By Jeffrey St. Clair

"Movement reporting on a par with Mailer's Armies of the Night"—Peter Linebaugh, author of *Magna Carta Manifesto* and *The Many-Headed Hydra*.

These urgent dispatches are from the frontlines of the war on the Earth. Gird yourself for a visit to a glowing nuclear plant in the backwoods of North Carolina, to the heart of Cancer Alley where chemical companies hide their toxic enterprise behind the dark veil of Homeland Security, and to the world's most contaminated place, the old H-bomb factory at Hanford, which is leaking radioactive poison into the mighty Columbia River.

With unflinching prose, St. Clair confronts the White Death in Iraq, the environmental legacy of a war that will keep on killing decades after the bombing raids have ended. He conjures up the environmental villains of our time, from familiar demons like James Watt and Dick Cheney to more surprising figures, including Supreme Court Justice Stephen Breyer (father of the cancer bond) and the Nobel laureate Al Gore, whose pieties on global warming are sponsored by the nuclear power industry. The mainstream environmental movement doesn't escape indictment. Bloated by grants from big foundations, perched in high-rent office towers, leashed to the neoliberal politics of the Democratic Party, the big green groups have largely acquiesced to the crimes against nature that St. Clair so vividly exposes.

All is not lost. From the wreckage of New Orleans to the imperiled canyons of the Colorado, a new green resistance is taking root. The fate of the grizzly and the ancient forests of Oregon hinge on the courage of these green defenders. This book is also a salute to them.

Available from CounterPunch.org and AK Press
Call 1-800-840-3683
$19.95

A Short History of Fear

By Alexander Cockburn

The idea that things are always getting worse, that Armageddon-in one form or another-is just around the corner, has been a common refrain since the very beginnings of Western culture. And, more often than not, the forces allegedlysending us to hell in a proverbial hand basket are shadowy conspiracies whose features are as murky as their nefarious power is supposedly Enter renegade journalist Alexander Cockburn to illuminate the darkest corners of our collective cultural unconscious. In his usual, take-no-prisoners-style, he battles an impressive collection of fear-mongers and the irrationalities they espouse. Likening the soul-saving indulgences sold by the medieval Catholic Church to today's carbon credits, Cockburn traces his subject through the ages, showing how fear is used to distract us from real problems and real solutions. Skewering doomsters on both the Left and Right, A Short History of Fear tackles: 9/11 conspiracy theories; the twentieth-century witch craze of "satanic abuse"; eugenics; the Kennedy assassination, Pearl Harbor, and other "inside jobs"; terrorism; the "Great Fear" of the eighteenth century; today's eleventh-hour predictions of planetary decline; and much more. Scathing, often hilarious, and always insightful, this is Cockburn at the top of his controversial game.

Coming in 2009 from CounterPunch and AK Press
Call 1-800-840-3683
$18.95